Part I

General LLOYD TILGHMAN
1816 - 1863
CSA

by
JAMES W. RAAB

Southern Heritage Press
Vol. 24

All rights reserved.
Copyright James W. Raab, 2001

LIBRARY OF CONGRESS CATALOGING-IN-PUBLICATION DATA.

Raab, James W.
p. cm.
ISBN 1-889332-07-0
1. Biography: Confederate Generals
Lloyd Tilghman, Frances Shoup
2. United States--History--Civil War
3. Confederate States of America, Army
Western Operations

Maps by Donald S. Frazier, Abilene Texas.
Adapted from the originals in
Vicksburg: Fall of the Confederate Gibraltar by Terry Winschel

Southern Heritage Press
4035 Emerald Dr.
Murfreesboro, TN 37130

Published in Tennessee

Table of Contents

Preface

Prologue ....i-iii

Profile..A1-A3

CHAPTERS

1. Paducah Kentucky..1 - 6
2. Hopkinsville Kentucky and Anna E. Carroll ....7 - 10
3. The Twin River Forts ....11 - 16
4. The Collapse of Fort Heiman..17 - 24
5. The Surrender of Fort Henry...25 - 30
6. The Surrender of Fort Donelson ....31 - 38
7. Prisoners of War...39 - 46
8. Iuka and Corinth...47 - 52
9. A Court of Inquiry for Earl Van Dorn...................................53 - 58
10. Coffeeville, Mississippi..59 - 62
11. Mississippi Duty...63 - 68
12. Grant's Yazoo Pass Expedition ....69 - 74
13. Pemberton - Tilghman Tent Flap ....75 - 78
14. The Siege of Fort Pemberton ....79 - 84
15. Grierson's Raid...85 - 88
16. Vicksburg and It's Approaches..89 - 94
17. The Fall of Jackson - The Army of Relief ....95 - 100
18. Fateful Champion Hill..101 - 106
19. In the Midst of Life There is Death ....107 - 110
20. Lloyd Tilghman's Monuments and Homestead.................111 - 116

END NOTES ....117 - 140

BIBLIOGRAPHY ....141 - 148

Illustrations

MAPS

Kentucky - Tennessee Frontier 7

The Twin River Forts 11

Fort Heiman - Fort Henry on the Tennessee River 19

Fort Donelson on the Cumberland River 32

Iuka and Corinth 48

The Theatre of War In The West, 1862-1863 65

Cutting The Yazoo Pass 69

Yazoo Pass to Fort Pemberton 71

Fort Pemberton at Greenwood, Mississippi 83

Grierson's Raid 86

Vicksburg and It's Approaches 89

Vicksburg and The Big Black River 91

The Move On Jackson, Mississippi 95

The Confederate Line of March at Champion Hill 98

Fateful Champion Hill 101

SKETCHES

Paducah Proclamation 4

Miss Anna E. Carol 9

The Gunboat St. Louis 18

Wartime Fort Henry 23

SKETCHES (continued)

Union Gunboats Advancing Up The Tennessee River 25

Gun Deck of Gunboat at Fort Henry 27

Reconstructed Log Hut - Fort Donelson 34

Newspaper - Fort Donelson Captured 39

Holly Springs, 1862 53

Railroad Depot at Holly Springs 61

A Confederate Prison at Jackson, Mississippi 63

The Southern News Illustrated - Tilghman 67

General W. W. Loring - 'Old Blizzards' 73

PHOTOS

Lloyd Tilghman - The Early Years A1

Lloyd Tilghman - The Colonel and The General 57

Lloyd Tilghman - The General 77

The Resting Place of Tilghman - New York City, N.Y. 111

Dedication of Tilghman's Marker at Vicksburg 112

Paducah - Monument to General Tilghman 113

The Tilghman House in Paducah, Kentucky 114

General Tilghman's Statue at Vicksburg ...... Cover Page

General Tilghman's Statue at Vicksburg 106

Preface

In the high drama of the conflict known as The American Civil War or War Between The States, Virginia has been popularized in film and fiction as the most prestigious theater of war for heroes and spectacular battles.

The vast land expanse west of the Appalachian Mountains cannot be overlooked or denied their legends and drama; especially the battles for the western rivers.

The events in the Western Theatre were spread over such a large area that it is difficult to record and provide a comprehensive account for the entire region.

Although these important facts and details are related, I have minimized them in a desire to produce a true narrative within the window of a single study that is easily read and understood by the average reader.

When the Southern homeland was invaded and the natural instinct was to protect home and hearth, the bugle was sounded. The 'cause' called Lloyd Tilghman and many brave comrades to follow it for practical and economic reasons, but most of all, these men fought to the end for the dream of States Rights.

Brig. General Lloyd Tilghman, CSA was a chivalrous and courageous Southern gentleman of the ante-bellum period and became the grandest embodiment of a gallant commander who ever graced or died upon a civil war battlefield.

James W. Raab
St. Augustine, Florida

Prologue

The United States of America was not far into the Eighteenth Century when men on both sides of the Mason & Dixon Line became sharply aware of two distinct and differing social-economic systems evolving side by side in their respective sections of the country.

The North was being thrust forward into the modern world of commerce, industry and finance and the acceptance of slavery simply no longer belonged in their new age.

The South was predominantly agricultural and saw no need to surrender their way of life or their chattels. The South, which had provided the nation with the author of the Declaration of Independence, Father of the Constitution and five of the Nation's first seven Presidents, could see its national role slowly eroding and consequently its very existence being threatened.[1]

In South Carolina the Charleston Mercury argued, 'The North and South are two nations, made by their institutions, customs, habits, as distinct as the English from the French.'[2]

In New York, Horace Greely of the New York Tribune said, "If the cotton states shall become satisfied that they can do better out of the Union than in it, we insist in letting them go in peace. The right to secede may still be a revolutionary one, but it exists nevertheless."[3]

By the summer of 1860, the southerners, demanding protection of their constitutional rights, decided on the peaceful expedient of withdrawing from the Union and resuming their sovereignty they had partially surrendered to the Federal government in 1776. They proposed no war upon the government in Washington nor upon any individual state.

It was a matter of fact that if Abraham Lincoln was to triumph in the fall elections, he would take initial action to keep the Union together.

When on November 5, 1860, Abraham Lincoln emerged victorious, the South Carolina House and Senate voted unanimously for a sovereign convention to be elected for the purpose of dissolving South Carolina's ties with the Union.

At Charleston on December 20, 1860, all one hundred and sixty-nine convention delegates voted for independence from the Union. This action of secession was followed closely by the states of Mississippi, Florida,

Alabama, Georgia, Louisiana and Texas, which summoned conventions of their own and adopted in their various ways, broke away from the Union.

By February 1861, the position of the general government in Washington was very difficult. They could either recognize the lawfulness of the acts of the seceded States or maintain the authority of the Federal government and compel the submission of these states to the Constitution and the laws of the land.

Conservative elements of both the North and South made great efforts to bring about a reconciliation. The State of Virginia called upon all the States to send delegates to an informal peace congress to meet in Washington in February.

Twenty states - thirteen northern and seven southern - were represented in it and ex-President Tyler was chosen to preside over its deliberations.

Various plans to settle matters peacefully were proposed; and after elaborate discussions, resolutions were adopted and were ordered to be presented to the rival governments.

The plans proposed by this body pleased neither side and the effort to close the breach was unsuccessful with both sides rejecting the proposal.

In the interim, the seceded states elected delegates to a convention which met in Montgomery, Alabama on February 4, 1861. The convention organized a new republic, The Confederate States of America. Its provisional government immediately entered upon their duties to enact measures for their common good.

Rapidly the forts, arsenals, post offices, and other public property of the United States were seized by the militia of the seceding states. The exceptions were Forts Moultrie and Sumter in Charleston, South Carolina harbor and Fort Pickens at Pensacola, Florida.

Abraham Lincoln was inaugurated on March 4, 1861. Determined to maintain the authority of the general government over the seceded states, he promised to continue to collect the public revenues at the ports and to hold and occupy the forts, arsenals and other public property seized by the Southern states.

An expedition consisting of seven ships, carrying two hundred and eighty-five guns and twenty-four hundred Federal soldiers, set sail from New York and Norfolk on its way to Charleston harbor with intentions to strengthen Fort Sumter. Before the convoy arrived at Charleston harbor, Pierre G. T. Beauregard, on April 12, ordered the Confederate batteries to open fire on Fort Sumter. The bombardment lasted over thirty-two hours, with the fort surrendering on April 13.

The proclamation of President Lincoln, issued soon after, calling upon the States for 75,000 troops to defend the Federal capital and enforce the laws, pushed the states of the upper South into secession.[4]

Burning with indignation and disbelief at the outrage committed against them by the Federal government, the Confederate government issued its own state call for volunteers to repel the threatened invasion of the Federal forces.

Are you for the South, or are you for the North? was the test question speciously put to all, thus appealing directly to the strongest passions of the heart, and at the same time, attacking the weakest points of man's nature.

Profile

General Lloyd Tilghman[1]

The Tilghman's genealogy in America can be traced back to 1659 when Dr. Richard Tilghman, an eminent surgeon and direct descendant of the great Duke, John of Gaunt, left London for the American colonies, where he obtained from the first Lord Baltimore a grant of one hundred acres of land in the colony of Maryland.[2] The Tilghman family were prominent in early American history. Lloyd's great, great, grandfather was Tench Francis Tilghman, a one time Attorney General of Pennsylvania, (1744-1752), and a confidant of George Washington. Lloyd's great grandfather was Matthew Tilghman, a member of the First Continental Congress of 1774. He would have been a signer of the Declaration of Independence but for the fact that he was called to Annapolis in June to preside over the convention which framed the first constitution of the State of Maryland. He was justly styled as the patriarch of the Maryland Colony.[3]

Lloyd was born at Rich Neck Manor near Claiborne in Talbot County, Maryland on January 18, 1816. He was the fourth child and only son of James and Anne Caroline Shoemaker Tilghman, and was named for his grandfather, Lloyd Tilghman.

Lloyd attended schools in Baltimore, and then entered the United States Military Academy at West Point, July 1, 1831, at the age of fifteen. He graduated July 1, 1836, forty-sixth in his class.

He was commissioned a Second-Lieutenant in the United States Army and assigned to The Dragoons, but resigned his commission on September 30, 1836 to accept the position of civil engineer of the Baltimore & Susquehanna Railroad. He was in that position until 1837.[4] He became an engineer in the survey of the Norfolk and Wilmington Canal. In 1838 he was engineer for the Eastern Shore Railroad and then with the Baltimore and Ohio Railroad until 1840. He afterwords supervised public improvement for the City of Baltimore.[5]

On May 26, 1843, Lloyd Tilghman married Augusta Murray Boyd. Her father, Joseph L. Boyd, had been the first Treasurer of the State of Maine and her aunt Elizabeth Southgate was married to Walter Browne, Mayor of the City of New York in 1833.

The couple were married in Portland, Maine. Their best man was Joseph Hooker, who later became Union General and one time Commander of the Army of Potomac.

With the beginning of the Mexican War in 1846, the thirty-two year old Tilghman enlisted as a volunteer aide-de-camp to General David E. Twiggs and accompanied him to Mexico. On May 8, 1846, Tilghman was engaged in the Battle of Palo Alto, and the next day the Battle of Resaca de La Palma.

During June of 1846, he supervised the construction of defenses at Matamoros, and on August 14, 1847 was made Captain of the Maryland and District of Columbia Volunteer Artillery, and remained with that unit until it was disbanded on July 13, 1848.[6]

Tilghman again left the Army, but soon found adventure and employment overseas. The discovery of gold in California in 1849 made the Isthmus of Panama an important link between the Eastern United States and California. All travelers by this route had to sail from the Atlantic Coast ports to Panama, and then cross the isthmus by boat, mule or on foot, and then board another vessel on the western side to set sail for California.

Panama was then part of Columbia and in 1850, the Columbian government granted permission to a group of businessmen from New York City to build a railroad across the isthmus. Tilghman was made principal assistant engineer of the Panama Division of The Isthmus Railroad, where he remained for over a year.

During this time, the Tilghman's were blessed with children. Upon returning to the United States in 1852, Tilghman, continued to follow railroad civil engineering opportunities, and moved his family to the river community of Paducah, Kentucky. Located on the southern bank of the Ohio River, at the confluence of the Tennessee River, it was a growing cosmopolitan community of about 3,000 people.

Robert Woolfolk built a two-story brick home for the Tilghmans at Seventh and Kentucky Avenues. By now the Tilghman's had eight children, including three sons: Lloyd, Jr.; Slidell and Frederick Boyd.

For the next eight years Lloyd was engaged in surveying and supervising the construction of southern railroads; one from Paducah to Memphis and another from Paducah to Mobile, Alabama.[7]

As the North and South became antagonistic on a great number of issues, Lloyd Tilghman became active in the Kentucky State Guard, and attained the rank of Lt. Colonel of the Western Kentucky Batallion, 3rd Infantry and 1st Battery.[8]

Keeping Kentucky neutral during the sectional crisis of early 1861 was ineffective. By June the direction of the state seemed to indicate that the majority incoming Legislature wished to stay in the Union.

The Kentucky State Guard, however, contained companies of southern sympathizers who favored the Southern position on secession. Both sides would soon test their beliefs in battle.

Chapter I

Paducah, Kentucky

The States of the Deep South were prompt in following the lead of South Carolina in passing ordinances of secession. However, in the early months of 1861 the states of Maryland, Virginia, North Carolina, Tennessee, Kentucky, Arkansas and Missouri were still in the Union.

Many people in the border states were reluctant to secede and break up the Union, although many of them believed in the constitutional right of secession and held that if the Deep South wished to leave the Union the Federal government had no right to keep them in the Union at bayonet point. It was generally believed that in the event of war the Upper South would cast their lot on the side of the Confederacy. With the firing on Fort Sumter at Charleston in April and Lincoln's call for volunteers to suppress the rebellion, these border states quickly held conventions of secession. Virginia seceded on April 17; Arkansas on May 6; North Carolina on May 20, and Tennessee on June 8; with conflicting sentiment continuing in Missouri and Kentucky.

President Abraham Lincoln requested four regiments of soldiers from Kentucky as part of his call for 75,000 volunteers for the Union, but Governor B. Magoffin refused, stating "I say, emphatically, Kentucky will furnish no troops for the wicked purpose of subduing her sister Southern States."[1]

Meanwhile political strife continued in the Legislature. Although the Kentucky legislature approved and endorsed the governor's refusal to send troops to President Lincoln, Magoffin's control over the state's military affair was tenuous.

In order to prepare to defend their state, the governor appointed Simon Bolivar Buckner as Inspector General of the State Guard. In a show of strength, Buckner ordered Colonel Tilghman with several State Guard companies to Columbus, Kentucky overlooking the Mississippi River, to guard the western water approaches of the state. Meanwhile, appropriations for the State Guard decreased drastically while the pro-Union voted money for a second militia to be called the Home Guard.

The Union newspapers in the state began to call for the disbanding of the pro-southern State Guard and for seizure of their weapons and arsenals. It was only a matter of time before Kentucky would declare her continued Allegiance to the Union.

Tilghman weighed his options and decided that the only avenue to pursue was to leave Paducah for the South. It had to be a momentous decision for the Tilghman family to decide to leave their home and friends of ten years. Their decision was to cast their lot with the new Confederacy. In the summer of 1861, Augusta with the children and five slaves, left Paducah and traveled up the Tennessee River on the steamboat *Dunbar* to Danville. Here they boarded the train that ran from Bowling Green to Memphis, and alighted at Clarksville, Tennessee, their new Confederate home.

Tilghman, remaining in Paducah, took time to recruit local citizens who wished to join the Southern cause. As an incentive, Tilghman paid from his own pocket the cost of transporting the men to Tennessee to enlist in the Confederate Army.[2]

When Tennessee seceded in June, hundreds of young restless Kentucky secessionists went singly or in small bodies over the state line into Tennessee to enlist at Camp Daniel Boone.[3]

The camp was located a few miles south of the Kentucky line and seven miles east of Clarksville and had only been open for a matter of weeks when Tilghman and his recruits arrived in the area. It was located within two miles of the Louisville & Nashville railroad, had wide flat fields, an abundance of water and ample forest for firewood. All pre-requisites for a training camp.[4]

Tilghman had arrived in the first week of July and was immediately put to the task of helping lay out the camp. Camp Boone was established for organizing the men into companies, and to begin their introduction to military life. The Kentucky enlistees were often organized on a town, county, or regional basis, thus Company D of the Third Kentucky Infantry was made-up entirely of men from Paducah.

Officers with experience were needed to organize and train these new recruits. Lloyd Tilghman with his military training and service was appointed Colonel of the 3d Regiment of Kentucky volunteers, Third Brigade, Second Division of Forrest Cavalry Corp.[5]

The regiment was organized July 5, 1861 and mustered into Confederate service the same day for a three-year enlistment period. Colonel Tilghman's appointment was confirmed July 19, and he accepted

Paducah, Kentucky

it September 1, 1861.[7]

The most serious weakness of the new companies were the lack of suitable weapons. Fortunately, weapons such as squirrel guns and double barreled shot guns had been carried along by the new recruits from their homes or they would have gone unarmed! Tennessee was stripped of its arms early in the year to be sent to Virginia; many of the newly formed units had few regulation firearms for training or fighting. This shortage of firearms plagued Tilghman for the next six months.

In the August elections in Kentucky, the secessionist party barely obtained a third of the members of the Kentucky House and thus the state remained in the Union.

Up to this time, General Buckner had remained neutral in spite of being enticed by both North and South with offers of a generalship if he went with their side. His decision, like Tilghman's, was to join the Confederacy. He, too, brought along many followers from the State and Home Guard.

Having lost Kentucky at the ballot box, the Confederate Government decided to seize Kentucky by force. Tilghman returned to Paducah in August with a recruiting Major and some staff to recruit for the Confederacy. Confederate occupation of the area, to some degree, was expected and this came to pass on the 4th of September. General Leonidas Polk moved into western Kentucky and seized Columbus and Hickman on the Mississippi River. The Stars and Bars now flew over the area and the secessionists hoped that the state would soon be taken by Confederate forces.

As the Confederates recruited men, built training camps and established supply depots, the Federals were doing the same thing on the opposite shore of the Ohio River. The Illinois Central Railroad collected troops and supplies in the north and brought them south to Cairo, Illinois. Cairo became the staging area of the new Federal Army and became headquarters for Brigadier General Ulysses S. Grant. He took command in September. This frontier boomtown was at the strategic confluence of the Mississippi and Ohio Rivers.

In response to the Confederates capturing Columbus and Hickman on the 4th of September, newly appointed Brigadier General Grant opted to move to check the Confederates advance by capturing Paducah. Traveling from Cairo by riverboat, his army of 5,000 soldiers debarked on the Illinois side opposite Paducah.

PROCLAMATION,
TO THE CITIZENS OF
PADUCAH!

I have come among you, not as an enemy, but as your friend and fellow-citizen, not to injure or annoy you, but to respect the rights, and to defend and enforce the rights of all loyal citizens. An enemy, in rebellion against our common Government, has taken possession of, and planted its guns upon the soil of Kentucky and fired upon our flag. Hickman and Columbus are in his hands. He is moving upon your city. I am here to defend you against this enemy and to assert and maintain the authority and sovereignty of your Government and mine. I have nothing to do with opinions. I shall deal only with armed rebellion and its aiders and abetors.

You can pursue your usual avocations without fear or hindrance. The strong arm of the Government is here to protect its friends, and to punish only its enemies. Whenever it is manifest that you are able to defend yourselves, to maintain the authority of your Government and protect the rights of all its loyal citizens, I shall withdraw the forces under my command from your city.

U. S. GRANT,
Brig. Gen. U. S. A., Commanding.

Paducah, Sept 6th. 1861.

In one of the greatest engineering feats of the war, Grant had a wooden pontoon bridge placed across the Ohio River! Constructed on 123 barges joined together the span was 3,000 feet long. When completed, Grant and his army marched across the Ohio River and entered Paducah on September 6.

The citizens were in awe. Grant said, "I never saw such consternation depicted on the faces of the people. Men, women, and children came out of their doors looking pale and frightened at the present of his troops. They had been expecting rebel troops that day."[9]

Grant added, "As we neared the city, Colonel Tilghman and a recruiting Major with a company raised in Paducah, left the city by railroad, taking with them all of the rolling stock."[10]

A parade of mounted bluecoats along with four military bands marched through the downtown Paducah and Grant issued a Proclamation to the citizens that they were now under northern control. The pontoon bridge remained across the Ohio River only until October 8. The Federals stayed for the balance of the war.[7]

On September 14, fifty-eight year old General Albert Sidney Johnston, second ranking general in the new Confederacy, arrived in Nashville to take over the vast frontier department that spread over 430 miles across Kentucky from the gaps of the Cumberland Mountains to the banks of the Mississippi River.

Johnston established the center of his defense at Bowling Green, Kentucky, seventy miles north of Nashville. S. B. Buckner, former commander of the Kentucky militia, was commissioned a Brigadier General in the Confederate Army and took command at Bowling Green with his Kentucky militia following him.

Johnston was taking command during a period of rapid change and had the misfortune to find himself with 15,000 untrained volunteers and few general officers. Johnston was called upon to organize, equip, train, and billet these newcomers as quickly as possible.[8] General Johnston appealed to Richmond for experienced general officers. Acting Secretary of War, Judah P. Benjamin replied, "There is an officer under your command whom you must have overlooked, whose claims in point of rank and experience qreatly outweighs those of others. I refer to Col. Lloyd Tilghman, whose record shows long and better service and who is besides a Kentuckian, especially appropriate to the command at Columbus. He, therefore, has been appointed Brigadier General; you will exercise your own discretion whether to place him in command at Columbus or not." Date October 18, 1861.[11]

Johnston did not assign Tilghman to Columbus, but rather used him at Hopkinsville to replace J. L. Alcorn who wanted to return to his native Mississippi. Tilghman now had a command as a Confederate General.

A Dual Biography: General Lloyd Tilghman & General Francis Shoup

Chapter II

Hopkinsville, Kentucky

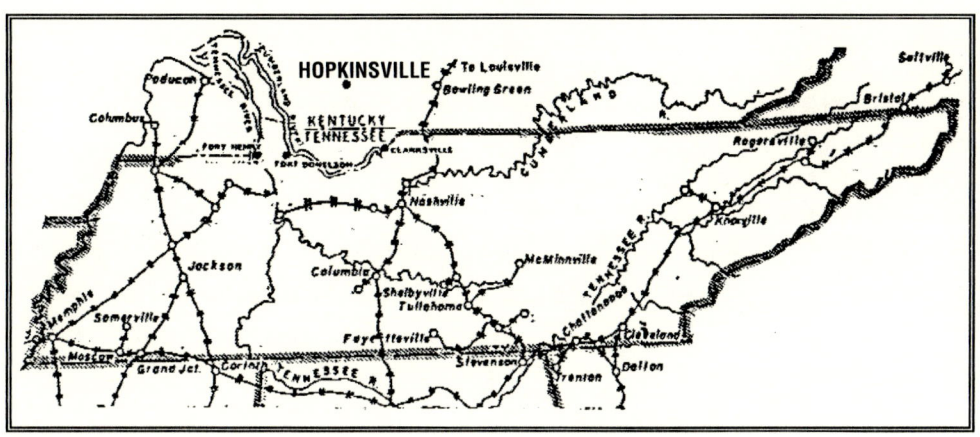

Hopkinsville, birth place of President Jefferson Davis, was the principle Confederate outpost in Kentucky and was located between Bowling Green and the Cumberland River. This small city was manned by a brigade of Mississippi volunteers who were a long way from home and with little knowledge of camp life in the field. General Tilghman, who arrived on the 28th, found the troops in a terrible state. Their morale was low and the poor boys were suffering from a ragging epidemic of diarrhea and pneumonia; not to mention 750 cases of measles.

In the filthy hospital at Hopkinsville, Tilghman, speaking from their bedsides, reported that "vermine could be seen and so offensive were their condition that it prevented the orderlies from attending to many of them."[1]

His infantry was so unfit for duty that the surgeon in charge stated that humanity demands these men should not be moved. Tilghman wired Johnston, "the raw troops are very raw, and it will take good handling to make them at all steady under the first fire in action. They are the poorest clad, shod, and armed body I have ever seen, but full of enthusiasm."[8]

Faced with a shortage of food, clothing and arms, Tilghman journeyed to Nashville seeking help in supplying his bedraggled troops. The task would not be simple.

A Dual Biography: General Lloyd Tilghman & General Francis Shoup

During the first nine months of 1861 the State of Tennessee borrowed over six million dollars from the State Banks to recruit, clothe and arm the Provisional Army of The Confederate States.[11] Nashville had been converted into a giant Confederate arsenal and depot with warehouses bursting with food, clothing, medicine, muskets, saddles, knapsacks and blankets. To his dismay Tilghman was turned away by the Nashville authorities. Now desperate, Tilghman attempted to purchase supplies on the open market at Bowling Green and elsewhere in Kentucky but soon discovered the farmers and merchants, badgered by both sides in the conflict, refused the Confederate and Tennessee paper money and demanded gold or Kentucky paper money which Tilghman did not hold.

Returning to Clarksville where his family was now living, he attempted to buy supplies on Confederate credit, but the Confederate line of credit had been halted in Tennessee when it became apparent that the State Banks were not receiving reimbursements for their monies from the authorities in Richmond.

A compassionate man, Tilghman had deep feelings about the suffering of the men in his command and accordingly took to the private sector to seek help. He approached the Benevolent Society of Clarksville to solicit their services for his men's needs. They agreed to make clothing and blankets at no cost provided the general would secure all of the material for them.

Tilghman learned of a clothier in town who had five bales of cloth of a jean material which totaled 1722 yards. It had been purchased earlier for Kentuckians quartermaster stores and was to be made into clothing for the 5th Regiment of the Kentucky volunteers. The cloth was in storage since August and the clothier said he knew of no one at Camp Boone to refer Tilghman to for further information about the material. The quick-thinking Tilghman said that most likely the material was forgotten and although he had no written authority, the persuasive Tilghman told them he wanted the material and must have it. The clothier accordingly delivered it over to him, and Tilghman quickly made good use of it.

Two hundred women of the Benevolent Society went to work making clothing and blankets for the men at Hopkinsville.[2] As fast as possible, Tilghman forwarded the finished works to camp and the beneficial efforts were soon seen in the improvement of the moral and physical condition of the whole command.

Hopkinsville, Kentucky

Undoubtedly, Tilghman's short stay at Hopkinsville was beneficial to the good of the service, but not beneficial for Tilghman as his depredations would be challenged by a higher authority at a later date.

On November 6, Gen. Ulysses Grant personally led a force of 3,000 bluecoats down the Mississippi River in transports and landed on the shore at Belmont across the river from General Polk's "Rock of Gibralter" at Columbus. In a day-long engagement, Polk's forces bested Grant and won a victory over the invaders. In spite of this win, Polk did not feel up to the task of also manning Forts Henry and Donelson in Tennessee, so he appealed to Richmond for some commander of large experience and military efficiency to be put in charge, adding "I beg to say that General Tilghman is better informed as to the military aspects and capabilities of the country and I would suggest he be put in charge of these defenses."[3]

Secretary of War Benjamin responded quickly and assigned Tilghman to the command of the two forts on November 14. Three days later, General Johnston ordered Tilghman to turn over his command at Hopkinsville and assume the command of Fort Donelson and Fort Henry and push forward to the completion of their works of completing them.[4] A significant piece of Johnston's defensive line hinged on the forts on the Cumberland and Tennessee rivers near the Kentucky border. If Kentucky did "fall" to the Union, Tennessee would be open to invasion on these watery corridors.

Union Military Strategy

Anna E. Carroll

Union strategy in 1861 was as muddled as was Confederates, but the Union had one advantage and her name was Anna E. Carroll.

Miss Carroll was born into a famous Maryland family. She lived on her father's plantation for most of her life. With the outbreak of the Civil War and after freeing her slaves, she began to write newspaper articles defending President Lincoln's war making power. In part because she was involved in the women's movement of that day, she was considered a controversial female figure of the war.

This reform activist wrote a series of pamphlets in the summer of 1861. One advocated Union forces to advance up the Tennessee and Cumberland Rivers rather than the Mississippi River.

In the fall of 1861, the Federal government prepared a gunboat fleet to go down the Mississippi River and begin the campaign in the deep south. Miss Carroll went to St. Louis and after a careful examination of the proposed plan, wrote to Union Attorney-General Edward Bates, the author of the expedition, that from her knowledge of the country and position of the Confederates, the mission would fail, and recommended that the fleet should, instead, be sent up the Tennessee River.

Miss Carroll sent letters and maps to the Federal War Department. She also sent a mass of information concerning the roads, bridges, towns and railway connections, which were very valuable to the Federals.

The papers were carefully examined, and the Federal authorities saw the importance of Miss Carroll's plans. Soon land and naval forces were massed on the Tennessee and Cumberland Rivers as she suggested.[5]

Miss Carroll received letters from many well-known public men of the day, and reported conversations with President Lincoln and Secretary Stanton.[6] All verified the existence of her plan.

Chapter III

The Twin River Forts

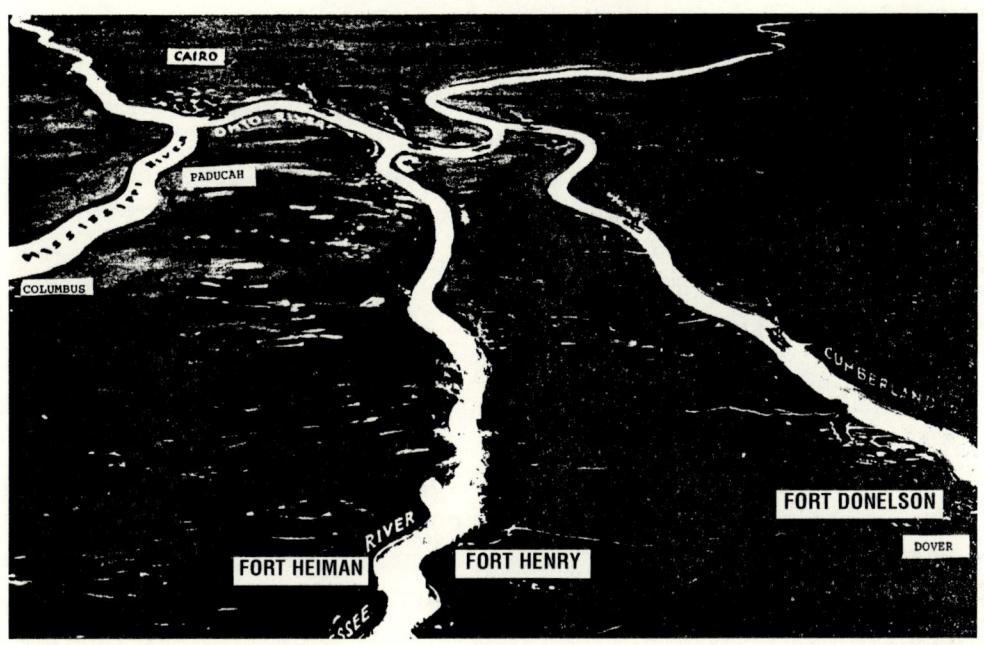

General Johnston at Nashville was faced with extremely limited resources and unseasoned troops. Along with Johnston, Tennessee's Gov. Isham Harris' primary concern was the defense of the Mississippi, Cumberland and Tennessee Rivers, in order to protect his state. Union forces, lacking strategic avenues of advancing into the south's heartland by railroad or overland, set their strategy to penetrating the Confederacy via these three waterways.

Any defensive Confederate forts to be built along the Tennessee and Cumberland rivers must be as far north in Tennessee as possible without violating Kentucky's neutrality. Selection of the best possible locations along these twin rivers was delegated to Daniel W. Donelson, a West Point graduate and engineer.

On the Cumberland River, Donelson reported that the strongest point was a high bluff on the west bank of the river a mile north of the village of Dover, Tennessee. This fort's purpose would be to protect Nashville, the capital of Tennessee, which was located down the Cumberland River. This fort was named Fort Donelson in honor of the engineer who was a member of the famous Donelson family which included the founder of Nashville, John Donelson, and also Rachel Donelson, the wife of Andrew Jackson.

In Donelson's judgement, there was no particularly good location for a fort on the Tennessee River near the Kentucky boundary. With some misgivings, Donelson selected a point on the east bank of the Tennessee River, located twelve miles west of Fort Donelson. This site was named Fort Henry in honor of Gustavus A. Henry, a Confederate Senator from Tennessee.

Next to control of the Mississippi, command of the Tennessee River was next in importance to that of the Mississippi River. It's main defensive purpose would be to obstruct and impede any invading Northern army or navy that was making a movement up the River to penetrate to Florence, Alabama.

Construction on the first of the twin forts was started at Fort Henry. In May of 1861, Adna Anderson, a civil engineer, chose the site for the fort south of Kirkman's old landing. The task of constructing Fort Henry was assigned to Col. Adolphus Heiman, along with a regiment of 10th Tennessee volunteers, a Confederate Irish Regiment. Construction was slow in the summer months of 1861 with inexperienced army volunteers, but some among the Irish of the Tenth were experienced railroad workers, use to heavy construction. The fort was located on a bend in the Tennessee River. It was to be a bastion that enclosed an area of about three acres, having an eighteen-foot dry moat surrounding earthen parapets. By the end of the summer, some breastworks had been completed by Colonel Heiman's Tennessee Volunteers.

At this time Albert Sidney Johnston gave Maj. Gen. Leonidas Polk the mission of fortifying and defending the Mississippi River. On September 4, violating the neutrality of Kentucky, Polk had seized Columbus, Kentucky. Governor Harris of Tennessee quickly transferred the command of Forts Henry and Donelson to General Polk.[2] Polk sent Cap. Jesse Taylor, a trained naval artillerist to take command of the guns to be mounted at Fort Henry. Taylor found that the fort was not in the right place and was a trap because it's highest point was far below the high-water mark of the Tennessee River and would be flooded by an ordinary spring freshet.[5]

The Twin River Forts

General Johnston, aware that the gateway to the heartland of the Confederacy was poorly guarded, sent a First Lieutenant Joseph Dixon, an engineer officer, to examine the two river positions. Dixon reported that Fort Donelson might have been better located, but, if the circumstances it would be better to retain it and strengthened it with outworks against it's landward approaches.[3]

In Dixon's opinion, "Fort Henry was not situated very favorably but he acknowledged that it was a strong works." He continued, "instead of abandoning it and re-locating to another point on the Tennessee," he suggested that it be completed and that an additional fortification be built across the river on the western banks atop Stewart's Hill."[4] This third fort was designated as Fort Heiman, named after the commander of Fort Henry, Col. Adelphus Heiman.

Maj. J. F. Gilmer, chief engineer for General Johnston inspected both fort locations on Oct. 26, and concurred with the others in their findings. At this time, Major Gilmer put into motion plans for the construction of Fort Heiman to be located opposite Fort Henry.[6]

The Federals in the middle of October sent the gunboat "Conestoga" up the Tennessee on a reconnaissance and threw several shells at the unfinished Fort Henry to measure location and range for their guns.[7]

The presence of Gilmer, Dixon and Taylor during the latter part of October saw a remarkable amount of energy put into both fortifications to bring them to completion.

By the 21st of November, Lt. Dixon reported that he had completed the new battery on the Cumberland River and was preparing to mount the cannon in it. He also laid out a small work on the ridge and mounted two nine pounders. Trees were felled around the encampment to clear fields of fire and to create obstructions to enemy attack.[8]

At Fort Henry on the Tennessee, J. F. Gilmer requested four eight inch Columbiads, four other heavy guns of long range and four thirty-two pounders. These were to be delivered with platforms, chassis, and carriages complete with fifty rounds of ammunition for each gun.[9]

General Tilghman hastened to his new assignment of bringing into "perfect shape" the fortifications on the Cumberland and Tennessee Rivers.[10]

After meeting with Gilmer, Tilghman reported to General Johnston that light batteries should be added to each fort and the absolute necessity of occupying the opposite bank of the Tennessee River, now designated as Fort Heiman.

Tilghman not only wanted the erection of Fort Heiman with several heavy guns, but also the occupation at an advanced point with a small force aided by a field battery. Later in the month the Twenty-Seventh Alabama Infantry Regiment was assigned to Fort Heiman to serve this purpose.[11]

Fortunately for Tilghman, he received some assistance from Brig. Gen. Gideon Pillow in Polk's command. It occurred that some citizens of North Alabama became concerned about the effectiveness of Fort Henry and approached Pillow for his opinion on the matter. Pillow told them directly that he did not consider the defense of the Tennessee River to be very adequate. The patriots then inquired of Pillow what could they do to help the cause? Pillow's reply to them was in the form of a request for several thousand volunteers, to be stationed on the Tennessee River; 5,000 if they can be raised, to help with the construction of the forts.[12]

General Johnston wired Gov. A. B. Moore of Alabama that as fast as they can be organized, equipped, and mustered in they will be transported down the Tennessee River to Fort Henry. "I recommend that the slave laborers shall be sent forward from the same point."[13]

S. D. Weakley was named side-de-camp to Pillow and in charge with the duty of mustering in the troops. Weakley announced he proposed to raise a regiment of men past middle life to serve during this emergency and the whole force would be armed with shot-guns and rifles.[14] Great credit must be given to now Captain Dixon of the Engineers whose unceasing labor enabled both Forts Henry and Heiman be completed by the end of January, not to mention through the efforts of The Soldier / Volunteers.

Tilghman reported to Richmond, "The strengthening of Fort Henry, the building of all the outworks around it, together with the advanced state of the new works at Fort Heiman, together with its line of outworks, of rifle pits, and abatis, was all thoroughly performed when re-enforcements arrived."[15]

Tilghman connected both Forts Henry and Donelson by a telegraph line from Cumberland City with a total distance of about thirty five miles, thus placing them in communications with Bowling Green and Columbus.[16]

On January 15, 1862, Lt. Col. M. A. Hayes, Chief of The Corps of Tennessee Artillery, arrived from Columbus to take charge of the artillery forces at all points. Tilghman directed him to Fort Donelson to take charge

The Twin River Forts

while he would remain in command at Fort Henry.

Every preparation to meet an attack at the three forts progressed favorably for Tilghman except for the most important, the much needed artillery. Efforts throughout the fall to procure cannon from Richmond, Memphis, and other points failed miserably.

It would appear that cannon which was not needed at Columbus, Bowling Green, Nashville and other Confederate positions, found its way slowly to the twin forts. "Many of the guns were defective and even dangerous declared one ordinance officer! One battery from the Memphis foundry lost three guns in a month by bursting, one of them in the battle of Belmont, November 7."[17]

When Tilghman inspected a battery of two iron 6-pounders and two bronze 9-pounders made at a Clarksville, Tennessee foundry, "He declared them to be worthless. The 9-pounders were of very little account and all the guns were mounted in a wretched manner. He fumed about a total ignorance of all mechanical principles evidenced in the construction of the carriages."[18]

During this ten week period, Tilghman had taken the three unfinished forts and molded them into a strong defensive system given the circumstances. The wretched military position of Fort Henry, compelled Tilghman to concentrate his efforts on land, within the riflepits. "In case I deemed it possible to do more than to operate solely against the attack by the river, I placed the 10th Tennessee and the 4th Mississippi regiments, around the camp and given instructions as to the exact ground each was to occupy.[19] The work itself was well built; it was completed long before I took command, but strengthened greatly by myself in building embrasures and epaulements of sand bags. Everything was arranged to make a formidable resistance against anything like fair odds."[20]

By this time Fort Henry was the position of first strategic value in Johnston's defensive line. It linked General Polk's position at Columbus with that of Fort Donelson and General Johnston's forces at Bowling Green and Nashville. If this line were broken, it would mean serious consequences for Johnston's overall defensive strategy.

Faced with dire circumstances, there still remained time for petty and trivial matters. Tilghman needed full co-operation from all departments, but a minor incident in the early days went back to his service at Hopkinsville.

When General Buckner at Bowling Green learned that Tilghman had requisitioned the cloth at Hopkinsville belonging to his Kentucky Commissary Department, he became vindictive and brought charges against Tilghman on January 3, 1862, claiming "conduct to the prejudice of good order and military discipline."[21] But it was Buckner's off the the cuff remark that revealed the truth. "I decided that this is probably the only course left to prevent the improper interference of General Tilghman with the command and administrative duties of other officers."

Perhaps Buckner was merely attempting to curtail Tilghman's abrupt manner and constant complaints of shortages whom irritated many who dealt with him. It only got worse after he was appointed a Brigadier General.

In a blistering handwritten letter to Buckner on January 26, Tilghman in no uncertain words outlined and defended his actions.

"My position was a critical one at Hopkinsville and nothing but good resulted from my action. As to any inconvenience of your 2nd Brigade, Kentucky Volunteers may have sustained the beneficial effects at Hopkinsville balances out to the bad against the other troops."[22]

Concluding, he told General Buckner "this trivial matter should have been resolved in Nashville with a personal meeting."[23] No Court of Inquiry was ever held and no personal meeting took place. There was not time for it as the bluecoats were advancing.

As trivial as this rift may appear, Tilghman later claimed he never received adequate support and that he was cast on his own resources and compelled him to "bend the rules" to accomplish an end.[24]

Chapter IV

The Collapse of Fort Heiman

General Johnston's thin line of defense held for only eight weeks before it began to unravel. On the eastern end of the line in late 1861, newspaperman and newly appointed Brig. Gen. Felix Kirk Zollicoffer with a small inexperienced force invaded southeastern Kentucky through the Cumberland Gap.

This rash movement brought the attention of the Federal command who gave battle to Zollicoffer's small legion at Logan Crossroad on January 18, 1862.

In a pouring rain storm, the nearsighted Zollicoffer, while trying to study the field of battle, rode by error into Col. Speed S. Fry's Fourth Kentucky Union infantry who fired upon the unwelcomed stranger.

Fifty-four year old Zollicoffer fell dead from his saddle. The leaderless and dispirited Confederates abandoned their position and guns and hurriedly crossed back over the Cumberland River, unhinging Johnston's defenses and shaking public confidence in him as the overall commander.

Meantime on the Western end of the new line, the Union strategy was simple. A joint attack by land and naval forces was agreed upon by U.S. Grant and his naval counterpart, Andrew H. Foote. Grant's invading force would be put ashore on the eastern bank of the Tennessee River and march south towards Fort Henry while at the same time, on the west bank of the river, Gen. C. F. Smith's infantry was to force its way down the Kentucky side of the river bank towards Fort Heiman.

Commodore Foote's flotilla of gunboats, teamed with steamboats used as troop transports, were the river force which would attack Fort Henry.

The build-up of Confederate forces on the Tennessee River over the six month period had been done sporadically, but by this time Tilghman had an aggregate of 2,600 forces scattered on the Tennessee River at Fort Henry, Fort Heiman, Paris Landing five miles south of the fort and at Bailey's Landing, three miles north of the fort. A light battery and rocket guard completed Tilghman's force.[1]

Throughout the month of January, 1862, heavy rains had been falling and the twin rivers began rising which would permit the Union strike force to sail up the rivers. Riding the flood waters of the river, the Union gunboat *Lexington* on January 21, came up the Tennessee and after chasing a small makeshift Confederate gunboat, fired twelve shells into Fort Henry.[2]

The next day the *Lexington* returned to reconnoiter the fort and again shelled the fort but this time the Tilghman's gunners returned the fire with shots from their thirty-two pounder.

General Tilghman was alerted by his cavalry scouts that General Smith's Union force had landed and were coming down the west bank of the river with 2,000 infantry and two hundred cavalry. The Bluecoats made camp on the Murray Road which led to Fort Heiman.[3]

The Union officers and men were equally untried and were no more experienced at warfare than were the Confederates. Thus the rain and mud slowed their advance and it became necessary for them to establish an encampment for the men and animals. This resulted in a two-week delay in their advance.

Meantime, Tilghman still waiting for cannon, tried to finish the uncompleted Fort Heiman.

Most of the fort's men were new to military life and had just volunteered for service with the Confederacy. They were not drilled properly,

The St. Louis, a vessel that saw action on the Mississippi from the battle of Columbus to Forts Henry and Donelson to Vicksburg.[4]

were poorly equipped and very indifferently armed with double barreled shot-guns and old Tennessee musket or rifles. None of the cavalry had

The Collapse of Fort Heiman

either sabers or pistols, and were only partly armed with whatever weapons they brought with them.

The appearance of the gun-boat *Lexington* in January, something never seen before on western rivers, undoubtedly instilled fear of the unknown into many of these new recruits. These iron-clad monsters were menacing and frightening. With a one hundred and seventy-five foot long superstructure, it was about the largest thing afloat the men had ever seen. The bows and bulwarks consisted of three feet of oak timber, bolted together and covered with wrought iron plates, two and a half inches thick. They were fifty feet in breadth, drew only five feet when loaded, and their very width in proportion to their length gave them a steadiness in action, almost that of a stationary land-battery. They had gun ports for nine to thirteen

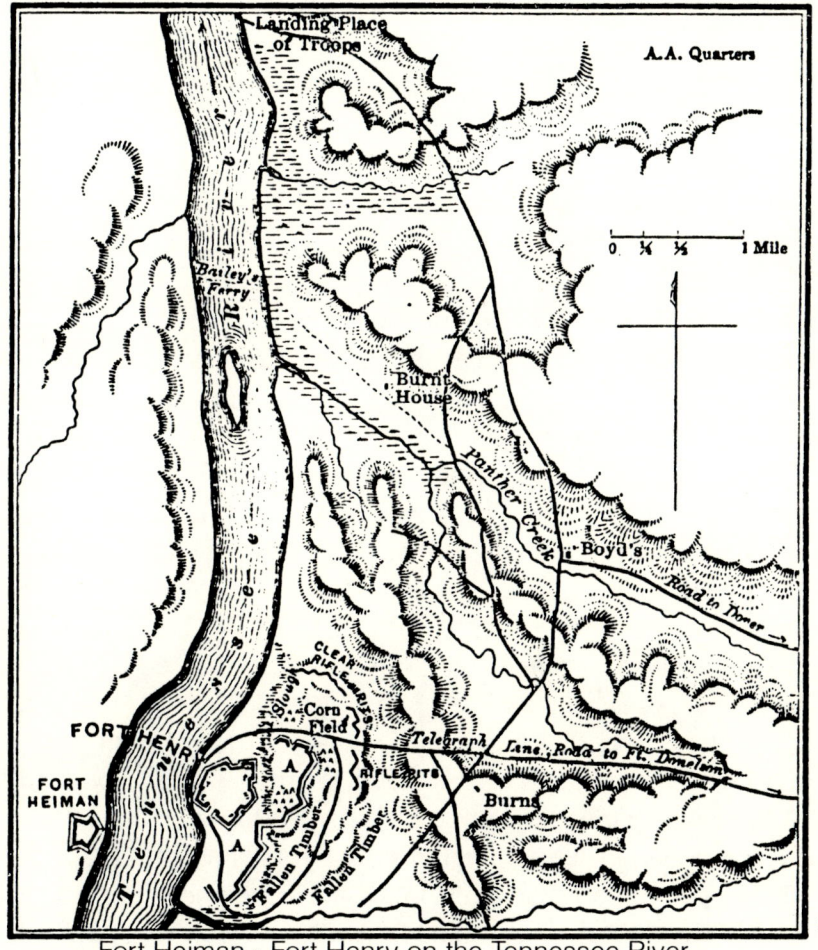

Fort Heiman - Fort Henry on the Tennessee River.

Columbiads and the bow gun was a rifled cannon. They packed a volume of fire-power never yet tested by the Union Navy.

By February 2, Flag-Officer Andrew H. Foote's Union floatilla was on their way from Cairo, Illinois for the coming invasion of Tennessee.

On the 4th at 4:30 a.m., the Confederate sentinel at Bailey's Landing down river sent up a rocket signal announcing the approach of the Union gunboats and transports. Heavy thunderstorms had raged the previous twenty-four hours making the roads thick with mud. The marching Bluecoats on land were getting behind schedule in advancing on the two forts. Inside Fort Henry, Colonel Heiman was experiencing the worst of military nightmares as the Tennessee River began rising and flowing into the lower part of the fort. Shortly after daylight the pickets on both sides of the river reported a large fleet approaching. The smoke from several gunboats became visible in the distance near Panther Island.

Colonel Heiman had a force of men at work on the epaulements at Fort Henry trying to keep the water out of the fort. The lower magazine was already under two feet of water. The ammunition had been removed to a temporary magazine above ground.

With the approach of the flotilla, the eleven guns in the fort bearing on the river were immediately manned and everything held in readiness for the attack. By 9 a.m., the gunboats commenced firing their shells at the quarters of the pickets and other buildings at Bailey's Landing. They also began landing cavalry. By noon five gunboats came into sight in the main channel. All Confederate troops, except the artillery force, were marched out of range of the Federal guns. The gunboats formed in line of battle across the channel about two miles below (north) of the fort. At about one o'clock, they opened fire with shell and shot, which was immediately returned by Heiman's rifled gun and the ten-inch Columbiad. The rifled gun was fired quickly and with good effect while the Columbiad on the fourth shot became disabled. As the gunboats advanced closer to the fort, Heiman's men opened with the eleven guns which were bearing on the river. The engagement lasted for half an hour. Some of the Union shots fell in and around the fort and others fell a quarter of a mile beyond the fort. After this heated exchange, the gunboats withdrew for the day.

Colonel Heiman wired Tilghman at Fort Donelson that the Federals were landing a large force three miles north of Fort Henry. The Colonel added that he was convinced that he could not hold Fort Heiman on the

The Collapse of Fort Heiman

opposite heights and he thought that it would be prudent to move these forces back to Fort Henry.

On Heiman's request, Tilghman came in person to the fort. He arrived at midnight with Major Gilmer's Corps of Engineers and three companies of cavalry. Lieutenant Colonel Hayes of the Artillery, joined them later.

On the 5th, Tilghman at Fort Heiman, directed the removal of all forces from Fort Heiman except the three companies of cavalry which would stay as scouts. His reasoning was that with heavy muddy roads, the Federal infantry could do little to harm Fort Henry if they ever did arrive at Fort Heiman. Without adequate cannon, Fort Heiman became an ineffective defense and thus had to be abandoned.

Tilghman was ferried back to Fort Henry at 8 a.m., bringing with him the Alabama brigade. He ordered them to take a position with the main body of troops outside of the backwater. They were detailed to throw up earth to keep the rising Tennessee out of the gunpowder magazine and to extend a temporary earthen bridge across the flooding backwater as an avenue of escape.

Soon the main body of the Federal advance guard, composed of a regiment skirmished with Tilghman's pickets. Tilghman moved out in person with ten companies of infantry and cavalry, but found that the Unionists had retired for the day. During the night Grant was reinforced by the arrival of a large number of transports.

That night Tilghman stayed aboard the steamer *Dunbar* which lay about a mile and a half south of the fort.[6] Early morning of the 6th revealed heavy black smoke rising over Panther Island, indicating that the Federal flotilla was in motion. Grant's and Smith's land forces were also on the move toward the fort. The Battle was about to begin.

Returning to the fort, Tilghman made a quick assessment of the situation. Grant on the eastern bank of the river had about 12,000 Bluecoats and cavalry between Bailey's Landing and the fort; Smith on the opposite west bank was moving south towards Fort Heiman with 7,000 infantry and cavalry. At the bend in the river, Commodore Foote had a gunboat with 54 cannon. In the fort, Tilghman had 2,600 unseasoned troops and 11 poor cannon. The situation was grim.

As the General Officer in charge of the forts, Tilghman had several options. He could abandon Fort Henry because of the overwhelming odds that graced him, or he could retire with his troops to Fort Donelson, leaving Colonel Heiman to defend the works. General Tilghman decided to remain at the fort with Colonel Heiman and a small company of rookie artillerists and fight until compelled to surrender. Realizing the precarious position of his forces in the fort area, he ordered them out of the fort and away from the range of the fleets powerful guns.

Tilghman had decided on the soldiery course to honorably conduct a defense against the coming attack. He and his men had been thrust into an untenable position because of the disparity of views between the Secretary of War and the Military Committee of the Confederate Congress in arming and defending the two forts.

The Collapse of Fort Heiman

Confederates built Fort Henry during the first year of the civil War on low ground beside the Tennessee River. From a wartime sketch.[7]

A Dual Biography: General Lloyd Tilghman & General Francis Shoup

Chapter V

The Surrender of Fort Henry

After the naval reconnaissance on February 4, it became apparent to Commodore Foote that the heavily wooded Panther Island located a mile north of the fort and off center in the river, created a "chute" or rapids on the west side of the island. Tilghman made the same observation. He ordered twelve torpedoes be placed in the "chute" on the western side of the island, hoping to force the gunboats to use the main channel on the east side of the island which was in range of the forts artillery. "Foote, taking into consideration the high stage of the river, caused by the recent heavy rains, deemed it best to attack up the western chute. If he were to do this, the torpedoes would have to be removed."[1]

Under orders from Grant to make a coordinated attack, the gunboats of Foote pushed forward towards the fort. Foote's first division of three wooden boats moved to the west of Panther Island, through the "chute". The *Tyler* and *Conestoga* succeeded in removing six torpedoes. The other torpedoes had been torn loose and carried down river by the swift current.

The wooden gunboats preceded the ironclads in moving through the "chute" at Panther Island on February 6, 1862.

Following the wooden ships was the second division made up of the ironclads. The *Cincinnati* was the flag ship; followed by the *Carondelet* and the *St. Louis*, each carrying thirteen guns and the *Essex*, carrying nine guns.[2] They successfully moved through the "chute" and emerged at the head of Panther Island. They were within a mile of the fort. Because of the swollen river, the guns of the boats and those of the fort were nearly on the same level, giving the Federals equal advantage.

The four ironclads formed a line of battle and the *Cincinnati* opened the firing, soon followed by the other three gunboats.

Inside the fort, General Tilghman and Colonel Heiman took position at the center battery to observe the gunboats as they approached. The Federals opened with shot and shell about noon. Their fire was returned by the forts heavy seacoast fortress cannon brought from Mobile. Then the gunboats came into range of the lighter guns. Soon all eleven guns of the fort were firing.[4]

The firing from both sides was furious, and the rookie gunners handled themselves well and stood by their guns but the combined fire of the Union fleet began to take its toll. First, the twenty-four pound rifled gun exploded, disabling every man at the piece; then a shell from the fleet exploded at the mouth of one of the thirty-two pounders, ruined the gun, and wounded all the men serving it. A premature explosion of a forty-two pounder killed three men and wounded others. A priming-wire accidentally spiked the ten-inch Columbiad. Use of the 32 and 42 pounders was lost when the gunners found that they had not the proper ammunition for them.

Within an hour and a half, General Tilghman had five men killed, eleven wounded, and five missing and four guns disabled. The gun captains were ordered by Tilghman to concentrate upon one particular vessel.[3] The *Cincinnati* which was in the lead, flying the Flag-Officer's pennant, took thirty-one shots, some of them passing through her completely.

The *Essex* was badly crippled by a missile that went into her side forward port, through her heavy bulkheads, and squarely through one of her boilers. Capt. W. D. Porter and his young aide, C. P. Britton, Jr. and his paymaster were standing in a direct line of the balls passing. Mr. Britton, being in the center of the group, was decapitated and his brains were scattered in every direction, thus earning him a place among Union heroes as the "Boy Britton" of Forcyethe Wilson's poem.[6] The exploding boiler killed the *Essex's* two pilots and several men, who were badly scalded, jumped over-

The Surrender of Fort Henry

board and drowned in the cold Tennessee. The disabled gunboat drifted down river carrying with it ten dead and twenty-three wounded and five missing from one Columbiad shot.

Gun-deck of one of the Mississippi gun-boats engaged in the attach on Fort Henry. – Sketched by Mr. Alexander Bixplot.[7]

In spite of the damage inflicted on the Union fleet, the shot and shell from the gunboats continued to fall upon the fort for over two hours. It was evident the fort could not hold out much longer. Gilmer and Heiman called Tilghman's attention to the state of affairs and said it was useless to hold out any longer. The Union gunboats were only 600 yards from the fort and their close-in fire was deadly. At 200 feet, knowing full well that the fort was finished, they began sweeping the entire fort with their guns ripping the fort's parapet to pieces.

When General Tilghman was advised of the state of affairs, he would not entertain the idea of a surrender, stating that he had as yet lost but few men and inquired the reason why some of the guns had ceased firing? He was told of the men being killed and wounded and the rest were exhausted, and that there were no men to relieve them. At this statement, General Tilghman threw off his coat, sprang on the chassis of the nearest gun, stating that he would work it himself. "I shall not give up the work," he replied and then ordered Colonel Heiman to get fifty men of his regiment to assist the remaining gunners in the fort. Heiman started out of the fort himself to find some men, but before he could reach his command, the huge gunboats were so close to the fort that further resistance was foolish. Tilghman was aware the rising Tennessee River was quickly turning his fort's levees of dirt into a ten foot high wall of mud. The odds were overwhelming. The gunboats fifty-four cannons continued to blast away and Grant's Army was expected at any time. Tilghman's mind turned to saving his infantry and cavalry encamped at the outside of the fort. He sent Colonel Heiman with instructions to his commanders to withdraw their forces as quickly as possible and move to Fort Donelson on the other side of the peninsula. By now, the volunteers were frightened. They soon retired, moving eastward, not on the Dover road, but along the telegraph lane.

While his army retreated, General Tilghman ordered his Captain to strike the colors and the flag was lowered. Commodore Foote ordered his vessels to cease firing and to stand by. A small yawl was put out from Fort Henry carrying Tilghman's adjutant. Approaching the flag ship, the Confederate officer relayed the message that General Tilghman wished to communicate with the flag officer and requested permission to come aboard. Two officers were dispatched to take possession of the fort while at the same time assuring Tilghman that his men would be permitted to retain their side arms and be treated with the highest consideration due prisoners-of-war. On February 6, General Tilghman, with twelve officers and sixty-six men in the fort, and sixteen men in the hospital boat surrendered Fort Henry unconditionally.

As the Union flag was raised over the fort, General Tilghman was escorted to the *Cincinnati* where he met Commodore Foote. Tilghman remarked, "I am glad to surrender to so gallant an officer."

Foote replied, "You do perfectly right, Sir, in surrendering, but you should have blown my boats out of the water before I would have surrendered to you."[8]

Because of the muddy road, Grant's floundering infantry did not reach the fort until after the naval bombardment was over. He ordered his cavalry to chase after Heiman's train and harass it as much as possible. Heiman's rear guard put up a spirited fight as the weary column made its way to Fort Donelson, arriving at 2:00 a.m. the next morning. They had marched twenty miles over a very bad road, through high creeks, while being harassed by the enemy.

After Grant's arrival, Commodore Foote turned the fort and its captured property over to him. On this same day, several of the Federal wooden boats continued up the Tennessee River and destroyed the railroad bridge of the Memphis & Ohio. They cleared all Confederate craft and shore resistance along the way until they reached Muscle Shoals at Florence, Alabama. The South had been pierced.

The abrupt collapse of Fort Henry stunned the new Confederate government at Richmond. It finally brought attention to the Richmond authorities that the western line of defense was in serious difficulty. "The authorities, both State and Confederate, are to blame for this disaster to our army," said Lt. Col. Randal W. McGavock.[9]

How could a fort, culmination of five months planning and construction, fall in a two-hour engagement? Tilghman, in his report to Col. W. W. Mackall at Bowling Green explained, "Against such overwhelming odds as 16,000 well-armed men (exclusive of the force on the gunboats) to 2,610 badly armed, in the field, and fifty-four heavy guns against eleven medium ones in the fort, no tactics or bravery could avail.[10] The rapid movements of the enemy, with every facility at their command, rendered the defense from the beginning, a hopeless one."[11]

"Had I been re-enforced, so as to have justified my meeting, the enemy at the advanced works, I might have made good the land defense on the east bank. I made no inquiry as to why I was not, for I have entire confidence in the judgement of my commanding general."[12]

Lt. Col. Milton A. Hayes reported, "I considered the defense of Fort Henry a military necessity in order to cover the retreat of our small army."[13] Also, Tilghman reasoned that a defense of Forts Henry and Heiman would aid Fort Donelson by buying time for reinforcements to arrive from Bowling Green, Clarksville and Columbus. He was correct in this assumption.

General Tilghman was praised by Colonel Heiman. He said, "I may be permitted to state that the self-sacrificing heroism displayed by Tilghman in this terrible and most unequal struggle challenges the admiration of all gallant men and entitles him to the gratitude of the whole people of the Confederate States. His tact and skill while in command of the defense of the Tennessee and Cumberland Rivers proved him a most skillful and gallant leader."[14]

On the other hand, there was much criticism of General Tilghman throughout the south. He was vilified for the surrender of the fort and men. Words such as treason, treachery and avoidance of duty were uttered by the uninformed public. General Tilghman was aboard the flag-ship *Cincinnati* as a prisoner of war. The ironclad returned downstream and put him ashore at Paducah, his old home town. But there was no cheering for him on his arrival as he was placed in the custody of Brig. Gen. W. T. Sherman.

General Grant, savoring the capture of his first Confederate general in the war, and in the absence of any firm Federal policy toward prisoners, suggested that Tilghman and the men be held incommunicado in confiscated Secessionist homes where they might have the freedom of the town while awaiting their paroles.[15] General Sherman told Tilghman that he and the other prisoners would be sent to either St. Louis or Cincinnati for parole.[16] When Federal authorities realized that Paducah was Tilghman's former home town, Grant suggested that Tilghman be sent to Cairo, Illinois, which was done. Secretary of War Edwin M. Stanton telegraphed his opposition to any parole and ordered Tilghman to be transferred to the Alton, Illinois prison north of St. Louis. Learning of this, Tilghman fired off a personal letter to Brig. Gen. T. L. Crittenden, USV, objecting to his removal instead of being paroled as promised by Sherman. This appeal was never answered and on February 17, General Tilghman was on his way up the Mississippi River to be incarcerated as a prisoner of war at the Alton prison. There was to be no parole.[17]

General Tilghman's report of the details and actions at Fort Henry is reproduced at page 122 in end notes.

Chapter VI

The Surrender of Fort Donelson

General Grant had driven a wedge into Johnston's line and Johnston, now at Nashville, was confronted with the problem of how best to utilize his untrained army.

Nashville, the Capital of the State of Tennessee, had not been fortified up to this time and it became Johnston's conviction that the fight to hold Nashville and Tennessee must be made at Fort Donelson.[1]

Even before he had received news of the surrender of Fort Henry, Johnston had sent telegrams to his commanders putting his strategy into motion. With the capitulation of Fort Henry, he ordered the evacuation of all positions in Kentucky and the forces be sent to Fort Donelson on the Cumberland River. On the 9th, Brig. Gen. G. J. Pillow arrived from Clarksville with 2,800 men. Before leaving Clarksville and again when he arrived at Dover he announced that the "watchword" for Fort Donelson was "Liberty or Death".[2] General Polk sent 1,800 men from Columbus. Brig. Gen. J. B. Floyd's regiments sent from Virginia arrived while Brig. Gen. S. B. Buckner's forces at Russellville joined, adding an additional 8,000 more Confederate reinforcements.

At Fort Donelson immediately after the capture of Fort Henry, there were, including the troops that Colonel Heiman had removed from Fort Henry, about six thousand effective men, now commanded by Brig. Gen. Bushrod Johnson, who had replaced the captured Tilghman. By the night of February 12, the fort was crowded with about 18,000 anxious Confederates ready to avenge the loss of Fort Henry.

Fort Donelson had been built by soldiers and leased slaves over a seven month period. North of the village of Dover it was a bastioned earthwork of logs and earth located on fifteen acres of the west bank of the Cumberland River. The earthworks was ten feet high, elevated one hundred feet above the shoreline.

Although Fort Donelson had been Tilghman's headquarters, he had few structural changes except to add armament when available. Within the fort there was one large howitzer and two small twelve pounders.

Water batteries had been constructed under the direction of Col. J. F.

31

A Dual Biography: General Lloyd Tilghman & General Francis Shoup

Gilmer. The lower battery had a ten-inch Columbiad and nine thirty-two pounders; the upper batter had a rifled piece with two thirty-two pound cannonades.

General Johnston, instead of traveling in person to the fort to assume command, sent three commanders of nearly equal rank which quickly became a divided and ineffective triumvirate.

The three generals came with divergent personalities, personal antagonisms and uncertainties of action, their motions would cancel whatever dim hope there may have been that General Johnston could defend Nashville by holding Fort Donelson.[3]

John B. Floyd, by virtue of his seniority and rank took command of the fort and was arguably the worst General the Confederacy would ever have; next in seniority was Gideon J. Pillow, definitely a bad general; and the junior of them was Simon B. Buckner, usually a competent officer.[4]

The arriving Confederates were given ample time to settle into their new position. The Federal flotilla needed seven days turnaround, i.e. to

Fort Donelson[5]

The Surrender of Fort Donelson

move back down the Tennessee to Cairo where they replenished supplies and ammunition, repair their damaged boats and then load additional infantry on board for Grant's invading forces. When loaded, the Federal flotilla ascended the Ohio River and entered the Cumberland River.

General Grant rode over from Fort Henry and made a personal reconnaissance of Fort Donelson, on the 7th, and discovered it next to impossible to move his infantry and cavalry because of the high water, rain and muddy bottomland. With a change in the weather on the 11th, Grant did begin moving his army across the twelve mile peninsula and marched virtually unopposed except for some limited skirmishing with Forrest's cavalry.

By evening, the Federal forces were firmly implanted on the land side of the fort's outer works and spread in a semi-circle upon the nearby hills.

An unexpected change in the February weather saw a cold front sweep in from the north over the Cumberland River and the mild rain turned to a blizzard of fine sleet and then wet snow. The temperature dipped to 10° F. The suffering began.

Within the fort's boundry the camped Confederates struggled to keep warm. One hundred log huts had been built earlier and this helped provide some relief but when the temperature got below freezing, many soldiers became frostbitten; others paced away the frigid night trying to keep warm. The men were forbidden to light fires because of the Union sharpshooters. The only food was hardtack and without fires there were no hot meals or coffee for the men to warm themselves. Soldiering began to look less glamorous.

The boys in blue had it no better. Aside from some seasoned troops from Missouri, Grant's regiments had come from the recruit depots in Illinois, Indiana and Ohio. They were so freshly formed that they had hardly changed their civil garb for soldier's uniforms before they were hurried on to the front.[6] They were not prepared for frigid weather and their shelter tents had not arrived. Confederate sharpshooters were also active so to light a fire at night was to invite a bullet. Some had abandoned their coats and blankets and then suffered from the bitter cold. With guns, caissons and wagons frozen to the earth on both sides it is surprising that the next day the Federal's were able to launch an attack. Grant had mustered a force of 15,000 men and eight field batteries for the affair. He had with him the brigades of Gens. Lew Wallace, C. F. Smith and John A. McClernand.

A Dual Biography: General Lloyd Tilghman & General Francis Shoup

The assault was beaten back by the Confederates in the outer defenses and Grant's men would have to be content to wait in the cold for another twenty-four hours until the Federal floatilla arrived.

Fort Donelson National Battlefield
Reconstructed Log Hut
This log hut is representative of the 100 huts built within the walls of Fort Donelson by the Confederate garrison. Here, a National Park Service Ranger portrays the life of the Confederate soldier at Fort Donelson.
FD-5   Photo by: © James P. Bagsby
© Eastern National Park & Mon. Assoc.

On the 14th, the ironclads and their wooden escorts appeared steaming up the Cumberland on schedule, and began to bombard the fort.

Their fire was immediately returned by the more powerful Confederate cannon mounted on shore, which due to the admirable position of these guns, enabled them to fire shells into the holds of the ships and cripple their machinery.[7] During the day-long battle, the Commodore's flagship was hit fifty-nine times, wounding Foote and incapacitating his boat. Two other ironclads lost their steering from direct hits and drifted aimlessly down the Cumberland. The more effective and powerful Confederate cannons had won the day as the gunboats retreated. For reasons known but to the timid General Floyd, who was in command of the fort, instead of being encouraged by the day's Naval victory, talked the other generals into the idea that the best thing for them to do was to cut their way out of the fort and retire

The Surrender of Fort Donelson

upon the Charlotte Road and make a move to Nashville. This would mean a stiff fight the next day but the plan was adopted. At 5 a.m. on the 15th, in freezing weather, G. Pillow moved forward to assault the Federal line. He was aided by Buckner's division and after a morning's fighting, the Federal line on Grant's right was broken and the avenue of escape was thus opened for the Confederates. But again, Floyd managed to snatch defeat from the jaws of victory.

Instead, General Pillow, flushed with his success, attempted altogether too much and attacked General Wallace's position in hopes of rolling his troop back into C. F. Smith's position and then turn the whole Federal line. In this he was aided by S. Buckner, but the combined advance made little headway during the afternoon. The men were worn out from the weather and the day-long battle.

Grant seized the opportunity and ordered the troops on his left, under C.F. Smith forward with the help of Wallace's men to hopefully close the gap. They seized the Charlotte Road back from the exhausted rebels and went on to occupy every yard of ground to the Cumberland's edge, making the situation far worse for the Confederates than it had been in the morning. They were trapped in their own fort.

The miserable soldiers, having spent days in snow and freezing weather without much sleep, little food and with no fire, were too worn out to continue the fight. In the heavy shelling and fighting of the past two days, they had lost 2,000 men and it was obvious their escape was cut off. They were surrounded.

In the evening the triumvirate of Generals again met to decide the fate of Fort Donelson. Pillow observed that the enemy's occupation of the rifle pits was an open gateway for them to the Confederates river battery and he thought that the army ought to cut its way through, carrying with them as many as possible and leaving the killed and wounded on the field.[8] General Buckner disagreed, stating it would cost three-fourths of the army to get the other out, and that he did not think any general had the right to make such a sacrifice of human life. General Floyd, who never wanted to come to Fort Donelson as he considered it a trap, began fearing for his life. Having been Secretary of War under President Buchanan, he believed he would be executed as a traitor if captured by Grant. He was running scared.

The situation seemed hopeless with such leadership.

General Pillow then rose up and said, "Gentlemen, as you refuse to make an attempt to cut our way out, and General Buckner says he will not be able to hold his position a half hour after being attacked, there is only one alternative left, that is capitulation," and then and there remarked that he would not surrender the command or himself; that he would die first.

General Floyd then spoke out, and said that he would not surrender the command or himself.

General Buckner remarked that, if placed in command, he would surrender the command and share it's fate.

General Floyd then said, "General Buckner, if I place you in command, will you allow me to get out as much of my brigade as I can?"

General Buckner replied, "I will, provided you do so before the enemy receives my proposition for capitulation."

General Floyd then turned to General Pillow and said, "I turn the command over, sir."

General Pillow replied promptly, "I pass it."

General Buckner said, "I assume it. Give me pen, ink, and paper, and send for a bugler."

General Pillow then started out of the room to make arrangements for his escape, when Colonel Forrest said to him, "General Pillow, what shall I do?" General Pillow replied, "Cut your way out, sir." Forrest said, "I will do it," and left the room.[9]

It didn't take General Floyd long to find a steamboat or two on the river, confiscate them, and remove his 3,000 Virginia troops from Fort Donelson and safely transport them to Nashville.

General Pillow and his staff got a smaller boat, crossed over like Floyd, and were freely on their way to Nashville. Col. N. B. Forrest, who was made of sterner stuff, led his cavalry and accompanying infantrymen, and

The Surrender of Fort Donelson

escaped across swollen Lick Creek south of the fort with horses wading in saddle-deep water and infantrymen clinging to their stirrups. He would fight another day.

This left Generals Buckner and Johnson in the fort with 14,000 demoralized rebels. White flags were placed on the works and by the time the sun rose above the horizon on February 16, the forces were surrendered.[10]

As the unworthy Generals forsook their obligations and fled, General Buckner at dawn sent a messenger to Grant to learn what terms would be accepted by him if he surrendered? "No Terms" answered Grant, "but unconditional surrender". This reply made Grant famous. The press corp, using Grant's initials had fashioned such monikers as "United States" Grant; "Uncle Sam" Grant and now "Unconditional Surrender" Grant.

General Buckner had no choice but to accept the terms. At his headquarters in the Dover Hotel, outside of the fort, he surrendered the Confederate field force. This was the first great Confederate defeat of the war.

No one will ever know the accuracy of how many surrendered that day. There was so much movement out of the fort all night long and the estimates of 12,000 captured must be suspect as it was most likely higher.

Bushrod Johnson said, "it is proper to state that many of the men and officers commenced to leave Fort Donelson as soon as they were aware of the proposed surrender, and hundreds of them made their way to their homes and to Nashville. I have not learned that a single one who attempted to escape met with any obstacle."[11]

Grant's victory with raw troops heralded his rise to power as he was immediately promoted to Major General to date from February 16, 1862, and assigned to the command of the Military District of Tennessee. Gen. W. T. Sherman succeeded to the command of the District of Cairo.

FRIENDS INDEED

Ulysses S. Grant and Simon Bolivar Buckner were classmates at West Point and good friends before the war. When Grant was down on his luck in the 1850s, Buckner loaned him money. But it was Buckner, in command of Fort Donelson after his superiors had fled, who received Grant's demand for "unconditional surrender." He felt that the terms were "unchivalrous," but had no choice other than to accept. Later he met with Grant and found his old friend more than magnanimous. Grant, remembering Buckner's help of years before, offered his own funds to ease the Confederate general's personal hardship.[12]

A Dual Biography: General Lloyd Tilghman & General Francis Shoup

Chapter VII

Prisoners of War

The surrender of the two forts so early in the war was a great coup for General Grant and his untried army. Even more impressive was the capture of 12,000 to 15,000 Confederates and their officers; along with about 20,000 stand of arms, 48 pieces of artillery, 17 heavy guns, from 2,000 to 4,000 horses and large quantities of commissary stores.[1] A huge loss for the Western Confederate Army.

The big prize, the one that the newspapers loved, was the capture of five Confederate generals.

CIVILIAN---Extra.

(BY TELEGRAPH.)

Glorious News!

Fort Donelson Captured!

15,000 Rebel Prisoners!

Generals Buckner, Johnston, Floyd and Pillow among those Captured.

The following dispatch has just been received from the West:

CINCINNATI, Ohio,
February 17th, 11.30 A. M.

Fort Donelson fell yesterday. Federal forces captured 15,000 prisoners, including Generals Buckner, Pillow, Johnston and Floyd.

Tennessee State Museum - photo by Stephen D. Cox
Time Life Books, Inc.
The Road to Shiloh, page 95

At first the newspapers reported that both Floyd and Pillow were among the captured, but it was soon learned that both had escaped. The North would have to content itself with the capture of three lesser Confederate generals. On the 18th, towards sunset, veteran Gen. Bushrod R. Johnson, not reported to be a prisoner, with another officer walked out of the fort entrenchaments and strolled toward the rifle pits on the hill. Finding no Yankee sentry to challenge them, they kept on walking beyond the fort's encampments and made their way to freedom and eventually to Nashville.[2]

It is difficult to determine how many Confederates were captured. In the confusion of surrender with many escaping, it is difficult to arrive at an accurate count of Confederate prisoners. The most reliable count may be that of the Federals at Cairo, Illinois, where 14,623 rations were issued for the arriving prisoners.

At the beginning of the hostilities, both sides used the old "parole of Honor" system for captives. Soldiers were paroled when captured and sent to a neutral place. The parole was a waiting period which could be spent outside a prison. When an official exchange of soldiers was made, the paroled soldier was free to return to his unit or home.[3]

As the war escalated and more men were captured, makeshift prisons were hastily occupied. Old forts, existing prisons, court houses and government buildings were all used. The most expedient way to quickly handle large numbers of prisoners was to construct a stockade around a tent city. All were equally hated by their inmates.

General Buckner's surrendered forces were collected as rapidly as practicable near the village of Dover, under their respective company and regimental commanders. They were permitted to keep their clothing, blankets and personal property and the commissioned officers were allowed to retain their side-arms.

Federal steamers were brought upriver to Dover. Each transport was loaded with six to eight hundred prisoners and guarded by two companies of Bluecoats. Herded on board, they quickly sailed down the Cumberland River on the 18th, passing Smithland and then Paducah. Reaching Cario, Illinois early in the evening they remained on board overnight. On the 19th after taking on coal and commissary stores, they proceeded up the icy Mississippi River enroute to St. Louis, Missouri which they reached on the 20th. Here they were received with great cordiality by the citizens who came out to see the prison boats.[4] On the 21st they left for Alton, Illinois and the 22nd they had pleasure of meeting General Tilghman[5]. It was a brief rendezvous as the prisoners were soon separated again.

Gen. H. W. Halleck issued General Order No. 50 which decreed that the officers should be separated as soon as possible from the privates. An attempt to control the men by depriving them of their leadership.[6] The privates were returned to St. Louis. General Tilghman did not join them as he was being sent east under separate guard and by a different route. On the 27th the prisoners boarded railroad cars and began moving eastward traveling thru Terre Haute, Indianapolis and finally arriving at Columbus, Ohio on the 1st of March. "The men were marched with much pomposity through the principal streets of the town and then four miles to Camp Chase."[7] On March 4, the officers were informed they were being sent to Fort Warren, Massachusetts. Leaving the capitol of Ohio, the officers passed through Cleveland and reached Buffalo early on the 5th. The snow was very deep on the ground as they passed through Rochester, Utica and Albany. They reached the depot in Boston on the 6th and then were conveyed by a small boat to their destination, Fort Warren, situated on a small island in Boston Harbor. When the trip was over "we broke ranks and took by the hands our two Generals, Buckner and Tilghman, who preceded us several days."[8]

Fort Warren was a depressing sight. Sitting on George's Island in the windswept Boston Harbor, the old fortress was constructed of thick granite walls and floors. Pentagon in shape, it had been a training base for Massachusetts Regiments, but was now designated a Federal Prison under the command of Col. J. E. Dimick. The prison housed a variety of inmates at the time. Early in the war it was a stockade for smugglers, blockade runners, persons of suspect loyalty to the Union, military offenders, spies and more recently it had been stocked with political prisoners from Maryland. The senior officers were processed according to the eighteenth century custom of treating captive officers as guests. The better know and wealthier, such as Generals Tilghman and Buckner, were formed into groups of eight for assignment to rooms in the officers quarters of the fort. The other officers with limited funds and lesser rank were assigned to a room seventeen by fifty feet in size and with double deck bunks.[9,10]

Iron cots, with mattresses and blankets and heat from an anthracit fire made the rooms comfortable. At this time, General Tilghman, Colonel Heiman, Colonel Gregg of Texas and Lieutenant Jackson of Alabama and

Lieutenant Colonel McGavock occupied the same room.[10] Officers with ample means feasted and fared excellently; those with not as much money at their disposal ate reasonably well and the less affluent had to be satisfied with regular U.S. Army rations.[11]

On March 7, General Tilghman and his companions were invited to join the Baltimore mess of the Maryland political prisoners. It had been formed for some time and had every thing properly arranged including French cooks and waiters, "as well served tables as can be found at any first class hotel in the country."[12]

On March 9, the prisoners of War were paroled upon their signing the following document:

> Head Quarters Ft. Warren
> Boston Harbor, Mass. March 8/62
>
> "We the undersigned having been granted the limits of this Post excepting the Barracks, the Warves and the beach beyond the sea wall, as far as that extends, and beyond the limits of the grass on other parts of the island do solemnly bind ourselves upon our honor, that we will not take advantage of the privilege thus granted; that we will not converse nor have any communication whatever with the sentinels or other soldiers of the Post, except as required by their duties in connection with us, or with citizens; that we will not attempt to communicate with nor connive at any attempt to communicate with the shore, nor utter any language militating against the Government of the United States in public or in a position to be heard by any of the soldiers of the Command or by citizens; and that between "Retreat" and "Reville" we will not leave the *sets* or *Quarters* assigned to us."
>
> [13]

Without any explanation the War Department on the 10th ordered Generals Tilghman and Buckner be placed in close confinement and denied any contact with the other officers or political prisoners. They were not even permitted to use the latrine at the same time others were in the area. This harsh treatment of Tilghman provoked his mother, who lived in Philadelphia, to travel to Washington, D.C. and gain from the Secretary of War, E. M. Stanton, permission for Generals Buckner and Tilghman to walk one hour daily on the ramparts for exercise and fresh air. On April 19, the restraining order on the two was modified. Although remaining in close confinement, they were permitted outside on the ramparts.

A local paper, *The Cape Ann Advertiser*, voiced hope that the two rebel leaders might be kept in close confinement so as to reflect upon their crimes against the Union.

Southern Editorial opinions were more strident. All over Dixie the newspapers demanded that the Donelson catastrophe be subject to investigation by the President. The Press sought to assign the blame within the army.

President Davis began looking for those responsible for the disaster. His wrath first fell on Gen. G. J. Pillow for deserting the fort. Some labeled Pillow as stupid, while others said he was a coward.

General Buckner told the story that when he met Grant to surrender the fort, Grant asked about Pillow? "Gone," replied Buckner. "He thought you'd rather get hold of him than any other man in the Southern Confederacy..."

"Oh," replied Grant. "If I had got him, I'd let him go again! He will do us more good commanding you fellows." Grant and Buckner, one time friends, shared a laugh.[14]

In Fort Warren, the Confederate Officers, the imprisoned victims of the Donelson debacle, closed ranks and agreed upon a common verdict, "Pillow deserted them and robbed them of a victory they had paid blood to win."[15] The other rascal on President Davis' hook was veteran Gen. J. B. Floyd, former Governor of Virginia. He was never again given a serious field command. He was assigned to recruiting the Virginia Militia. In failing health the fifty-seven year old politician and disgraced General, died on August 26, 1863.

"A cry of condemnation arose against General Johnston, upon whom, as commander of the Western Department, rested the responsibility of these irreparable disasters. Why hadn't he sent the 14,000 troops at Bowling Green to attack Grant when there was adequate time? Why had the works at Columbus on the Mississippi been made for a garrison of 13,000 men and armed with one hundred and forty heavy guns and the twin forts had only 30 cannon? Had a reasonable portion of the time and labor been misspent upon Columbus? Whatever the fault, Johnston retained the trust of President Davis and kept his command.[16]

Pillow and Floyd became the scapegoats for the surrender while Buckner emerged the martyr. The aristocrat Tilghman, who commanded both of the forts, was protected from the damaging public accusations or future rewards, since he had been captured earlier.

As the spring months passed into summer, the officers at Fort Warren kept busy reading the daily newspapers, writing letters, playing cards, and singing, but their minds focused always on exchange and home.

It was becoming impossible for both sides to continue to hold the growing number of prisoners, yet efforts for an effective exchange system had been held up for months because of rancorous disputes, mainly involving the tacit recognition of the Confederacy implied in a prisoner exchange. Finally through the efforts of Maj. Gen. John A. Dix, USV and Maj. Gen. D. H. Hill, CSA, the Dix-Hill Exchange Cartel was signed at Haxall's Landing on the James River in Virginia on July 22, 1862. Under the cartel a system was adopted where the transfers would take place, officer for officer, private for private or a certain number of privates for commissioned officers depending on rank.

The 28th of July was a glorious day for the prisoners in Fort Warren. Colonel Dimick received an order to have the prisoners ready to start for the main locality of exchange which would be City Point on the James River outside of Richmond.[17] Generals Tilghman and Buckner were immediately turned out of close confinement. "The scene of meeting between them – and their fellow prisoners was wonderful. Many of them shed tears of joy."[18] With the Cartel in place, there was no time lost in emptying the overcrowded prisons.

July 31st was the day of departure from Fort Warren; many having been there for five months. "The prisoners were drawn up in line in the shade of the fort and the roll called. Amid the sweet strains of the fort's band, the prisoner bid adeau to set sail on the *Ocean Queen*, one of the largest Union transports afloat."[19]

On August 3, they cast anchor below Fortress Monroe, Virginia. In a short time a transport called *The Knickerbocker* came along side and took the men off and then moved them to a point above the fort where several other transports were lying loaded with other Confederate prisoners. While here, some five or six additional transports arrived, crammed with Federals.[20] On the 5th, the prisoners were landed at a point called Eakin's Landing, some fifteen miles below Richmond. The debarkation was as rapid as possible. "Nearly every man as he stepped off the boat seemed to draw a long breath and looked like he felt better and happier."[21]

General Tilghman was officially exchanged for Union Gen. J. F. Reynolds, who had been captured at Gaines Mills, Virginia, during the Peninsula campaign.[22] General Buckner was exchanged for Gen. C. A.

Prisoners of War

McCall. The return of so many soldiers significantly aided the manpower-deficient Confederates who were having trouble recruiting new men to the ranks.

On August 7, General Tilghman and other officers called upon Secretary of War G. W. Randolph who informed them that they would proceed to Vicksburg, Mississippi and reorganize their Regiments.[23]

Meanwhile, Buckner traveled to meet with Gen. Braxton Bragg at Chattanooga where on the 16th of August Buckner was promoted to Major General to serve under General Bragg.

Tilghman was afforded no reward or promotion for his earlier service at the two forts or for his imprisonment. Departing quickly from Richmond with his staff, he passed through Knoxville, Dalton, Tunnel Hill and Mobile on his way to Jackson, Mississippi for his new assignment.

A Dual Biography: General Lloyd Tilghman & General Francis Shoup

Chapter VIII

The Returning Confederates
– Iuka and Corinth –

Long trains filled with returning prisoners began arriving in Vicksburg. On the 7th of September, 3,000 rebels were received; on the 10th, an additional 4,000 forces reached Vicksburg. Some exchanged prisoners were sent to General Bragg; some to Western Virginia and a regiment to Port Hudson. Others were discharged on surgeons' certificates, and the balance organized into regiments, battalions, and companies, in accordance with special instructions from General Bragg.[1]

A parole camp was set up at Clinton outside of Jackson, Mississippi. Here General Tilghman took over for the purpose of supervising the exchange under the Cartel Agreement. Col. R. W. McGavock, one of the officers held at Fort Warren with Tilghman rejoined his Regiment, the 10th Tennessee, and recorded in his diary:

> "General Tilghman made speeches to three Regiments encamped here. The burden of his remarks to my Regiment was in regard to their reorganization. He proceeded to recommend some half dozen of his Kentucky friends for Captains. He then told them that he had provided everything for them...from a tenpenny nail to a locomotive if they needed such a thing and that if they did not get everything that they were entitled to – it would be the fault of the Regimental officers and not his fault. In his speech, he pitched into General Pillow pretty severely – and charged him with having caused all our misfortunes at Ft. Donelson."[2]

Colonel McGavock remarked, "He is quite a demagogue – and lets off a great deal of gas."[3]

The currently released officers were brought up to date. They knew that with the fall of the two forts in February, the Federal advance became relentless. Johnston was forced to evacuate Bowling Green and move his main body of forces from Nashville while General Polk on the Mississippi evacuated his fort high up in the bluffs of Columbus. They retreated to a small country church at Shiloh.

In April at Shiloh, Tennessee, 62,000 Federal soldiers battled 40,000

Confederates. Total carnage on both sides resulted in a staggering 23,000 killed, wounded and missing. Among the dead was the beloved Commanding General A. S. Johnston, who was shot in the leg and bled to death before he could be helped. His surgeon was off treating Union wounded.

Union Gen. H. W. Halleck arrived to take personal command of the huge Federal Armies and decided to consolidate their gains. Rather than push into Mississippi pursuing the Confederates, he scattered his forces for more routine duties like guarding the many rail lines leading into Corinth.

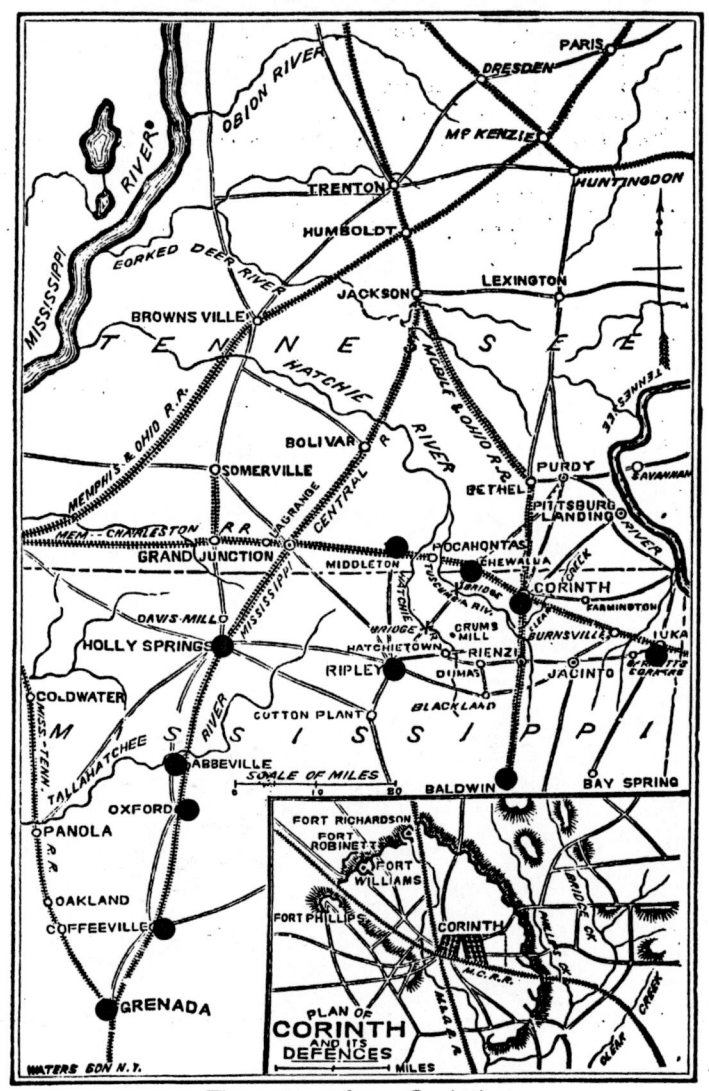

The retreat from Corinth.

The Returning Confederates

The incoming prisoners and their officers were now to reinforce Gen. Earl Van Dorn at Holly Springs, Mississippi and Gen. Sterling Price, who had come across the Mississippi River with his Arkansas troops and was at Tupelo, Mississippi with orders from Gen. B. Bragg at Chattanooga to prevent the movement of Federal forces out of Corinth to reinforce the Federal forces in middle Tennessee.

In early August, Van Dorn proposed a combined attack on Corinth to General Price. An agreement was reached on such a plan by both of the generals. On September 13, the impatient Price, not waiting to join with Van Dorn on a movement on Corinth, attacked Iuka, west of Corinth in an attempt to block the Federals move towards the middle of Tennessee. General Grant knew that Van Dorn was not on the scene. He ordered an attack on the spirited Arkansas troops under Price. The strength of Grant's forces and the surprise on September 19 was too much for Price's forces and after an all-day battle, again with heavy losses, Price saw it was a hopeless situation and removed his battle weary men from the field, barely making his escape westward beyond Corinth to Ripley, Mississippi.

Coping with the erratic southern supply system, Tilghman armed and equipped the returned forces at Clinton as quickly as possible. In Gen. Van Dorn's eyes, Tilghman was to shape-up the men and then, when properly exchanged, ship them out to him as rapidly as possible to Holly Springs in northern Mississippi.

Unfortunately for Van Dorn, his thinking did not coincide with Tilghman's. His pleas for a speedy exchange by Tilghman and forwarded to him fell upon deaf ears of an honest disciplinarian who kept to the letter of the Cartel's rules. "Though I was urged frequently by Generals Van Dorn and Sterling Price to send forward the troops allotted to their several commands, I was forbidden to do so by my orders until the Exchange was ratified."[5] Both commanders wanted fresh troops. They knew the prisoners were angered for being incarcerated for the past five months and would fight like angry hornets and incite the new volunteers to do likewise less they end up in a Federal prison pen again. On September 22, Tilghman sent a part of the first 2,000 exchanged soldiers to Sterling Price at Ponchatoula, Mississippi which helped fill Price's depleted ranks from his recent disaster at Iuka.

Van Dorn's army succeeded in joining with Price on the 28th, now with a combined strength of 22,000 men. The consolidation of the commands had an inspiring effect on the troops as they now felt that they were a sufficient force to make effective headway against the enemy.

Van Dorn was the overall commander. The two Corps would be led respectively by Gens. Mansfied Lovell and Sterling Price.[6] Their goal was still to capture Corinth. It would be a plume in Van Dorn's hat to retake the valued railroad center.

General Tilghman did not join Van Dorn at Holly Springs nor did he catch up with them at Ripley. He remained at Jackson with 8,000 replacements awaiting to be exchanged. He would not participate in the battle of Corinth. Both Generals Van Dorn and Price continued to request that these troops be released and added to their commands. On September 19, Tilghman wired Price, "the exchange must be ratified first. I shall thoroughly equip except arming, and if I had your arms, could drill the raw men.[7]

Van Dorn ordered a combined movement of his command eastward toward Corinth without the benefit of Tilghman's 8,000 replacements remaining at Jackson awaiting the Exchange. General Price categorically opposed Van Dorn's movement and was not hesitant to express his opinion. He agreed that the taking of Corinth was important, yet he felt that the attack should be delayed until the veteran prisoners at Clinton could join the army. "Without their added numbers, Price failed to see how the Confederates could hold Corinth, much less exploit its capture.[8]

Van Dorn replied, "Surprise, not added numbers, is the key to success."[9] Nevertheless, the two commanders were being watched by higher authorities.

A concerned President Davis at Richmond did not want a repeat of the command disaster at Fort Donelson. On September 30 he appointed Maj. Gen. J. C. Pemberton to move west and assume command of the Department of Mississippi and East Louisiana, while leaving Van Dorn in command of the field forces and exchanged prisoners at Jackson.[10]

The small dapper forty-three year old Van Dorn began the attempt to recover Corinth by marching from Ripley to Pocahontas on the M. & C. Railroad, threatened Bolivar, Tennessee to confuse the Federal troops stationed there and then turned suddenly and marched against Corinth hoping to attack before the Federals could concentrate their forces.

On October 3, a battle line was formed. Gen. M. Lovell's corps was placed in line of battle, south of the railroad in the following order: J. B.

The Returning Confederates

Villepigue's brigade on the right with cavalry flankers; J. S. Bowen in the center and A. Rust on the left, with left flank resting on the railroad while Price's corps was deployed on the north side of the railroad.[11]

As the attack commenced, the charging Confederates raised the "rebel yell" and made a dash for the outer works. Lovell's forces drove the Federals into the forts surrounding the town, but were met by rapid fire from the forts artillery. They managed, however, to gain ground until within several hundred yards of the fort when the bluecoats abandoned the fort. Their gain was not exploited, however, as they remained in this position for hours.

The ever colorful Price rode the battle line and with him was the mounted headquarters band, which paused now and then to encourage the men with popular tunes, such as "Listen to The Mockingbird."[12] He also spoke to his troops and "With a wave of his hand, old Woodpecker as the Federals sometimes called Price, said, 'Boys, if they are many, we will take them, and if they are but few, we will take them the quicker.'"[13]

Price, with his gallant forces, engaged the Federals in and around the town as he pushed the bluecoats back from position to position. A Confederate victory was in sight. On the 4th, Van Dorn arranged the entire army in full view of the earthworks and the Federal brigades inside.

Retaining no reserves, Van Dorn began his advance as he thought in unison with Price and Lovell. By noon the Indian summer gave way to heat and the temperature rose to around ninety degrees and the men began falling out with heat exhaustion. To worsen matters, Grant's reinforcements arrived and Price was compelled to yield the ground he had gained the day before.

Strangely, Lovell's division remained inactive all day while Price's command was making a desperate effort to hold the line. The battle had been short, sharp and for the time, decisive as the losses were heavy on both sides. After this obstinate battle, the Federals had rallied because they had been heavily reinforced and met the attack with firmness. General Price said his troops were too much fatigued, too hungry and thirsty to risk a final attack. Van Dorn agreed.[14]

By this time the army was wracked with staggering casualties. Van Dorn had lost 2,470 killed and wounded with 1,763 missing. The Federals faired no better, losing over 2,500 men. It was another blood bath for both sides.

A Dual Biography: General Lloyd Tilghman & General Francis Shoup

Fearing additional Federal reinforcement by rail, Van Dorn ordered a general withdrawal. Villepigue's brigade was marched out and formed across the line of withdrawal and through their ranks passed the retreating troops, warily and downcast, plodding slowly to the rear towards Chewalla where they halted at nightfall. At Chewalla a courier brought a dispatch to Van Dorn that the Federal force at Bolivar was moving south quickly with 9,000 troops and the Hatchie River bridges were in danger of being captured, thus cutting off Van Dorn's command.

Van Dorn managed to extract himself, thanks to the hard-fighting Texas Cavalry of Colonels Davis and Hawkins, or less he would have lost his wagon train and much of his army may have been trapped.

The Confederate withdrawal had become a retreat as the Federal Cavalry became very aggressive in their pursuit. The rebels passed slowly through Ripley along the same route they had used a few days earlier, and ended up back at Holly Springs.

President Davis, learning of the latest squabble among the Confederate generals, promoted the late-comer, J. C. Pemberton to become a Lieutenant General, thus crushing Van Dorn's hopes of further advancement.

Chapter IX

A Court of Inquiry for Van Dorn

Harper's Weekly
Holly Springs at the time of the Civil War.

General Tilghman's assignment in Jackson was coming to an end. It had been an enjoyable stay in the capital city after having spent months in a northern fort as a prisoner. His duty and responsibility of handling the exchange of prisoners had become taxing when it became apparent these replacements were urgently needed by Van Dorn and Price for their advance on Corinth.

The Cartel specified, "Prisoners of war will be paroled and delivered at some point within the lines. A receipted list must be taken in duplicate, and one copy sent to the Adjutant-General in order to effect an exchange."[1] Tilghman had to deny access to these troops until the Exchange had been ratified by the Adjutant General and it put him in a very awkward position with the leadership of his own army.

Tilghman would do the honorable thing and live by the letter of the Cartel agreement by refusing to release these 8,000 prisoners. Generals Van Dorn and Price had to go it without these men at Corinth and it cost them dearly.

A Dual Biography: General Lloyd Tilghman & General Francis Shoup

As soon as the announcement was made of the ratification of the exchange, Tilghman lost no time in equipping and sending forward as fast as railroad transportation could be found, every available man. The last of the troops reached Holly Springs on October 14.[2] With the exchange completed, Tilghman himself left Jackson and made the two hundred mile rail journey north to Holly Springs to join Van Dorn and receive a new assignment.

Arriving at Holly Springs, the general found that the disaster of Corinth hanging like a heavy cloud over the dejected and scattered brigades. The only positive note was the arrival and assimilation of his replacement troops into the depleted brigades. Tilghman himself reported to Major General Lovell for duty.[3] He would be needed to help repel the coming Federal advance.

General Pemberton, new to the situation in Mississippi, ordered Van Dorn's army out of Holly Springs to take the stage road and move south towards Abbeville, Mississippi, where entrenchments had been constructed on the south bank of the Tallahatchie River and at the Mississippi Central railroad tracks. It was a fine place for the Confederates to make a firm stand against the invading Federals.

The alarmed citizens in northern Mississippi, believing the army was abandoning them, panicked and began fleeing with the soldiers, carrying every bit of moveable personal property, slaves and livestock. They clogged the road so that Van Dorn's brigades lost valuable time in escaping the pursuing Federal juggernaut.

The heavy casualties and the loss of the battle of Corinth had to be blamed on someone. The early scapegoat was General Lovell. His unpardonable sin of being born in the north made him an ideal scapegoat, and generally the nicest things he was being accused of were imbecility and incompetency, although the less generous were thinking more in terms of cowardice and treachery. Slowly he redeemed himself when other events and facts were reviewed. Replacing him as a subject of blame was no less than General Van Dorn. He became the object of ridicule and the camp rumor was that he was negligent for his part in the battle. The many accusations included that he, General Van Dorn was without proper maps of the area; that he refused the services of available artillery; that he went into battle without proper food for his men; that he needlessly delayed the attack; that he permitted the enemy to run reinforcement trains and that he was guilty of cruel treatment of officers and men. Added to these charges was a personal one by Brig. Gen. J. S. Bowen's insulting remark that he thought that the Mississippian had been drinking.

Van Dorn earned a reputation as a daring young officer. He was wounded three times in the Indian wars and once in the Mexican War. During the first year of the war his heroic conduct had been rewarded by several promotions. Stunned by these charges, he demanded a court of inquiry into the matter as soon as possible to clear his good name.

On November 15, at Abbeville, Pemberton directed that the allegations against Van Dorn be heard by Military Court. The court was constituted as follows: Gen. Sterling Price, Gen. Lloyd Tilghman and Gen. D. H. Muray and Cap. E. H. Cummings. After hearing the charges, witness, and testimony, every point against the cavalier was disproved and he was acquitted, and the court recommended the matter be closed.[4] No further proceedings were held on the charge.

On news that the Federals had landed on the eastern shore of the Mississippi River opposite Helena, Arkansas was enough for General Pemberton to order the defensive line at Abbeville to be abandoned and another withdrawal be made southward towards Oxford, Mississippi. It was now December. The Confederates withdrew across the Tallahatchie and Col. A. L. Lee's Brigade consisting of the Seventh Kansas, the Fourth Illinois, and a battalion of the Second Iowa followed them across the river. The Federals pressed forward on the direct road toward Oxford and skirmished with Col. H. W. Jackson's cavalry which made a strong stand about a mile north of Oxford. The Union's Seventh Kansas made a mounted charge but was checked by the heavy Confederate fire. The entire regiment then deployed and made an attack, dismounted, with its revolving rifles and carbine, and drove the rebels through and beyond Oxford. The fighting was sharp, the Confederates lost eight killed and many taken prisoner.[15]

Mississippi was beginning to feel the effect of Federal occupation and the Jayhawking that came with it. Jayhawking meant to prey upon your enemy and steal property such as food, draft animals, grain, cattle and personal effects.

Although both sides practiced it throughout the war, the Seventh Kansas Cavalry were often named the predicators and were credited with many atrocities.[6]

The Seventh Kansas remained long enough at Oxford to lay in a bountiful supply of tobacco at the expense of the Oxford merchants. Their pursuit continued until they reached Water Valley. Here the Seventh was given the job of guarding the nearly one-thousand Confederate prisoners and stragglers who had been gathered during the past few days.

It is said, "discovering that the prisoners were destitute and fainting for a 'chaw', the jaykawking Kansasians began to pitch whole plugs of 'flats' to the suffering Johnnies. It is said it created a transformation; despondency disappeared and three cheers for the Jayhawkers were given with a gusto by the rebels.[7]

A Court of Inquiry for Van Dorn

The Colonel

Tilghman's best-known uniformed portrait, taken when he was colonel of the 3rd Kentucky in 1861. *(Ernest Haywood Papers, Southern Historical Collection, University of North Carolina, Chapel Hill).*

The General

CARTES DE VISITE
Calling Cards

A Dual Biography: General Lloyd Tilghman & General Francis Shoup

Chapter X

Coffeeville, Mississippi

The Federal Army occupied the Water Valley and the persistent Colonel Lee's Kansas Jayhawkers continued to harass the Confederate rear guard.

By December 5, General Lovell's division with Tilghman had retreated to Coffeeville, nearly thirty miles south of Oxford. Lovell's scouts alerted him to the fact that a gap of several miles existed between Lee's aggressive cavalry and the slower infantry. The two West Pointers decided to take advantage of the opportunity presented to them and laid a trap for the over-confident Jayhawkers. Lovell observed it was impossible for Lee's cavalry to see the Confederates or their strength because the muddy stage road was narrow and lined along the way on both sides by a dense growth of oak trees and underbrush.[1] Lovell sent Tilghman back up the stage road to form a screened front upon the road at Red Hill, a mile north of the town. Tilghman posted his infantry in timber on a ridge running perpendicular to the road and behind his infantry he placed four pieces of artillery, while 300 yards to the rear of this battery, two Parrott guns were placed on still higher ground. Lee's cavalry now south of Water Valley, pressed down the muddy road as one column, forming a broad front and moved within two miles of Coffeeville. Hauling two cannons with them, they probed Tilghman's front with artillery fire which was answered by Tilghman's screened artillery. Four companies of the Seventh Kansas were at once ordered to dismount and go forward as skirmishers. The other six companies of the Seventh dismounted and were deployed in support of the skirmish line. Sending their horses to the rear, the four companies advanced across an open field toward the Confederate infantry; they were met by a withering volley and were forced to fall back on their support.[2]

With the Confederate "yell" from Tilghman's men, the Southerners moved forward to attack the heavily outnumbered cavalrymen who fell steadily back for a mile and then mounted their horses, galloped across the clearing to the next patch of woods, dismounted and took position. Although the Federals were armed with Colts, Smiths and Sharps, nothing could halt Tilghman's onward Confederate movement. The Federals held on as long as they could before retreating two miles. The fighting went on until dark, when Lovell called a halt and a cease-fire. Confederate losses were seven killed and forty-three wounded with ten men missing. The Federals had thirty-four killed, sixteen wounded and left on the road with thirty-five captured. Twenty-nine graves at Water Valley are marked as unknown Federals that were buried after the battle.[3]

Tilghman remarked, "the whole affair was a complete success and taught the enemy a lesson I am sure they will not soon forget."[4] Among Tilghman's personal staff present for the affair was Lt. Lloyd Tilghman, Jr., Aide-de-camp, and the General's son. On the 7th, General Lovell was relieved of his Corps and would await orders. He was to face a court of inquiry about the fall of New Orleans in the spring of 1862. Van Dorn was transferred latterly, and reduced to Commander of the cavalry of the First Corp.

Grant's forces in northern Mississippi extended from Holly Spring, now their main supply depot, all the way south to Coffeeville, a distance of fifty miles.

Grant had to supply and feed eighty-thousand men and animals, via a one-track railroad that extended over one hundred eighty miles from Columbus, Kentucky. It also meant that the Federal supply line was vulnerable to the attacks of the roaming Confederate cavalry.

Grant's forces were moving in northern Mississippi and advancing towards the rear of Vicksburg while General Sherman was already proceeding down the Mississippi River with an invasion force to besiege Vicksburg in a pincer movement. It seemed that Anna E. Carroll's strategy was being used.

Some Confederates remained positioned in Coffeeville while the main part of he army, with its refugees, crossed over the rain-swollen Yalobusha River at Grenada and took up positions along the south bank of the river, where Tilghman and his brigades joined them.

Soon a form of co-operative Confederate offensive strategy was devised by Generals Pemberton and N. B. Forrest in these last days of 1862. Their Christmas gift to the boys in blue would be to cut Grant's supply line of food, clothing, gifts, mail and sutler's supplies.

On December 11, Forrest, with a combined cavalry of twenty-five hundred horsemen and ten cannon, left Columbia, Tennessee and began to operate northward against Grant's rail line in western Tennessee.

With twenty-five hundred cavalry threatening his rear, Grant ordered a

Coffeeville, Mississippi

Railroad Depot at Holly Springs

Harpers Weekly

concentration of troops at Jackson, Tennessee by calling other mounted infantry and cavalry from the garrisons at Columbus, Forts Heiman, Henry and Donelson, Oxford, Boliva and Cornith to intercept the raiders movements. In so during, Grant reduced his cavalry strength in and around Holly Springs.

On December 15, Pemberton ordered his main body of Confederate cavalry in Grant's front, to cross south of the Yalobusha River and form into three brigades made up of Col. John S. Griffith's Texas Cavalry; Col. Wm. "Red" Jackson's Tennesseans; and Col. Robert "Black Bob" McCulloch's Mississippians. This twenty-five hundred man detachment of Confederate Cavalry would be led by no less than the Earl Van Dorn whose goal was to plunder Grant's new supply depot at Holly Springs.

Van Dorn's force was poorly mounted and badly armed with shot guns, squirrel guns, captured Yankee weapons, and with whatever animals they could find, horse or mule! They headed northeast towards Ripley at a great speed and cut west to Holly Springs where on December 20, they captured Grant's huge supply depot with a minimum of effort.

Here they found tons of medical, quartermaster, ordinance and commissary stores, what they could not take they put to the torch. Van Dorn's raiders helped themselves to boots, hats, saddles, food, and weapons. By sunset the destruction had been completed and the horsemen raced out of town.

The long trek back to Grenada was treacherous since they had to elude the enraged pursing Union cavalrymen. Van Dorn, however, made good his retreat. The spectacular round trip of 400 miles took two weeks to complete. The raid was a wonderful Christmas gift for the cause. Van Dorn's force, with little bloodshed, accomplished more to stop Grant's invasion of

Mississippi in the last two weeks of the year than the combined Confederate Army had done in the past three months.

The loss of over a million and a half dollars worth of war material plus the burnt-out depot buildings and store houses at Holly Springs were a serious set-back for Grant. Simultaneously, he was informed that at the other end of his supply line, Forrest's cavalry had shut down the Mobile and Ohio Railroad in western Tennessee for the past ten days; not only disrupting communications but tearing up track into Kentucky.[6]

While Grant was taking inventory of his losses, General Sherman moved on to Vicksburg on Christmas eve. Brig. Gen. S. D. Lee, with less than 3,000 Southerners, repelled Sherman's men and sent them packing back up the river shortly after the New Year at the Battle of Chickasaw Bayou.

The raids of Van Dorn and Forrest and Lee's successful defenses of Vicksburg, had a most decisive effect upon the Federal high command, in deciding to abandon the invasion of northern Mississippi.

General Grant was ordered to join General Sherman's and Admiral D. D. Porter's operations. The 1863 Vicksburg Campaign would commence on the Mississippi River.

Chapter XI

Mississippi Duty

Since the beginning of the war the Confederates had occupied and defended an assortment of river forts on the long and winding Mississippi River. Many of them had already been captured, destroyed or abandoned. By 1863, the Union forces controlled all of the vital Mississippi River except for a stretch from Vicksburg, Mississippi to Port Hudson, Louisiana. Grant's Federal juggernaut was positioned north of Vicksburg and preparing to assault one of the last river bastions.

Vicksburg's crowning bluffs were so high that the invading ship's guns could not be elevated sufficiently to inflict any damage. The town had been fortified earlier by Generals Van Dorn and Pemberton. With scores of cannon on the bluffs overlooking the winding river, the rebels controlled the river traffic. The task of taking this city would not be easy.

Twenty-five miles below Vicksburg along the river was another well armed fort at Grand Gulf. Anchoring these two northern strategic locations some one hundred and fifty miles further down the river was Port Hudson.

Harpers Weekly
A Confederate Prison over Pearl River at Jackson,
where Union prisoners were confined.

A Dual Biography: General Lloyd Tilghman & General Francis Shoup

North of Port Hudson was the great Red River which emptied into the Mississippi from Louisiana. The Red River was the last west to east waterway which connected the Trans-Mississippi region with the rest of the Confederacy. The Red River provided a supply line over which arms supplies and ammunitions were transported from the Mexican and Texas seaports, after being run through the blockade.

On January 2, 1863, general orders were issued, reassigning commands in the army. Maj. Gen. W. W. Loring, who had arrived from the east in early December and who had been in command while Van Dorn was on his Holly Springs raid was assigned to be commander of Van Dorn's First Division.[1] Tilghman reported to Loring.

General Tilghman took command of the First brigade previously led by Brig. Gen. W. E. Baldwin. Baldwin was one of the exchanged officers from Fort Donelson.

The Second brigade was placed under Brig. Gen. A. Rust, who had served with Loring for the Cheat Mountain campaign in western Virginia in the fall of 1861. Rounding out the division was Col. T. N. Waul's Texas Legion of infantry, artillery and cavalry.[2] The Division was stationed at Grenada guarding the northwest approaches to Vicksburg and protecting the supply line of foodstuffs coming from the rich Mississippi delta country.

General Tilghman was sent to Jackson on temporary duty to handle the exchange of the Federal prisoners that had been captured and imprisoned from the December engagements. In the prison pens were over seven hundred bluecoated prisoners including twenty officers.[3] Tilghman showed little compassion for the Federal prisoners – especially for those of the Seventh Kansas, who had wrought such devastation in Mississippi. Captured Col. A. L. Lee denounced Tilghman for his treatment and said bitterly that some of his officers were held in close confinement and on hard fare. "I desire to call attention to one fact. There are among these prisoners three men of the Seventh Kansas Cavalry. General Tilghman ordered them in irons, and they are chained together, hand and foot, by heavy irons. This is only because they are connected with that regiment."[4]

Colonel Lee sent his complaint to General Grant, saying, "Is there any method of righting this wrong or of retaliation? If our policy will permit it, I will capture three Confederate officers within the fortnight and put them in irons in the camp of the Seventh Kansas, and then open up a correspon-

Mississippi Duty

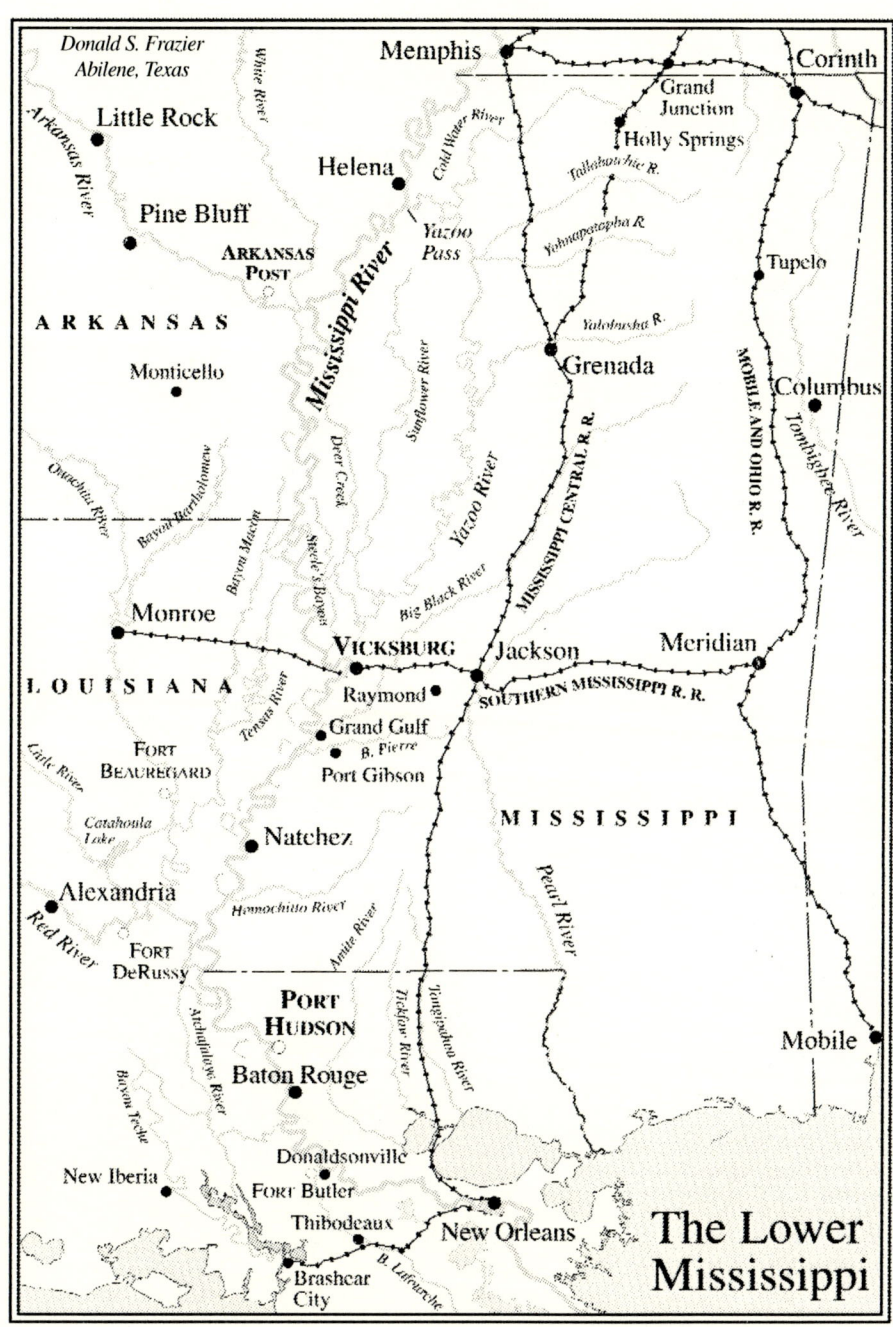

The Theatre of War in the West, 1862-1863.[7]

dence with General Tilghman."[6]

Grant advised Colonel Lee that if he was perfectly satisfied that some of his men were being punished as described by him, by rebel authorities, he may serve in the same manner, an equal number of the enemy and then open a correspondence with General Tilghman as he proposed.[8] If any such retribution was accomplished by Colonel Lee, it is not recorded in the Official Records.

On January 20, 1863, the flamboyant and prominent General Van Dorn was appointed permanent commander of Pemberton's cavalry forces in the Mississippi Valley. This excellent horseman flourished as a cavalry officer, but seemed to fail when given a significant command of a larger army.[9]

Soon thereafter General Bragg requested from Pemberton that Van Dorn's forty-five hundred experienced cavalrymen be loaned to him in Tennessee for the coming Tullahoma campaign. Pemberton acquiesced to Bragg's request, but it was a mistake. In effect, he had given his eyes and ears away, let alone his most effective defensive land fighting force. He was now left with virtually no cavalry to protect the entire state of Mississippi. The Confederacy would pay for Pemberton's errors!

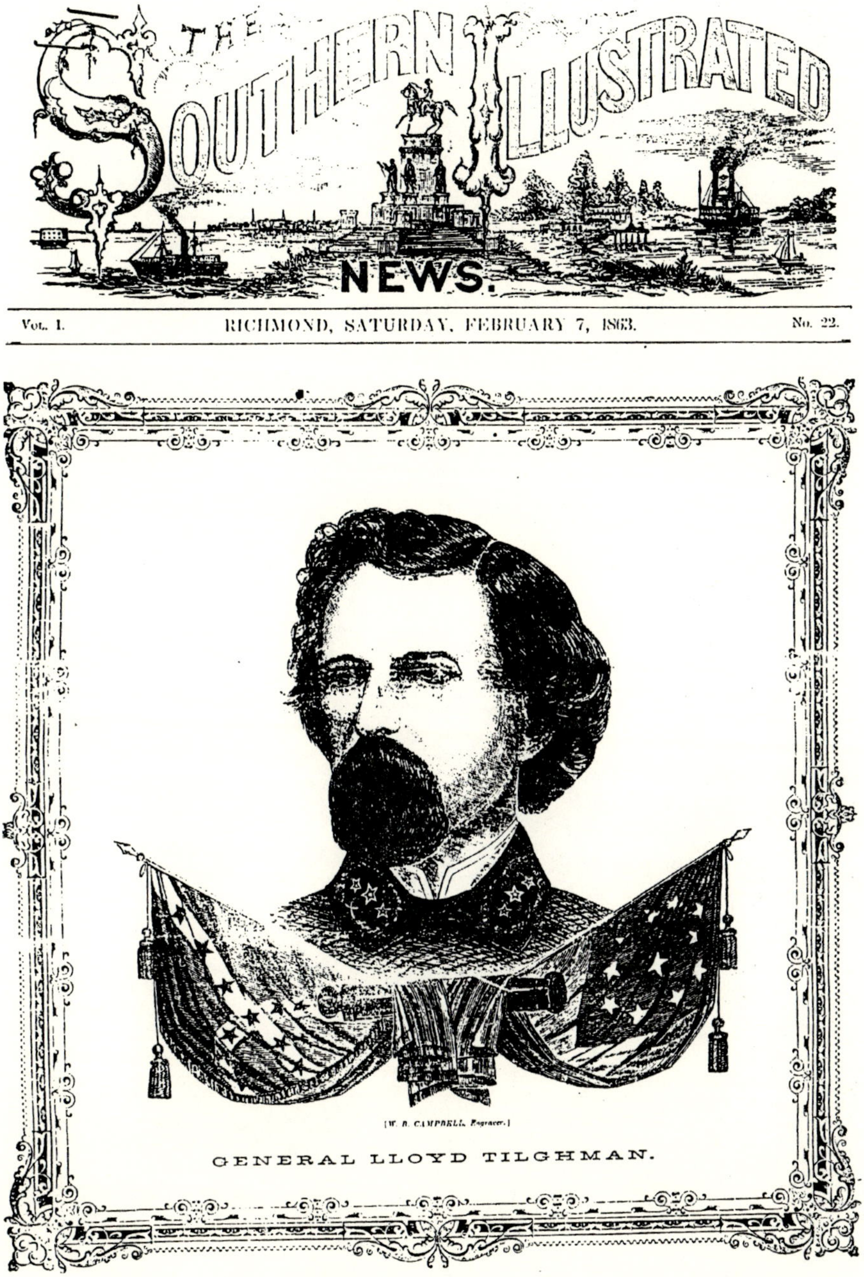

Mississippi Duty

General Tilghman was the subject of a front page biography in early 1863. The Richmond newspaper finished it with "A few months ago he was exchanged, and passed through this city in company with General Buckner, on his way to the West, where he is now in active service."

A Dual Biography: General Lloyd Tilghman & General Francis Shoup

Chapter XII

Grant's Yazoo Pass Expedition

The Mississippi River was lined with swamps, dense forests and creeping vines, which made it next to impossible for a naval force to make a successful landing of Federal troops along it's banks.

The Federal strategy focused on getting below Vicksburg without having to travel the heavily guarded river. Their first attempt was to try to cut a series of canals to bypass the Vicksburg stronghold. The plan was to dig a mile-long, nine foot wide canal through the bayou on the Louisiana side opposite Vicksburg. This was in vain as the Confederates immediately established a battery of heavy guns opposite the mouth of the canal, to bombard the Unionists. Next, an attempt was made to cut a canal at Duckport Landing on the Louisiana side to connect a winding route through the bayou. Later, a four-hundred mile route from Lake Providence,

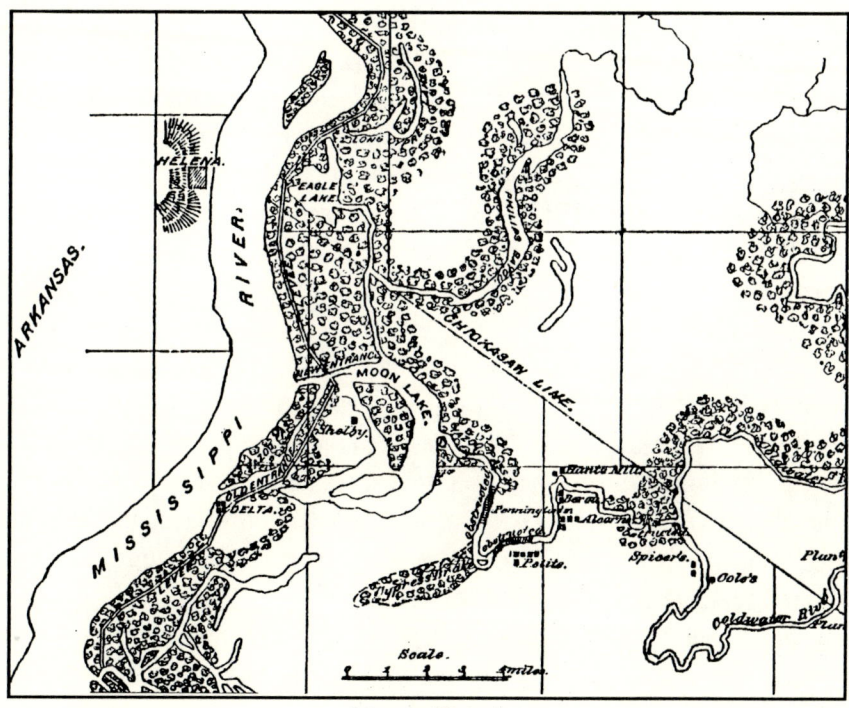

Yazoo Pass[1]

Louisiana through the swamps was started, but all failed. As many as 3500 soldiers toiled away at excavating these ditches in the swamps. These schemes inflicted incredible hardship and suffering on the young bluecoats. Snake bites, foul water, wretched sanitary facilities lead to diarrhea and fever, all took their toll. In all cases, the changing Mississippi River either receded or flooded and negated these early attempts of the Federals to get below Vicksburg.

By the middle of January, Grant began switching from ditch-digging to an amphibious war and the engineers of the canals would now give-way to the officers and sailors of the Union Navy. The new attempt would be the Yazoo Pass expedition.

Five miles below Helena, Arkansas, on the eastern bank of the Mississippi was the sealed Yazoo Pass. Used earlier in the Century as the shortest route in traveling to Memphis, it had been sealed up because the rich bottomlands of the delta were lower than the surface of the Mississippi by eight feet at high water.

To protect these fertile fields from periodic flooding, a levee eighteen feet high and one hundred feet thick had been constructed across the mouth of the pass that led into Moon Lake. If this pass could be reopened it would permit access to Moon Lake for the Federal Navy.

Once on Moon Lake a floatilla of gun-boats, steamers, and transports could enter into the Coldwater River, and float down this stream into the Tallahatchie River, which, when it joined the Yallobusha River, became the headwaters of the Yazoo River which continues south to Yazoo City and eventually to Haines Bluff which was the northern approach to Vicksburg. This was a two-hundred mile mission being proposed by Grant in order to get at his goal.

On January 21, General Pemberton ordered Loring at winter quarters in Grenada to send a party of civil engineers and overseers with two hundred slaves up the Tallahatchie and Coldwater rivers to locate and then fortify a position that would stop Grant's latest experiment. The detachment proceeded all the way to the Yazoo Pass, where the overseers and slaves were landed on both sides of Moon Lake. The Blacks commenced felling the huge trees leading into the Pass to obstruct it.[2]

On February 3, Union pioneers operating on the Mississippi side of the pass, cut two ditches through the embankment and sappers then buried a fifty pound barrel of gunpowder under the earthen dike and exploded it, opening a gaping forty yard wide ditch into Moon Lake. It took four days for the rush of water on the Moon Lake to subside, but it was deep enough for the passage of some Union tugs and light draft gunboats.

As they entered the breach, they encountered the obstacles of fallen trees and in some places the water was too shallow for boats. Slowly they moved toward the cut into the Coldwater River, taking three days to make the twelve mile trip.

Lt. F. E. Shepperd's Confederate Navy dispatch on February 14 said "the enemy have driven us off the works on the Pass, and are coming through. I have done my best; worked under their noses till their pickets came in 100 yards of me."[3]

On February 17, Pemberton shifted Generals Loring and Tilghman to Yazoo City to prepare for the Federal advance. Loring went up the Yazoo River to Greenwood. Upon landing, he was conducted by Major Merriwether to an area two and a half miles above the town where fortifications were being constructed at Beck's

The Yazoo Pass and Big Sunflower Experiments
February and March, 1863[4]

Ferry landing. Gangs of soldiers and impressed slaves had started work on another inland fort which Loring had approved.

The site for the fortification was a neck of high land looping the two rivers, the Yazoo on one side and the Tallahatchie on the other. Located on the Clayton Bayou, the site was named Fort Pemberton while the Federals referred to it as Fort Greenwood. The fort would become a typical Mississippi cotton-bale fortification constructed under the direction of Capt. Powhatan Robinson of the Confederate engineers. Robinson ordered a boat up the Tallahatchie River to Dr. Curtiss' Plantation where a load of cotton bales were obtained to be used to build the breastworks while a similar boat of cotton bales were obtained from the Purnell plantation down the river. The four-hundred pound cotton bales were partially sunk and the breastworks were made by putting three to five bales of cotton on top of one another and some four to five bales wide. These were joined together with sheet iron. After this, five to six feet of earth was thrown on the bales, finishing off a formidable breastwork. The parapets of the stronghold were built of logs, mud and cotton bales covered with rawhide so the shells would bounce off. The flanks of the position rested on both sides of the water barriers; they zig-zagged to the right on the Tallahatchie and zig-zagged to the left on the Yazoo.

Capt. J. D. Myrick was in charge of the seven guns mounted en barbette. The guns were emplaced in partially sunken redans 35 feet long with the gun platforms one foot below the surface. They were emplaced to command either river. Within the fort were three well protected powder magazines. The cotton bales were watered down to prevent them from burning from the Federals shelling of red hot cannon balls that were heated on the gun-boats. General Tilghman sent a regiment of infantry and a field battery to the fort and ordered Col. R. McCulloch with his cavalry force to the vicinity of the Coldwater River to operate against the Federal fleet at such points as might be practicable.[6] General Loring's next move was to assign Thomas Weldon, a Civil Engineer and ship builder from Yazoo city who was acquainted with the locality to supervise the obstruction of the Tallahatchie River.[7] Weldon and his men had the captured U.S. *Star of the West*, towed to the head of the Yazoo and then into the Tallahatchie. At the site of the fort, it was swung squarely across the channel and sunk, thus blocking the channel and becoming an integral part of the fort's defense. The fortification had been completed. The Federals would soon test them.

Grant's Yazoo Pass Expedition

"Old Blizzards"

A Dual Biography: General Lloyd Tilghman & General Francis Shoup

Chapter XIII

Pemberton-Tilghman Tent Flap

While Grant and Sherman were developing their strategy to reduce Vicksburg, Pemberton managed to alienate General Tilghman.

In November when the Confederate Army was making a hasty move from Abbeville, Mississippi, there was not sufficient transportation belonging to General Tilghman's Division to haul the soldier's wet and muddy tents. Upon a verbal order from Maj. Gen. M. Lovell, Tilghman burned and abandoned the tents.

Pemberton, upon hearing of this, requested a court of inquiry for the purpose of investigating the circumstance attending the destruction of valuable property. On February 1, 1863, a court of inquiry was assembled at Grenada, Mississippi. The point in question was the interpretation of Pemberton's order, which on November 30, read in part... "required stores that could not be transported to be destroyed."[1] At the inquiry it was brought out that there was not sufficient transportation belonging to Tilghman's division to haul the tents and that they were then burned and destroyed in compliance with a verbal order issued by Major General Lovell, i.e. "to throw out sufficient tents, as they were wet and heavy, to enable wagons to pass over the bad roads and keep up with the train."[2] The court of inquiry findings were that "Brig. Gen. L. Tilghman was fully exonerated from all censure in relation to the burning and destroying of the tents and they recommended that no further proceedings be brought against him.[3]

General Tilghman was officially cleared, but not apparently in Pemberton's mind. After this court of inquiry, there was a coolness and almost spiteful attitude in Pemberton's dealings with Tilghman throughout the winter and spring campaigns.

In spite of the fact that Tilghman's mother was living in Philadelphia at this time which was Pemberton's home town, Pemberton the Quaker from Pennsylvania, served his cadetship at West Point at the same time as Tilghman. "These future generals were schooled and spanned the years together at the Point."[4] Even more binding in spirit was the fact that "the most distinguished ancestor of Pemberton's wife-to-be Martha Thompson, was Elbridge Gerry, a signer of the Declaration of Independence.[5] General Tilghman was the great-grandson of Matthew Tilghman, who was the President of the revolutionary convention of Maryland and a member of the Continental Congress, and undoubtedly knew Gerry.

These considerations and the fact that they both served in the Mexican War should have created an amicable relationship between the two generals, but it did not. Pemberton was undoubtedly a difficult commander.

GENERAL ORDERS, } HDQRS. DEPT. OF MISS. AND EAST LA.,
No. 33.   }   Vicksburg, February 1, 1863.

I. A court of inquiry having assembled at Grenada, Miss., pursuant to Special Orders, No. 21, current series, Headquarters Army of Mississippi, for the purpose of investigating the circumstances attending the burning of tents in General Tilghman's division at the time of the retreat of the army from Abbeville, Miss., &c., and having found as follows—

> That there was not sufficient transportation belonging to Brigadier-General Tilghman's division to haul said tents, and that they were burned and destroyed in compliance with and in obedience to an order issued by Lieutenant-General Pemberton, dated "Headquarters Department of Mississippi and East Louisiana. Abbeville. Miss.. November 30, 1862;" and those that were destroyed on the march in compliance with and in obedience to a verbal order issued by Major-General Lovell to Brigadier-General Tilghman to throw out sufficient tents, as they were wet and heavy, to enable the wagons to pass over the bad roads and keep up with the train; and in the opinion of the court Brig. Gen. L. Tilghman is fully exonerated from all censure in relation to the burning and destroying of said tents, and we recommend that no further proceedings be had in relation thereto against him—

the decision of the lieutenant-general commanding the department is as follows:

> That the order dated "Headquarters Department Mississippi and East Louisiana. Abbeville, Miss., November 30, 1862," required the stores that could not be transported to be destroyed, and it does not clearly appear to him that the transportation of the stores was impracticable, and their destruction consequently necessary.

II. The court of inquiry appointed by Special Orders, No. 21, Headquarters Army Mississippi, "for the purpose of investigating the circumstances attending the burning of tents in General Tilghman's division," is hereby dissolved.

By order of Lieutenant-General Pemberton:

J. R. WADDY,
Assistant Adjutant-General.

Pemberton-Tilghman Tent Flap

Gen. Lloyd Tilghman[7]

A little-known portrait of Tilghman taken after October, 1861, and specially noteworthy for displaying probably more buttons on his uniform than any other Confederate brigadier.

A Dual Biography: General Lloyd Tilghman & General Francis Shoup

Chapter XIV

The Siege of Fort Pemberton

On March 1, Tilghman was informed that some of the Federal boats had gone back to Helena to bring down the fleet to pass through the breach at Yazoo Pass, now also known to the Federals as Grant's Pass.[1] The next day Tilghman learned that the Federals had two large iron-clads, the *Chilicothe* and *De Kalb*, two rams and six light-draught gunboats that had passed through Grant's Pass on to Moon Lake and were ready to enter the cut into the Coldwater.[2] "The tug has passed into Coldwater and returned; intention to bring gunboats through evident" was next wired to Tilghman.[3]

In addition, 5000 Federal troops were on Moon Lake in twelve transports. They were carrying Brig. Gen. L. F. Ross with a division of Gen. J. A. McClernand's Corps from Helena, and the 12th and 17th Missouri of Sherman's Corps.[4]

Lt. Com. W. Smith who had charge of the Union flotilla was by now in a state of distress. This two hundred and fifty mile water journey was going to take much longer than he expected. Coming through Grant's Pass on to Moon Lake to the cut at the Coldwater River had cost him valuable time. The heavy March rains brought strong currents to the rivers. It was very difficult for the floatilla to maneauver and navigate the flooded river.

The river banks and low lands were underwater and with the weather beginning to warm, there appeared buffalo gnats, which swarmed and drove the horses, mules, cattle and even the soldiers into a frenzy from their bites.

The dense and tangled growth formed barriers on the river which delayed the floatilla. In one spot large trees, reaching from bank to bank had been felled by the Confederate engineers. The soldiers, in parties of 500, debarked from the transports and worked furiously in chopping the boughs and hauling the massive tree trunks out of the river.[5]

On March 6, Tilghman was informed by his cavalry scouts that the floatilla was 15 miles below the mouth of the Coldwater now on the Tallahatchie. "The Yankee boats are here; four of them are lying at E. V. Dickens; and two went below and landed at George McRaie's place."[6]

Confined for weeks at a time, life aboard a Union transport was often likened to being on an early slave ship. The soldiers were packed aboard along with the horses, mules, rifles, wagons, camp equipment, ammunition and food. Disease and sickness prevailed and the bodies of the unfortunate soldiers who died were buried on the shore in unmarked graves.

Colonel McCulloch's cavalry continued to shadow the Federal Floatilla as it moved down the Tallahatchie. On the 10th he wrecked the steamer *Parallet* and a barge in the river. The barge, loaded with 3,000 bales of cotton, were set on fire and left to drift into the path of the gunboats. It did well the job of slowing and harassing the Federals.[7]

In spite of these efforts, the Federals that night tied up along side of the bank, only 32 miles above the fort. Tilghman was ordered to take the balance of his command from Jackson and proceed to Yazoo City as rapidly as possible.[8] At Yazoo City, Tilghman requested more ammunition for Fort Pemberton in preparation for the coming siege.[9]

The Confederates stationed in the fort were not surprised at the appearance of the Federal gun-boats on March 11, having observed the steady approach of the expedition for the last eight to ten miles as it came down stream with curling black smoke rising high above the forest. As fast as the current would permit, the large gun-boat *Chillicothe* advanced into open space in the river wishing to inspect the fort's defenses, especially the newly sunk *Star of the West*. The heavy cannon of the fort had an open front of the Tallahatchie for about a half-mile. When the *Chillicothe* got within range, the Confederates greeted the Union tars with a five gun salute; two shells striking hard on the turret and portside of the gunboat, forcing it to back up the river.

While the firing took place on the gunboats, the transports had tied-up at Shell Mound Plantation on the right bank of the river. Gen. L. F. Ross ordered his Indiana troops to disembark and explore the rebel position. The flooded countryside prevented the Hoosier's from making much of an approach on Colonel Waul's Texans, who were in place in their main line of resistance. Frustrated and soaking wet, the Union troopers retired to the transports.

The *Chillicothe*, ironclad *Baron De Kalb* and the ram *Lioness*, again floated down the river to investigate the defenses of the fort. At 4:15 PM, the fort's cannon erupted with a heavy fire on the *Chillicothe* and within ten minutes the trio of boats again backed out of range. In this encounter, four tars were killed and nine wounded. The heavy guns in the fort had done

The Siege of Fort Pemberton

good service in holding the Federals at bay.

As night approached, the Yankees landed a fatigue party on the edge of the woods about 700 yards from the Confederate fort. Here they placed a make-shift cotton-bale battery by removing one of the 30 pounder Parrotts from one of their gunboats. On the 12th, a second Parrott was landed as well as a 12-pound Howitzer.[10]

Meanwhile, Union soldiers toiled reinforcing with bales of cotton the bows and bulwarks of the *Chillicothe*, *Baron De Kalk*, and the mortar-boat, transforming them into cotton-clad boats.

Tilghman had come up to the fort from Yazoo City and he wired General Pemberton that the ammunition for the heavy guns had just arrived.[11]

On the 13th, the Federals commenced a coordinated attack. The three cotton-clads appeared from around the bend firing their bow guns while the land battery on the shore opened fire simultaneously on the fort. And as Tilghman later reported, "They kept it up with great spirit until after sunset."[12]

In this five hour battle, the *Chillicothe* was hit by 38 projectiles, the cotton bales were set on fire and six sailors on board were wounded. The *Baron De Kalb*, which fired on the fort at 15-minute intervals, was struck six times, sustaining casualties of three dead and three wounded. The mortar vessel had lofted 49 shells into the fort during the day, exhausting their supply of 200 pound shells.

The large gunboats moved slowly through the narrow, tree lined stretch of river. Unable to maneuver, they became sitting ducks causing them to take a terrible pounding from the forts artillery. The only thing the navy men accomplished was to bounce their big projectiles off the resilient parapet of cotton bales and earth inflicting but minor damage on the fort. During battle, General Loring was seen prancing back and forth on top of the cotton-bale parapet, shouting to his men, "Give them a blizzard of shot, boys. Give them a blizzard of shot." Thereafter his troops nicknamed him "Old Blizzards."

The following day Tilghman and Loring kept the men in the fort busy repairing the damaged parapets while the navy men on their cotton-clads were busy patching their badly crippled boats.

The Federal infantry, awaiting debarkation upriver found the banks still flooded and were unable to land any men.

A Dual Biography: General Lloyd Tilghman & General Francis Shoup

The best the Federals could do on the 14th was to fire the twin Parrotts of their land battery for a thirty-minute shower of shell. This same day the Confederates 8-inch naval gun arrived by steamer from Yazoo City and undercover of darkness on the 15th, the gun was placed in the battery. With the gun came much needed ammunition requested by Tilghman.

The Federals resumed their attack on the 16th. They decided that the cotton-clads would close rapidly on the fort and smother the defenders under a storm of shot and shell. As the *Chillicothe* closed within 1100 yards, the Confederate gunners registered eight direct hits within 15 minutes, sealing both gun ports so neither could be opened. This was enough for Commander Smith to call it quits, turn over his command to Com. J. P. Foster and begin a movement of the fleet and transports back up the river with the intention of returning to Helena. The Yankees had been defeated.

This move was aborted when Foster learned Gen. I. F. Quimby was coming through the Yazoo Pass with additional infantry for the campaign. Arriving on the scene, General Quimby deemed it best to order the troops and transports back towards Greenwood. After experiencing much difficulty in turning the boats about, the floatilla headed back downstream towards Fort Pemberton.

With the Federals withdrawing, Loring and Tilghman greatly strengthened their fortifications, constructing a number of secondary fortifications. The strength of the defenders was augmented by the arrival on March 29 of Gens. W. S. Featherston and J. C. Moore's brigades, bringing the fort's command to over 7,000. They now out-numbered the approaching enemy.

On the 23rd the *Chillicothe* appeared and the Confederates detonated a torpedo near her bow, requiring her to withdraw up the river. The aggressive Quimby went ashore and established headquarters at a farm house. He believed that his forces could be landed south of the fort and attack it from the rear. By the 28th, the rebs had thrown up new field works and they covered the reach of the Tallahatchie where Quimby intended to cross the river. Heavy rains continued to fall, greatly hampering the work of the Federal engineers charged with the construction of advanced artillery emplacements.

On April 1, Maj. Gen. D. H. Maury arrived from Vicksburg and the newcomer was assigned to the command of the Confederate Left Wing. On the 2nd, the fort shelled Quimby's farm-house headquarters. Tilghman made a map showing the position of Quimby's headquarters which was a

The Siege of Fort Pemberton

mile away from the fort, hidden in the dense forrest. Tilghman trained his guns by a compass while General Maury and Tilghman's staff, the 37th Mississippi Infantry, the 1st Mississippi sharp-shooters and the 2nd Texas Infantry made a reconnaissance of the position.[14]

General Maury could scarcely find dry land enough on which to form a line of battle for his force. Fires were lit all along the line so that the smoke might relieve the men and horses from the swarming buffalo gnats. "I lost twenty-four mules one night from their poisonous bites," reported Maury.[15]

At the appointed signal, Tilghman opened up with his artillery and the infantry and sharp-shooters went to work. This surprised the crowded camp of bluecoats and sent them scattering in all directions toward their transports for protection.

The Federal expedition loaded their infantry on board, packed up their equipment, guns and supplies, and began withdrawing their transports up the river back toward Moon Lake and Grant's Pass. Grant had given up on this invasion route. The two-month siege and expedition was another failure. The persistent Federals would try again!

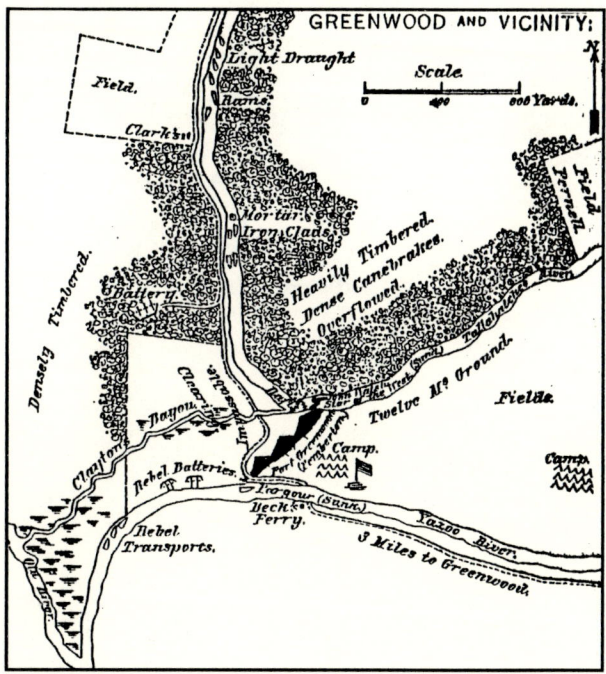

As the Union floatilla of gun-boats and transports retreated slowly

83

toward the Pass, detachments of Confederate units posted along the Tallahatchie fired upon the passing boats from ambush, but caused little damage.

General Pemberton did not order any pursuit. Instead he abandoned Fort Pemberton and returned the forces to their various assignments proclaiming he needed the men to defend Vicksburg.

General Grant was at the lowest point in his Western career as the northern newspapers attacked him for one failure after another. In these months of delay, thousands of casualties occurred and there were thoughts of recalling him. Fortunately for the Union, it never happened.

THE YAZOO EXPEDITION.

The Truth Concerning the Yazoo Expedition—Gen. C. C. Washburne's Energetic Opening of Yazoo Pass—Unwarrantable Delays of the Naval Force—Criminal Negligence of the Naval Commander—Eight Days Lost in Consequence—Rebel Fort Built in this time—The Expedition Brought to a Stand — The Greatest Opportunity of the Movement against Vicksburg Thrown Away—Where the Blame Rests—Affairs at Vicksburg — State of Things at Helena.

Correspondence of The N. Y. Tribune:
HELENA, Ark., March 28, 1863.

A complete roster of the Union and Confederate Forces that participated in this battle can be found in the Appendix to Chapter XIV at the End Notes, pages 133-136.

Chapter XV

Grierson's Raid

Confederate forces were elated in March when it was learned that the invincible Van Dorn and his cavalry force achieved a stunning victory over the Union cavalry at Thompson's Station, Tennessee on March 4. Battlefield success aside, Van Dorn would meet his end, not on the battlefield, but at the hand of an irate husband.

On May 8 at Spring Hill, Tennessee where Van Dorn made his headquarters, the General was assassinated by an angry husband who claimed Van Dorn had violated the sanctity of his home and wife. In addition to the loss of Van Dorn, Pemberton never got his cavalry back.

On April 13, upon Bragg's request, Pemberton ordered Generals Rust, Buford and Tilghman's brigades to Tullahoma, Tennessee to bolster Bragg's Army.[1]

Not deterred by his failures for the past three months, Grant ordered General McClernand to open a road for his army from Milliken's Bend on the Louisiana side of the river to a point on the river south of Vicksburg. At the same time, he ordered Admiral Porter to run the Vicksburg batteries with his floatilla and rendezvous with McClernand south of the city.

During the night of April 16, Porter got eleven boats safely past the river batteries at Vicksburg and succeeded in joining McClernand's forces at a village called Hard Times, Louisiana. With this news, Pemberton abruptly counter-manded his orders to Tilghman and the other brigades. They were to remain in their positions at Jackson and Clinton as reserve units waiting in readiness to support Vicksburg.

The Union navy continued to run the Vicksburg defenses by sailing six transports and twelve barges to bring supplies to McClernand; although almost every boat in the floatilla was hit repeatedly, this did not stop the invaders.

In order to divert Pemberton's attention from his movement down the river to Hard Times, Grant called for help from his cavalry. He proposed a series of combined cavalry raids in northern Mississippi that he hoped would distract General Pemberton and scatter his infantry reserves waiting north of Vicksburg.

A Dual Biography: General Lloyd Tilghman & General Francis Shoup

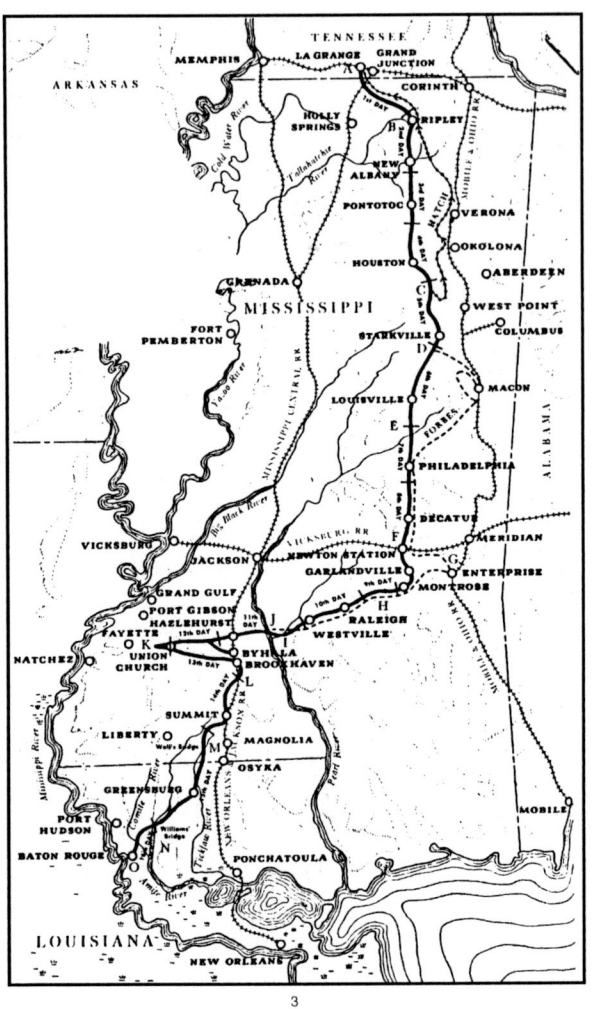

To accomplish this goal, Col. B. H. Grierson, with 1700 cavalrymen and six two-pounder cannons rode out of La Grange (near Memphis) at dawn on April 17, proceeding south towards Pontotoc, Mississippi. Here the command split, and Grierson, with his own regiment went towards the Jackson Railroad near Meridian.[2] At Starkville on the 22nd, 500 men left Grierson's main column and rode east towards Macon and Enterprise thus effecting another division in hopes of confusing Pemberton. With limited cavalry Pemberton's headquarters received contradictory reports of where the Yankee Cavalry was headed.

General Pemberton, not realizing at the time there was more than one column of Federal cavalry, devised an ambush for Grierson which he thought would entrap the invader.

Pemberton sent Loring to Meridian to command all troops in the vicinity and to try and contain Grierson's movement. Likewise, Col. J. Adams and three infantry regiments were sent to Morton to prevent Grierson from making a move on the capital at Jackson. He ordered Tilghman who had moved to Canton to have his trains put in readiness to move to Winona sixty miles north of Canton to block any retreat towards the northwest.[4] Pemberton was fairly confident that he now had the Yankee cavalry cornered. He next ordered Tilghman to send one-half of his command to

Grierson's Raid

Carthage. On the 25th, a courier from Carthage reported that seven hundred yankee cavalry had been at Philadelphia the day before. This was southeast of Starkville which meant they had slipped Pemberton's trap. On the same day, Loring informed Pemberton that the enemy was raiding the Mobile & Ohio Railroad at Enterprise and demanded the surrender of the town. When no surrender was forthcoming, the Federals rode off. Old Blizzard's Loring, who by now was disgusted with Pemberton ineptness closed the episode with the remark, "I have no hope of catching them on foot!"[5]

Since the Confederates were unable to defend every railroad station on the road with infantry, Grierson's columns struck at will and destroyed the roads, bridges and the telegraph lines. Moving southward, Grierson smashed the vital Southern Railroad at Newton and then rejoined Colonel Forbes brigade at the crossing of the Pearl River. They re-entered Union lines on May 2 at Baton Rouge, Louisiana, thus completing a very successful foray.

Grierson's men had traveled six hundred miles in sixteen days. They had cut through the center of the state of Mississippi and wrecked havoc on communications and destroyed vital military material. Colonel Grierson was rewarded by being promoted to Brigadier General on June 3, 1863.

In his futile effort to stop Grierson's raid, Pemberton had worn down his weary and scattered strategic reserves.[6] More importantly, Grant had diverted Pemberton's attention with the raid, and permitted Grant to set in motion the chain of events that would culminate in the fall of Vicksburg.

A Dual Biography: General Lloyd Tilghman & General Francis Shoup

Chapter XVI

Vicksburg and It's Approaches

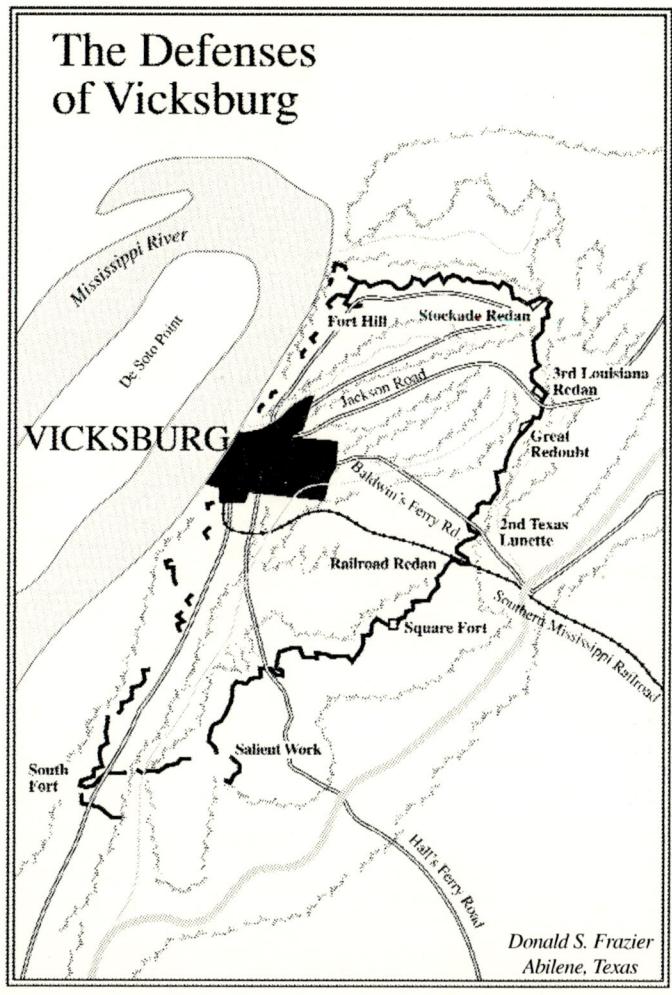

Operations by General Sherman's forces at Snyder's Bluff north of Vicksburg brought pressure to bear on Pemberton while the Federal naval squadrons, loaded to the gunwales with expeditionary supplies, fought and sailed successfully south beneath the guns of Vicksburg between April 16 and 22. [1]

With the change of season, and the drying of the roads, Grant's army began marching south on the Louisiana side of the river. On the 29th, his advance Corps reached the hamlet of Hard Times, Louisiana. He was now south of Vicksburg and opposite Grand Gulf, waiting for the balance of his land forces.

Pemberton repeatedly requested General Bragg to return his cavalry of 4500 horsemen. Bragg refused.[2] Receiving no help from Bragg, Pemberton turned to Gen. Richard Taylor across the river in Louisiana for re-enforcements. But Taylor had his own problems.

Meanwhile, Gen. J. S. Bowen, who commanded the Grand Gulf fort twenty-five miles below Vicksburg observed the Union gunboats and transports as they moved past his fort. The Union squadrons began to ferry McClernand's Army from the Louisiana shore at Hard Times to Bruinsburg on the Mississippi side, six miles below Grand Gulf. If Pemberton had not spread his forces all over Mississippi he may have been able to trap Grant's divided forces as they were ferried from one side of the river to the other. Bowen, with limited forces telegraphed Pemberton to send him re-enforcements.

On short notice, Gen. E. D. Tracy troops moved out of camp at Warrenton on the 27th and marched twenty-seven hours non-stop to join Bowen. Likewise, General Baldwin's forces, north of Vicksburg, marched all the way to Port Gibson to join the others. Bowen ended up with 8,000 fatigued Johnnies and little more. The Federals had slipped the noose.

After the establishment of the beachhead at Brunisburg, General McClernand's XIII Corps came ashore and were closely followed by the divisions of J. B. McPherson and J. A. Logan, presenting a Federal front of 22,000 troops to join the battle. On May 1, after an afternoon of severe fighting at Port Gibson, General Bowen had to withdraw from the field and give ground to McClernand's Corp. In the fray, General Tracy fell near the front line, pierced through the breast and died without uttering a word.[3]

Looking to remedy the situation, Pemberton ordered Tilghman to take his field battery and troops and move rapidly to the Big Black River bridge at Vicksburg and to assume command of the troops in the vicinity. On his arrival, Tilghman wired Pemberton he had an effective aggregate strength of 1,550 men.[4]

On May 1, Loring, at Jackson, received many contradicting orders. "You will proceed at once to Port Gibson with Tilghman's two regiments, which have gone from Edwards Station. Your troops from Jackson to come via Vicksburg." Later in the day, "Proceed to Edwards Depot; from thence with General Tilghman to Port Gibson. You will take command of operation there. General Tilghman will be placed in command of Tracy's bridge (he was now deceased) and his own regiments there."[5] More orders to Tilghman by Pemberton directed, "Hurry on your two regiments as rapidly as possible. Wait yourself for General Loring…take no artillery and send your two regiments with greatest dispatch to Grand Gulf by dirt road…Loring will take the Point Coupee Artillery from Jackson." Now a countermand, "Do not march by Grand Gulf, but go the most direct route to Port Gibson."[6] Pemberton wired Richmond, "unless very large re-enforcements are sent here, I think Port Hudson and Grand Gulf should be evacuated. I will required at least 6,000 cavalry to prevent heavy raids and to keep railroad communications on which our supply depends."[7] Richmond promised that heavy re-enforcements would be sent from General Beauregard's department; he spared two brigades totaling 5,000 men. From Gen. J. E. Johnston he received word that "Forrest is moving west with his cavalry."[8] All of these requests were too late. With the broken down and patched Southern Railroad System, any re-enforcements coming from the east would take two weeks or longer to arrive. Frantic with worry, Pemberton began switching infantry units from one location to another in hopes of containing Grant's movements so that he could hold Vicksburg until re-enforcements could arrive.

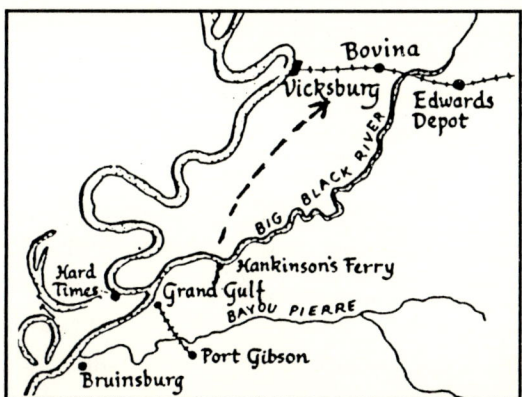

General Bowen, meanwhile, was attempting to maintain his position below Bayou Pierre. On May 2, he was relieved to see Generals Loring and Tilghman riding into camp. His hope was that the re-enforcements they would be bringing would be sufficient to halt the tide of bluecoats. Unfortunately, the 3500 additional men hardly filled Bowen's need to defend Port Gibson and Grand Gulf. At midnight Bowen issued orders to abandon their positions and to begin the retreat to Hankinson Ferry on the Big Black River. The vanguard reached the flatboat bridge on May 3rd, and began crossing the Big Black. By mid-afternoon, the soldiers and their baggage, ammunition and a supply train had crossed the river. A formidable rear guard of Tilghman's, Reynolds' and Cockrell's units harassed the pursuing Federal cavalry.

Admiral Potter's gunboats took possession of Grand Gulf on May 3, and the Big Black River was open to the Union Navy. Once over the Big Black, Loring wired Pemberton, "The troops are prostrated by constant marching and want of sleep."[9] The Confederate forces were west of the Big Black and moving towards Mont Alban and then Bovina. Loring continued, "The enemy is now at Hankinson's Ferry and with pontoons are preparing to cross the river."

At 10 PM the rear guard of Bowen's depleted division passed through Mont Alban followed by Tilghman, who was five or six miles behind him. Earlier in the day, Tilghman's brigade held the enemy in check on the road from Gridstone Ford to Hankinson's Ferry.[10]

The defeat of General Bowen at Port Gibson and the subsequent withdrawal to the north bank of the Big Black made it necessary for the concentration of Pemberton's whole force for the defense of Vicksburg.

On May 4th, Loring and Tilghman were ordered to Big Black Bridge and Edwards Depot, establishing headquarters at N. B. Lanier's plantation, three miles south of Mount Alban on the Baldwin-Ferry road west of the Big Black River.[11] Officers in command at Grenada, Columbus, and Jackson were to move all available forces to Vicksburg as rapidly as possible.[12]

General Grant established his base of supplies at Grand Gulf while the troops remained three days in bivouac at Willow Springs and Hankinson's ferry, awaiting the arrival of Sherman's corp from north of Vicksburg.

Grant's first intention had been to establish himself there and then detach a corps to cooperate with Gen. N. P. Banks in Louisiana in reducing the bastion at Port Hudson. His plan went awry when a letter from General Banks revealed that he was in the interior of Louisiana, and could not reach Port Hudson before the 10th of May.

This delay was all that Grant needed to decide his movements. To wait would permit Pemberton to receive re-enforcements. Grant's sources had already informed him that General J. E. Johnston was on his way from Chattanooga with substantial re-enforcements.

Grant decided to cut loose from his present supply base at Grand Gulf, to feed his troops on what they could carry in their haversack and what they

Vicksburg and It's Approaches

may pilfer along the way, and moving with all possible speed, unencumbered by heavy wagons, to attack Jackson, the Capitol of Mississippi.

At Jackson, Gov. John J. Pettus began moving the state archives. Staff, state records and all valuable stores were sent to northeastern Mississippi to establish a government in exile at Columbus. As soon as Sherman crossed over the river from Hard Times on May 7, the invading Federal force was made up of three corps or about 45,000 bluecoats.

Grant began moving in the direction of Jackson. The centre wing under Sherman headed for Bolton Station; the right wing under McPherson was directed toward Raymond and the left wing under McClernand marched up the eastern bank of the Big Black River, threatening Tilghman and Loring at Edward's Depot.

Tilghman reported he saw plainly about sixty cavalry on the opposite bank of the Big Black River, moving toward Edward's Ferry. "The man at the ferry says the enemy stated their number to be 4000 to 5000, all cavalry, bound for Edward's Depot.[13] This was part of a feint by Grant, in hopes of confusing Pemberton.

A Dual Biography: General Lloyd Tilghman & General Francis Shoup

Chapter XVII

The Fall of Jackson

Union J. A. McClernand's corps, eleven miles west of the village of Raymond made contact with Loring's outposts guarding the crossings of the Fourteen Mile Creek. Sharp skirmishing ensued as the Federals drove Loring's pickets back across the creek. Grant then ordered McClernand to disengage his force along the creek and contain Tilghman's and Loring's brigades, thus eliminating some of the Confederate force.

Union General McPherson's advance skirmish line on the 12th encountered 5000 grayclads in a strong position at the village of Raymond. Pemberton received the news, "A courier just in from Raymond talked with General Gregg on the battlefield. His troops are falling back before greatly superior numbers." Gen. W. H. T. Walker is within four miles of Gregg with 1000 men and will join him."[1]

Gregg and Walker, after a furious battle with Logan's Division, fell back toward the capitol, hopefully to find General Johnston there with reenforcements from the east.

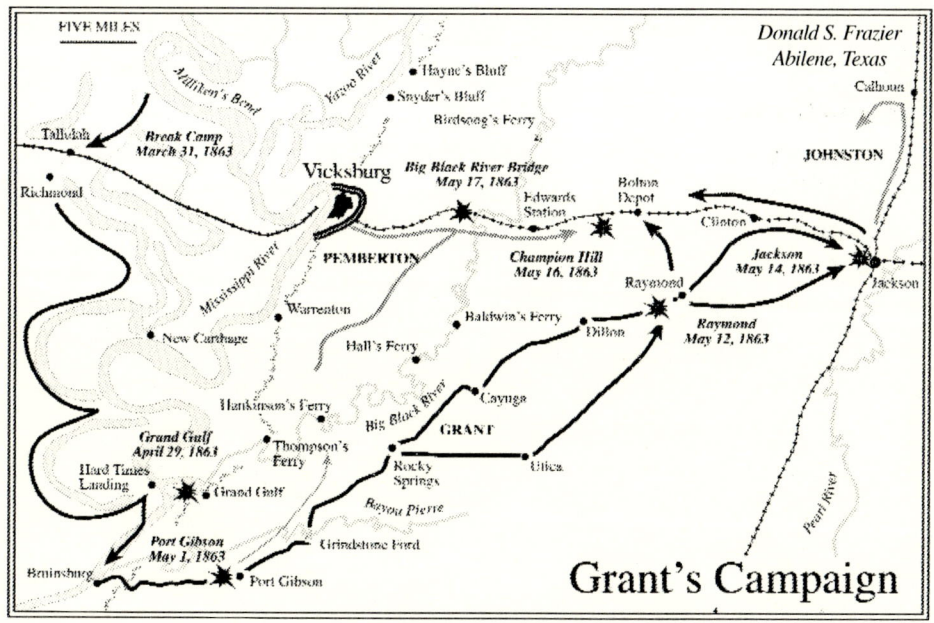

The move on Jackson.

A Dual Biography: General Lloyd Tilghman & General Francis Shoup

The popular Joe Johnston had been rushed west to support Pemberton. Departing Tullahoma, Tennessee, he was fifty miles east of Jackson by the 13th when he received word that elements of the Union Corps were moving rapidly towards Jackson. Upon his arrival at Jackson, Gregg told him that just 6000 Confederate forces were available to defend the capital city. Out of necessity, Johnston decided to retreat from the capital before any pressure would be put on him to do battle in defending it. He would leave Gregg behind to defend Jackson until the evacuation was completed.

Johnston then fired off his famous message to President Davis, "I arrived this evening finding the enemy in force between this place and General Pemberton, cutting off the communication. I am too late."[2]

Although Gregg and Walker put up a stubborn fight in a pouring rainstorm, the Federals finally entered Jackson. This was the second Confederate State Capital to fall since the war began, Nashville being the first in 1862.

Gregg and Walker and their troops retreated on the Canton Road and joined Johnston who was ten miles north of the burning capital. In a fortnight, Johnston would have over 20,000 troops in his command, but these would not help Pemberton now.

General Grant, leaving Sherman to burn the bridges, factories, arsenals and government buildings at Jackson, faced his column west and started for Vicksburg. The red bearded Sherman did not dally in Jackson more than a day. Once the city was fired, he followed Grant to the west and camped his troops at the town of Clinton.

Along with Grierson's raid and the loss of the railroad and telegraph at Jackson, Pemberton found himself isolated and denied valuable military information. Without the cavalry still with Bragg's Army, his position was untenable.

Johnston, near Canton, north of the flaming capital, composed a written order to Pemberton outlining plans for a proposed joint offensive against Sherman's Corp encamped at Clinton. Johnston's message to Pemberton was clear, "It is important to re-establish communications. If practicable, come up on Sherman's rear at once. The troops here could cooperate. All the strength you can quickly assemble should be brought."[3] This written message was made out in triplicate and handed to Capt. Wm. S. Yerger and two other couriers. The hope was that one of them would get through to Pemberton's headquarters.

Captain Yerger, by moving around McPherson's flank, did deliver these instructions to Pemberton on May 14 at 9 AM. At about the same time, one of the other duplicate messages of Johnston's orders was delivered to Union Gen. J. B. McPherson! One of the trusted couriers was a southern traitor. This valuable information was dispatched to Grant.

The absence of Van Dorn's cavalry now became critical as the need for communication and co-operation between Pemberton and Johnston's Army would be necessary for survival.

Who commanded the department had been growing unclear in the past ten days. The newly arrived General Johnston and President Davis repeatedly warned Pemberton not to surrender Vicksburg, not to get trapped in the city and not to permit a siege of the garrison by General Grant.

As Pemberton journeyed to join his army at Edwards Depot, he had second thoughts about attacking Sherman's corps as had been ordered by Johnston. Upon arrival at the Depot, he decided against the move and rescinded Johnston's orders. He then called a council of his field generals. The council adopted a plan of divide and conquer. Their strategy envisioned a Confederate advance along the Raymond road as far as Mrs. Ellison's place. Here the army would turn south and strike the Port Gibson-Raymond Road, Grant's line of communication at Dillon's plantation. Pemberton's united Confederate forces would then overwhelm and destroy the isolated A. J. Smith's division at Dillon's before the Federal troops which had advanced on Jackson could come to Smith's aid.[4] Having resolved to move on Dillons, Pemberton sent the courier back to General Johnston with his revised plans.

On May 15, leaving 10,000 troops in the Vicksburg garrison, Pemberton began moving his field army of approximately 17,000 men. The artillery and ambulances followed in the rear of each brigade of men; the ordnance wagons followed in the rear of the division; while the wagons of supplies followed in the rear of the train. The entire train was two and a half miles long.

Col. Wirt Adam's cavalry formed the advance guard and rode at least one mile ahead of the main body. Loring's division with Tilghman constituted the right in the line of march; Bowen's division constituted the center and Stevenson's division constituted the left and brought up the rear of the column. Continuing heavy rains had made Baker's Creek impassable by the ordinary ford on the main Raymond Road, where the country bridge had

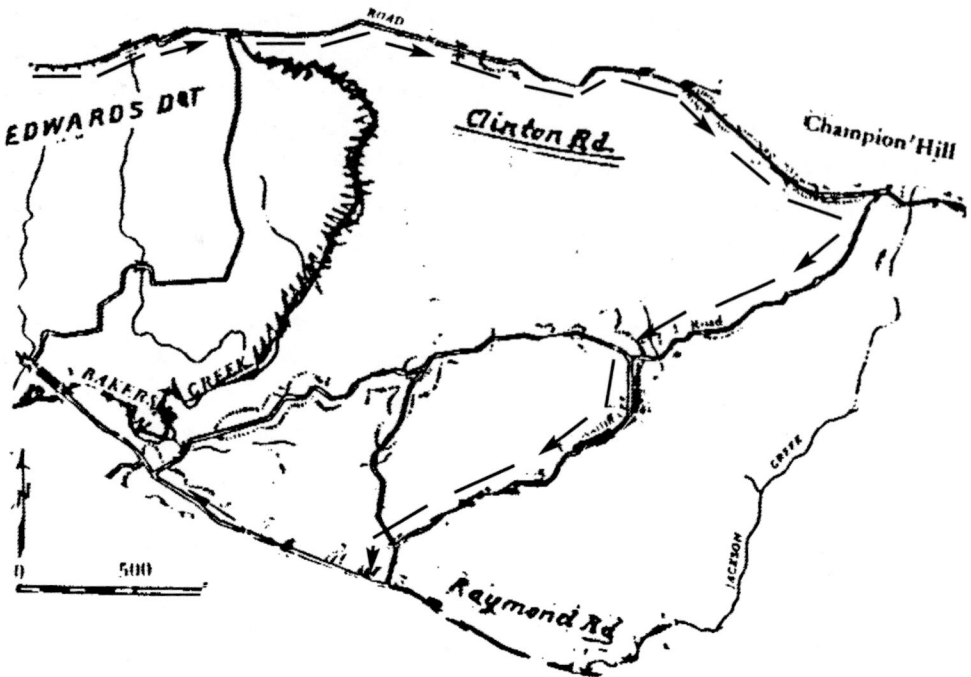

been washed away. The column had to detour to the Clinton Road where there was a good bridge. Once over Baker's Creek, the van traveled a mile and a half to Champion's Hill and then turned right on to a local road, so as to strike towards the main Raymond Road. This was a narrow country road that was hedged on either side by dense woods. The column continued on the narrow back road until the front column of Lorning and Tilghman came back to the main Raymond Road. Here they turned left and continued to the Elliston's house where they halted and the troops bivouacked for the night of the 15th.[5]

During the day, one of Pemberton's couriers arrived at Johnston's headquarters with his message. When General Johnston read the plan, he was distressed, since Pemberton's move was away from Clinton, thus increasing the distance between the two Confederate commands. Johnston dashed off a reply, "Your dispatch of yesterday received and your plan impracticable. The only mode by which we can unite is by your moving directly to Clinton." Without the benefit of adequate cavalry, neither Johnston nor Pemberton were aware that Grant, with seven divisions of about 32,000 bluecoats, were between Bolton and Raymond and were converging toward Champion Hill. Early on May 16, Pemberton received Johnston's message. Pemberton then ordered a countermarch towards Clinton. This change of orders brought on wholesale confusion among the men and officers. The tail of the van resting partially on the Clinton Road now became the head of the column; while the head of the column resting on the Raymond Road would become the rear. The whole army would have to reverse itself in order to make the move. It could not be done on this narrow country road. Pemberton's Army was boxed into a frightful predicament.

By sunrise it became evident that the Confederates along this long narrow country road had come into such proximity of the advancing Federal corps that the bluecoats on the Raymond Road had begun skirmishing with Loring's advance skirmishes at the Elliston's place.

A Dual Biography: General Lloyd Tilghman & General Francis Shoup

Chapter XVIII

Fateful Champion Hill

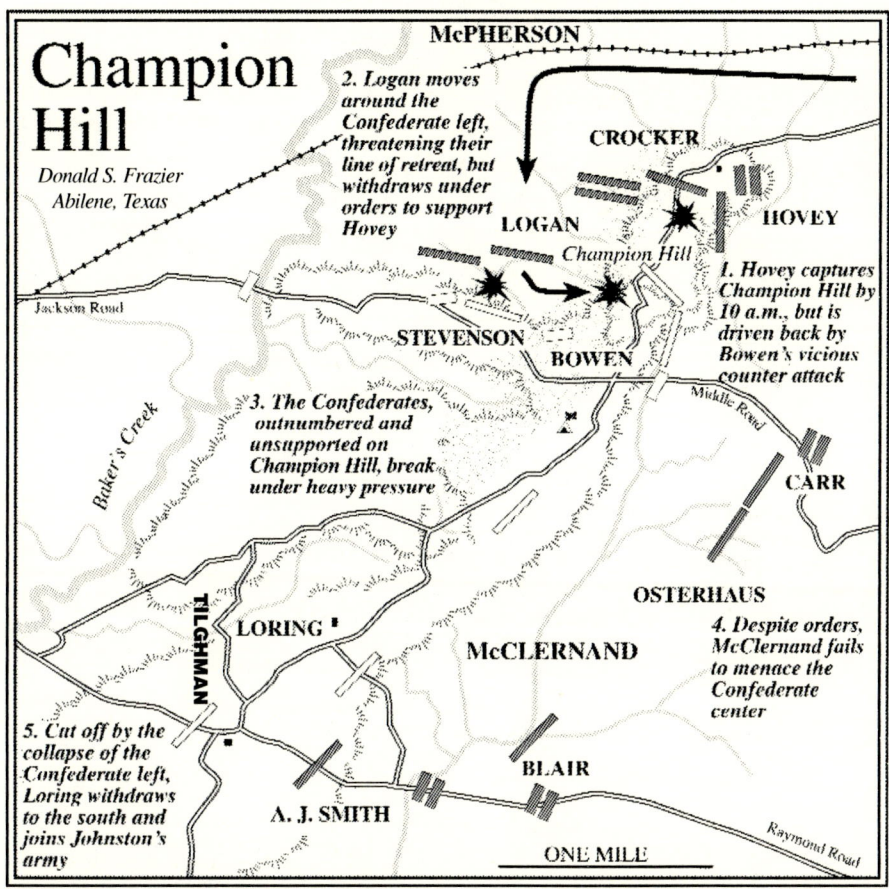

Within the twenty-four hour period before May 15, over sixty-five thousand soldiers from the Union and Confederate armies had converged on a two-and-a-half mile stretch of country outside of Edward's Depot, known as Baker's Creek or Champion Hill.

The battle line at Champion Hill happened by accident. No earthened levy had been erected or trenches dug and only a smattering of unsurveyed ravines and bushes would separate the tide of the blue and the gray. Prior to Pemberton's countermarch orders, Tilghman surprisingly received an order from General Pemberton's headquarters relieving him of his command and directing the senior Colonel of the brigade to take its command! The only plausible explanation could be Pemberton's continuing feud with Tilghman.

At Loring's headquarters at the Ellison's house, Lt. W. A. Drennen of Gen. W. S. Featherston's staff wrote to his wife, "I sat down under a tree and listened to Generals Loring, Tilghman and Featherston engage in quite an animated conversation, the principal topic being General Pemberton and the affairs of the country in general. They all said harsh, ill-natured things, made ill-tempered jests in regard to General Pemberton and when an order came from him, the courier who brought it was not out of hearing, before they made light of it and ridiculed the plan he proposed." [1]

Lt. F. W. Merrin of McLendon's battery later wrote, "Here was a pretty kettle of fish. The whole army right close up, face to face, with Grant's army, twice or three times as strong, and our officers are all in a stew!" He continued, "General Loring, who acted as a breakwater between the two on past occasions now again cut the Gordeon knot. This one-armed general rode squarely up to the pompous Pemberton and in language more forcible than elegant, more caustic than clever, informed Pemberton that unless he then and there revoked the order of the day before in reference to Tilghman that he might dispense with his (Loring's) service for the day's battle. Then and there, an order was hastily written by Pemberton on the pummel of his saddle, restoring General Tilghman to his command." [2]

Pemberton's movement towards Edwards Depot had hardly begun when at approximately 6:30 a.m., Col. W. Adams reported that his pickets were skirmishing with the Federals on the Raymond Road some distance in front of Tilghman's position.[3] Colonel Goodwin rode to the front and conferred with Colonel Adams about the strength of the foe. "The Federal cavalry were drawn up in an open field at intervals of 40 to 50 yards and were slowly advancing, driving in the vindettes. Behind the cavalry a long battle-line of infantry moving to the right."[4] This was General McClernand's Seventeenth Army Corp. that had been ordered by Grant to day before to move forward cautiously, "feeling the enemy if he encountered him, but not to bring on an engagement unless he felt entirely able to content with him." [5]

After reconnoitering the front himself, General Loring ordered the line of battle to be changed to a high hill on a continuous ridge some 600 yards in the rear of his present line. This defensive position became known as the

Fateful Champion Hill

Coker House ridge. Upon this ridge, Tilghman's artillery was advantageously posted on both sides of the Raymond Road. The field to the front was entirely open as far as Mrs. Ellison's house. This new line of resistance facing eastward offered the army a stronger position as it permitted coverage of the plantation road which could be utilized by Pemberton to shift troops rapidly from one threatened sector to another.[6]

The Tenth Division of the Union XIII Corps, spearheaded by Gen. S. G. Burbridge's 1st Brigade, advanced down the Raymond Road but was halted when the vanguard reached Jackson's Creek and discovered the bridge had been destroyed by Colonel Goodwin's men.

Efforts by the Union pioneers to repair the bridge were frustrated as Tilghman's artillery with a range of 1200 yards roared into action.

General Burbridge eye-witness account reveals, "I pushed my brigade rapidly ahead until the skirmishers began to find it a hot contest, and as we rode to the crest of the hill, they poured in a most terrific fire of shot, shell, grape, and canister. My sharpshooters kept the enemy annoyed and they had to abandon some of their guns. After a lively artillery duel for an hour or more, the attack was relinquished."[7]

The battle for Champion Hill started quickly. As the demonstrations of the Union Army became more serious, orders were set to the Confederate Division Commanders to form in line of battle on the cross-road from the Clinton to the Raymond Road. This cross-road was likened to that of a one-and-a-half mile string of fireworks. It was ignited early by Tilghman's artillery and soon spread across the narrow country road and then to the Clinton Road where it let go with one big explosion at 10 A.M., when a large Federal force was thrown against Gen. C. L. Stevenson's front at Champion Hill.

Pemberton soon became uneasy of having the swollen Baker's Creek to the rear of his army and the bridge being washed out. He sent instructions to Tilghman to collect all the spades and picks and move some men down the Raymond Road and cut down the side of the banks at the ford. Maj. S. H. Lockett had a pioneer company construct a bridge as soon as possible across Baker's Creek.[8] This move saved Pemberton's forces later in the day.

By 11 a.m. the engagement became general all along the lines and began to rage with increasing fury as General Stevenson's rebels were driven back with great slaughter from Champion Hill.

General Bowen was now moved to Stevenson's aid, thus leaving a gap

103

in the Confederate line. By 2 p.m., Loring received orders to move to the left to fill this gap. He refused to move because of the large Federal force to his front. His division was the only one in the area to contain McClernand's Army.

Subsequently, after much bantering from Pemberton's subordinate officers, Loring decided to move without receiving Pemberton's order in person. Taking Gen. W. S. Fatherston's brigade with him, he left Tilghman's single brigade alone on the Raymond Road to cover the right and center of the original Confederate line, a position previously held by five brigades.[9]

By early afternoon the Federals had succeeded by their vastly superior numbers in completely turning the Confederate left, and Stevenson's and Bowen's division began to break and fall back in considerable disorder. The battlefield was littered with the wounded and dead of both sides.

The Jackson Road crossing at Baker's Creek was one of the open avenues of escape. By mid-afternoon this route, too was closed, leaving the Confederates the Raymond Road make-shift bridge crossing the Baker's Creek as the only avenue of escape.

Tilghman brigade began following Loring's move to the left when they met up with Maj. S. H. Lockett, who had been directed by Pemberton to inform Tilghman, "that the position he occupied was one of vast importance in securing the Confederate retreat, and that he must hold the Raymond Road at all hazard."[10]

Tilghman halted his command, and facing about, returned to the Raymond Road, and took a new position on a ridge some six hundred yards in rear of his first position and just in front of the cross road which the shattered Confederate forces began using. This ridge was known as Cotton Hill. Here, Capt. J. Cowan's Battery of Artillery and Company G, Col. W. F. Wither's Regiment straddled the Raymond Road.

About 3:00 P.M., General Loring, withdrawing his division from the battle, rode up to Captain Cowan and said, "I intend to save my Division as I have been cut off by the defeat of General Stevenson. I want your Battery to hold this position until sun down, fall back, following my line of retreat."[11]

The Federal troops, pursuing the earlier withdrawal of Tilghman's troops from the ridge west of the Coker House, took possession of this ridge. The Chicago Mercantile Battery went into position with six ten-pound Parrot guns, four six-pound guns and two ten-pound Howitzers. The

Fateful Champion Hill

Federal battery opened up and firing accurately began assaulting Tilghman's brigade.

By inspiration and personal courage, Tilghman's brigade contained the Federals from charging his woefully undermanned position on Cotton Hill while the country road filled up with men in gray fleeing with their horses, wagons, and artillery, all bent on escaping the pursuing bluecoats. Bedlam had broken out as Pemberton called for a retreat towards Vicksburg.

An eye witness relates, "General Tilghman came to our position in an open field on foot. He was in a particularly good humor and wore a new fatigue uniform. He ordered his son, Lloyd Tilghman, Jr., who was his aide-de-camp, to go with a squad of men and drive some Federal sharpshooters from a gin house on the left of the Raymond Road who were annoying Wither's cannoners."[12]

Captain Cowan and his officers were mounted, making them a conspicuous target for the Federal sharpshooters. Tilghman said in a pleasant manner, "I think you and your Lieutenants had better dismount. They are shooting pretty close to us, and I do not know whether they are shooting at your large gray horse or my new uniform." The officers promptly obeyed and dismounted. General Tilghman then went to one of the twelve-pound Napoleon's and remarked to the gunner, "I think you are shooting rather too high," and sighted the gun himself. He returned to a little knoll within a few feet of the gun, and was standing erect, his field glasses to his eyes, watching for the effect of the shot from the gun, when there was a thud and Tilghman suddenly collapsed to the ground. A piece of an incoming exploding Parrot shell had struck Tilghman in the upper part of his stomach. The three inch solid piece of metal passed through him and nearly cut him in half. As he lay unconscious, men raced to find his son who was brought back to his fallen father.[13]

"I shall never forget the touching scene when, with grief and lamentations, his son cast himself on his dying father.[14] The soldiers who witnessed this distressing scene shed tears of sympathy for the bereaved son and of sorrow for their fallen hero, the chivalrous and beloved Tilghman."

He was struck at 5:20 o'clock on Saturday, May 16, and lived about three hours after being carried to the shade of a peach tree. He died in the arms of his adjutant general, Powhatan Ellis.

His body was carried on a litter from the field of honor by four of his men. Tilghman's mortal remains were taken to Vicksburg for burial in

A Dual Biography: General Lloyd Tilghman & General Francis Shoup

Searles family plot in the city cemetary.[15]

General Tilghman's death spared him the sight of the defeat of his soldiers. The rebels abandoned their cannon and wagon to escape into the darkness and confusion perhaps to fight another day. Some followed Loring to Crystal Springs and eventually to join Johnson's Army at Jackson. Others, unluckily, followed Captain Cowan into Vicksburg. (See page 175 for additional details of Vicksburg battle.) They would help in the gallant defense of the city, throwing back repeated Federal assaults, but disaster awaited them. Grant could not carry the garrison by storm but, eventually, after hard times on rations of rat and mule meat, the Confederates were starved into submission. Pemberton, whose blunders had contributed greatly to the Confederate defeat surrendered his command on July 4, 1863. In sorrow and disgrace, Pemberton would finish out the war as an obscure Lieutenant Colonel. The Father of the Waters now flowed unvexed to the sea as Lincoln would say, but for the Confederate States of America, the sun was setting.

General Tilghman at his moment of death at Champion Hill is the finest statue in the Vicksburg National Military Park.

Sentiment Inscribed on the Monument
BRIGADIER GENERAL LLOYD TILGHMAN C-S-A
Commanding First Brigade of Loring's Division
Killed May 16, 1863
Near The Close Of The Battle Of Champion Hill, Miss

Chapter XIX

In The Midst Of Life There Is Death

Ah! Fearless on many a day for us
They stood in front of the fray for us
And held the foeman at bay for us
　And tears should fall
　Fore'er o'er all
Who fell while wearing the gray for us. [1]

"Poor Tilghman" lamented Lieutenant Drennan. "Three hours before I had sat and listened to him talking and jesting – full of life and gaity – and now he has gone to that place from whence no traveler returns."

A saddened Loring spoke out, "he repulsed the enemy on several occasions and thus kept open the only line of retreat left to the army. The bold stand of his brigade saved a large portion of the Confederate Army."

Loring's condolence for his loyal friend continued, "it is befitting that I should speak of the death of gallant and accomplished Lloyd Tilghman. Quick and bold in the execution of his plans, he fell in the midst of his brigade that loved him well, after repelling a powerful enemy in deadly fight, struck by a cannon shot. The brigade wept over the dying hero, alike beautiful as it was touching." [2]

Col. A. E. Reynolds who succeeded to the command of Tilghman's brigade paid this high tribute to his memory. "As a man, a soldier, and a general, he had few superiors. Always at his post, he devoted himself, day and night, to the interests of his command. Upon the battlefield collected and observant, he commanded the respect and entire confidence of every officer and soldier under him, and the only censure ever cast upon him was that he always exposed himself too recklessly." [3]

****

WHAT PRESIDENT DAVIS SAID OF GENERAL TILGHMAN.

Evidence of his great merit to the homage of his people of the Southland may be had in an address delivered by Jefferson Davis at Mississippi City, Miss., in 1878, when he said: "Martyrdom has generally been considered, and with reason, a fruit of the sanctity of the cause in which the martyr died. You know how many examples your army furnished of men who piously served and piously died from wounds received in battle. The proofs of martyrdom, if I were to attempt to enumerate, would exceed your time and my strength on this occasion. Yet I am not willing to pass by as silent memory some of those examples of heroism, of patriotism, of devotion to country which the Army of Tennessee furnished. The Greek who held the pass, the Roman who for a time, held the bridge have been immortalized in rhyme and story. But neither of these more heroically, more patriotically, more singly served his country than did Tilghman at Fort Henry, when approached by a large army, an army which rendered the permanent defense of the fort impossible, with with a handful of devoted followers went into the fort and continued the defense until his brigade could retire in safety to Fort donelson; then when that work was finished, when it was impossible any longer to make a defense, when the wounded and dying lay all around him, he, with the surviving remnant of his little band, terminated the struggle and suffered in a manner thousands of you who have been prisoners of war know how to estimate. All peace and honor to his ashes, for he was among those, not the most unhappy, who went hence before our bitterest trials came upon us."

4

The avenues of communication was always open between both sides.
    On August 28, 1863, Gen. W. T. Sherman communicated to Mrs. Augusta Tilghman still living in Clarksville, Tennessee the sad news of the death of her son Lloyd, Jr.

In The Midst Of Life There Is Death

HEADQUARTERS FIFTEENTH ARMY CORPS
Camp on Big Black, Miss., August 28, 1863.

General W. H. JACKSON,
   Commanding Division of Cavalry, C. S. Army, Canton:
GENERAL: I had the honor to receive on the 24th instant at the hands of Captain Moorman your letter of the 23d. 'The lady, Mrs. Cotton, was sent to Vicksburg by cars. I also according to the request of captain Moorman communicated to Mrs. General Tilghman, at Clarksville, Tenn., the sad news of the death of her son Lloyd.

I have noticed by your newspapers that General Stephen D. Lee has been assigned to command the cavalry forces in the State of Mississippi, and that he entered on his duties about the 20th instant. Our official advices from Washington come down to a much later period, and we have no notice that the Vicksburg prisoners or any of them have been exchanged. Such a notice is universally required in war, and is specifically required by the Dix-Hill cartel, article 5. If General Lee is in command I request this letter be considered as addressed to him, and that he communicate to me the simple fact that he has received notice of his exchange from the proper quarters in Richmond, and if possible the name of the officer or officers taken as his equivalent. This information will enable me and General Grant to repress a growing belief that your authorities design to disregard the Vicksburg paroles, which I cannot suppose.

I send this communication by the hands of my aide, Captain Dayton, and escort of twenty-five men, accompanied by Colonel Coolbaugh, who is well acquainted with many of your officers, and I authorize them to carry along a budget of newspapers, full of the current gossip of the world, in which I know you feel more interest than you would have us outside barbarians believe.†

With great respect, your obedient servant,
W. T. SHERMAN,
Major-General, Commanding.

OR Series II, Vol. 6, p. 234

A Dual Biography: General Lloyd Tilghman & General Francis Shoup

Chapter XX

Tilghman's Monuments and Homestead

When General Tilghman offered his life in defense of the cause of the South, he wrought with his own blood an epitaph which would not be forgotten as long as bronze statues last to remind all who see them of his courage and gallantry.

In 1902 his two sons, Sidell Tilghman and Frederick B. Tilghman, who lived in New York City, came to Vicksburg to recover their father's remains. While on this mission the two successful stock brokers selected a

New York City
(The Bronx)
Woodlawn Cemetery

Grave of General Lloyd Tilghman.[1]

A Dual Biography: General Lloyd Tilghman & General Francis Shoup

site for the erection of a Tilghman equestrian statue and also marked the site at Champion Hill where their father was mortally wounded.

The general's remains were disinterred at Vicksburg and at the request of his sons, were taken to New York City where they were reburied in Woodlawn Cemetery.

In 1907 the two sons returned to Vicksburg and dedicated a monument on the spot where their father was killed at Champion Hill.

On May 16, 1909 (same month and day that General Tilghman was

Present for the dedication of their father's monument on the spot where he was killed on Champion Hill were the Tilghman brothers (kneeling), of New York City. Other identified in the 1907 photograph found in the Mississippi Dept. of Archives and History were: "Artist" no name , extreme right, J. W. Ratliff, next to him; Capt. W. T. Ratliff, next to his brother; and Capt. Rigby, next to Capt. Ratliff. Mrs. Sid (Matilda) Champion is the lady.

Mississippi Dept. of Archives and History

killed) his two sons in co-operation with the Paducah Chapter of the United Daughters of The Confederacy, unveiled a fitting monument in Lang Park in Paducah, Kentucky. It was designed by sculptor Henry H. Kittson.

In 1921 Lloyd Tilghman's two sons donated the site where the new Augusta Tilghman High School was constructed in Paducah.

Tilghman's Monuments and Homestead

PADUCAH MONUMENT
TO GENERAL TILGHMAN

SENTIMENT INSCRIBED ON THE MONUMENT AT
PADUCAH, KY.
Brig. Gen. Lloyd Tilghman, C. S. A.
Killed in the Battle of Champion Hill, Miss.
May 16, 1863
"To the faithful sons of the Confederate States of America who gave all to uphold the constitutional liberty and States rights."

ENLARGED VIEW OF THE STATUE

A Dual Biography: General Lloyd Tilghman & General Francis Shoup

In 1919, specifications for the erection and completion of a granite pedestal with an equestrian statue of General Lloyd Tilghman was proposed by the Vicksburg National Military Park Commission. F. Wm. Sievers of Richmond, Virginia was commissioned as the sculptor and Frederick and Sidell Tilghman, his two sons, would pay for the monument. The monument was dedicated on May 19, 1926. Sidell Tilghman, now the only son surviving, made the presentation and the acceptance was delivered by Governor Harry L. Whitfield at Vicksburg, Mississippi.[3] (page 106).

This single family dwelling was occupied by Lloyd Tilghman and his family in 1852.

It was a single family home for fifty-four years and then became a boarding house and later an office building.

Growth, Inc. saved the house from demolition in 1986 and then in 1992 it became the Tilghman Heritage Foundation.[4]

General Lloyd Tilghman House
Seventh & Kentucky Avenue
Paducah, Kentucky

Tilghman's Monuments and Homestead

Today, the Sons of Confederate Veterans is preserving the history and legacy of these heroes, so future generations can understand the motives that animated the Southern Cause.

The SCV is the direct heir of the United Confederate Veterans, and the oldest hereditary organization for male descendants of Confederate soldiers. Organized at Richmond, Virginia, in 1896, the SCV continues to serve as a historical, patriotic, and non-political organization dedicated to insuring that a true history of the 1861-1865 period is preserved.

GENERAL LLOYD TILGHMAN CAMP 1495
Sons of Confederate Veterans
Paducah, Kentucky
1989

A Dual Biography: General Lloyd Tilghman & General Francis Shoup

End Notes

Prologue
[1] Grady H. Howell, Jr. *For Dixie Land I'll Take My Stand*. Introduction, page VI

[2] A. B. Bender. *New Mexico Historical Review*, page 102.

[3] Henry George. *History of the 3d, 7th, 8th & 12th Kentucky C.S.A.*, page 13.

[4] J. H. Battle, W. H. Perrin and G. C. Kniffin. *Kentucky: A History of the State*. Part II, page 81.

Profile
[1] Picture courtesy of Philip L. Phillips, The Tilghman Heritage Center, Paducah, Kentucky.

[2] Fred Neuman. *Paducans in History*, page 35.

[3] Ibid, page 36.

[4] Ibid, page 37.

[5] Bryan S. Bush. *The Civil War Battles of the Western Theatre*, Page 23.

[6] Fred Neuman. *Paducans in History*, page 37.

[7] Ibid.

[8] Additional material for this section from *Confederate Military History*, Volume II, Maryland, page 163.

A special thank you to Philip L. Phillips of Paducah, Kentucky, who took time to provide this profile of General Tilghman's life in Paducah.

Chapter I

[1] Hall Allen. *Center of Conflict.* Local Civil War History Timeline, Paducah, Kentucky.

[2] William C. Davis. *The Cause Lost*, page 14.

[3] John Fiske. *The Mississippi Valley in the Civil War*, page 42.

[4] William C. Davis. *The Cause Lost*, page 13.

[5] Confederate Service Record of General Tilghman.

[6] OR Series I, Vol. 4, page 197.

[7] Paducah McCracken County booklet.

[8] Robert Selph Henry. *First With The Most Forrest*, page 38.

[9] OR Series I, Vol. 4, page 479.

[10] Ibid.

[11] Ibid, page 453.

[12] Ibid, page 472.

Chapter II

[1] Confederate Service Record of General Tilghman.

[2] OR Series I, Vol. 4, page 479.

[3] Ibid, page 491.

[4] Ibid, pages 552, 560, 687.

[5] *Encyclopedia of American Biography*, page 193.

End Notes

⁶In 1891, Sarah Ellen Blackwell published "A Military Genius; Life of Anna Ella Carroll, the Great Unrecognized Member of Lincoln's Cabinet," giving documentary evidence to prove that Miss Carroll planned the Campaign of the Federal Army in Tennessee. *Encyclopedia of American Biography*, page 125. Blackwell, Sarah Ellen.

Chapter III

¹Fashioned and altered from the National Park Service map painted by Sidney King.

²Thomas L. Connelly. *Army of the Heartland, The Army of Tennessee*, page 64.

³Stanley F. Horn. *Tennessee' War 1861 - 1865*, page 77.

⁴Ibid.

⁵Ibid, page 78.

⁶OR Series I, Vol. 4, page 476.

⁷Stanley F. Horn, *Tennessee' War 1861 - 1865*, page 80.

⁸OR Series I, Vol. 7, page 699.

⁹Ibid.

¹⁰OR Series I, Vol. 7, page 144.

¹¹*Confederate Military History, Kentucky*, page 143.

¹²OR Series I, Vol. 7, page 695.

¹³Ibid, page 733.

¹⁴Ibid, page 733.

[15]Ibid, page 144.

[16]Ibid, page 145.

[17]Larry J. Daniel. *Cannoneers in Gray*, page 16.

[18]Ibid.

[19]Alfred Roman. *The Military Operations of General Beauregard*, page 494.

[20]Ibid, pages 494-495.

[21]Confederate Service Records, Broadfoot Publishing Co.

[22]Ibid.

[23]Ibid.

[24]OR Series I, Vol. 7, page 145.

Chapter IV
[1]OR Series I, Vol. 7, page 148.

[2]Ibid, page 73.

[3]Ibid, page 74.

[4]David G. Martin. *The Vicksburg Campaign*.

[5]M. F. Force. *From Fort Henry to Corinth*, page 29.

[6]Herschel Gower. *Pen and Sword*, page 584.

[7]Wartime Sketch from *Harper's Weekly Newspaper*.

End Notes

Chapter V

[1] Edwin C. Bearss. *The West Tennessee Historical Society.*

[2] M. F. Force. *From Fort Henry to Corinth*, page 29.

[3] *Harper's Weekly*, February 22, 1862, Vol. 6, page 269.

[4] OR Series I, Vol. 7, page 151.

[5] Benjamin Franklin Cooling. *Forts Henry and Donelson*, page 103.

[6] Ibid, page 106.

[7] *Harper's Weekly*, February 22, 1862, Vol. 6, page 269.

[8] Ibid.

[9] *Pen and Sword*, page 586.

[10] OR Series I, Vol. 7, page 143.

[11] Ibid.

[12] Ibid.

[13] Ibid, page 147.

[14] Ibid, page 152.

[15] Benjamin Franklin Cooling. *Forts Henry and Donelson*, page 220.

[16] Confederate Service Record, Broadfoot Publishing Co.

[17] Ibid.

A Dual Biography: General Lloyd Tilghman & General Francis Shoup

APPENDIX TO CHAPTER V.

Feb. 12th, 1862.

Col. W. W. Mackall, A. A.- Geul. C. S. A., Bowling Green:

Sir,–My communication of the 7th instant, sent from Fort Henry, having announced the fact of the surrender of that fort to Commodore Foote, of the Federal navy, on the 6th iust., I have now the honor to submit the following report of the details of the action, together with the accompanying papers, marked A, B, containing list of officers and men surrendered, together with casualties, etc.

*   *   *   *   *   *   *   *   *

The wretched military position of Fort Henry, and the small force at my disposal, did not permit me to avail myself of the advantages to be derived from the system of outworks, built with the hope of being reinforced in time, and compelled me to determine to concentrate my efforts, by laud, within the riflepits surrounding the 10th Tennessee and 4th Mississippi regiments, in case I deemed it possible to do more than to operate solely against the attack by the river. Accordingly, my entire command was paraded and placed in the riflepits around the above camps, and minute instructions given, not only to brigades, but to regiments and companies, as to the exact ground each was to occupy. Seconded by the able assistance of Major Gilmer, of the Engineers, of whose valuable services I thus early take pleasure in speaking, and by Colonels Heiman and Drake, everything was arranged to make a formidable resistance against anything like fair odds. It was known to me, on the day before, that the enemy had reconnoitered the roads leading to Fort Donelson, from Bailey's Ferry, by way of Iron Mountain Furnace; and at 10 o'clock A.M., on the 5th, I sent forward, from Fort Henry, a strong reconnoitering party of cavalry. They had not advanced more than one and a half miles in the direction of the enemy, when they encountered their reconnoitering party. Our cavalry charged them in gallant style, upon which the enemy's cavalry fell back, with a loss of only one man on each side.

Very soon the main body of the Federal advance guard, composed of a regiment of infantry and a large force of cavalry, was met, upon which our cavalry retreated. On receipt of this news I moved out in person, with five companies of the 10th Tennessee, five companies of the 4th Mississippi, and fifty cavalry, ordering, at the same time, two additional companies of

APPENDIX TO CHAPTER V.

infantry to support Captain Red at the outworks. Upon advancing well to the front I found that the enemy had retired. I returned to camp at 5 P.M., leaving Captain Red reinforced at the outworks. The enemy were again reinforced by the arrival of a large number of transports. At night the pickets from the west bank reported the landing of troops on that side, opposite Bailey's Ferry, their advance pickets having been met one and a half miles from the river.

* * * * * * * * *

To understand properly the difficulties of my position, it is right that I should explain fully the unfortunate location of Fort Henry, in reference to resistance by a small force against an attack by land co-operating with the gunboats, as well as its disadvantages in even an engagement with boats alone. The entire fort, together with the intrenched camp spoken of, is enfiladed from three or four points on the opposite shore, while three points on the eastern bank completely command them both – all at easy cannon range. At the same time the intrenched camp, arranged as it was in the best possible manner to meet the case, was two thirds of it completely under the control of the fire of the gunboats. The history of military engineering records has no parallel to this case. Points within a few miles of it, possessing great advantages and few disadvantages, were totally neglected; and a location fixed upon, without one redeeming feature, or filling one of the many requirements of a site for a work such as Fort Henry. The work itself was well built; it was completed long before I took command, but strengthened greatly by myself in building embrasures and epaulments of sand-bags. An enemy had but to use their most common sense in obtaining the advantage of high water, as was the case, to have complete and entire control of the position. I am guilt of no act of injustice in this frank avowal of the opinions entertained by myself, as well as by all other officers who have become familiar with the location of Fort Henry. Nor do I desire the defects of location to have an undue influence in directing public opinion in relation to the battle of the 6th instant. The fort was built when I took charge, and I had no time to build anew.

* * * * * * * * *

The case stood thus: I had, at my command, a grand total of two thousand six hundred and ten men, only one third of whom had been at all disciplined or well armed. The high water in the river, filling the sloughs, gave me but one route on which to retire, if necessary; and that route, for some distance, in direction at right angles to the line of approach of the enemy, and over roads well nigh impassable for artillery, cavalry, or infantry. The enemy had seven gunboats, with an armament of fifty-four guns, to engage the eleven guns at Fort Henry.

* * * * * * * * *

I argued thus: Fort Donelson might possibly be held, if properly reinforced, even though Fort Henry should fall; but the reverse of this proposition was not true. The force at Fort Henry was necessary to aid Fort Donelson, either in making a successful defence, or in holding it long enough to answer the purposes of a new disposition of the entire army from Bowling Green to Columbus, which would necessarily follow the breaking of our centre, resting on Forts Donelson and Henry. The latter alternative was all that I deemed possible. I knew that reinforcements were difficult to be had; and that, unless sent in such force as to make the defence certain, which I did not believe practicable, the fate of our right wing at Bowling Green depended upon a concentration of my entire division on fort Donelson, and the holding of that place as long as possible; trusting that the delay, by an action at Fort Henry, would give time for such reinforcement as might reasonably be expected to reach a point sufficiently near Donelson to co-operate with my division by getting to the rear and right flank of the enemy, and in such a position as to control the roads over which a safe retreat might be effected. I hesitated not a moment. My infantry, artillery, and cavalry, removed, of necessity, to avoid the fire of the gunboats, to the outworks, could not meet the enemy there. My only chance was to delay the enemy every moment possible, and retire the command, now outside the main work, towards Fort Donelson, resolving to suffer as little loss as possible. I retained only the heavy artillery company to fight the guns, and gave the order to commence the movement at once. At 10 o'clock Lieutenant McGavock sent a messenger to me, stating that our pickets reported General Grant approaching rapidly, and within half a mile of the advance work; and movements on the west bank indicated that General Smith was fast approaching also.

* * * * * * * * * *

At 11:45 A.M. the enemy opened from their gunboats on the fort. I waited a few moments, until the effects of the first shots of the enemy were fully appreciated. I then gave the order to return the fire, which was gallantly responded to by the brave little band under my command. The

APPENDIX TO CHAPTER V.

enemy, with great deliberation, steadily closed upon the fort, firing very wild until within twelve hundred yards. The cool deliberation of our men told from the first shot, fired with tremendous effort. At twenty-five minutes of 1 o'clock P.M the bursting of our 24-pounder rifle gun disabled every man at the piece.

This great loss was, to us, in a degree, made up by our disabling entirely the *Essex* gunboat, which immediately floated down stream. Immediately after the loss of this valuable gun we sustained another loss still greater, in the closing up of the vent of 10-inch Columbiad, rendering that gun perfectly useless, and defying all efforts to reopen it.

* * * * * * * * *

It was now plain to be seen that the enemy were breaching the fort directly in front of our guns, and that I could not much longer sustain their fire without an unjustifiable exposure of the valuable lives of the men who had so nobly seconded me in the unequal struggle. Several of my officers, Major Gilmer among the number, now suggested to me the propriety of taking the subject of a surrender into consideration.

Every moment, I knew, was of vast importance to those retreating on Fort Donelson, and I declined, hoping to find men enough at hand to continue awhile longer the fire now so destructive to the enemy. In this I was disappointed. My next effort was to try the experiment of a flag of truce, which I waved from the parapets myself. This was precisely at ten minutes before 2 o'clock P.M. The flag was not noticed, I presume from the dense smoke that enveloped it, and, leaping again into the fort, I continued the fire for five minutes, when, with the advice of my brother officers, I ordered the flag to be lowered, after an engagement of two hours and ten minutes with such an unequal force.

The surrender was made to Flag-Officer Foote, represented by Captain Stemble, commanding gunboat *Cincinnati*, and was qualified by the single condition that all officers should retain their side arms, that both officers and men should be treated with the highest consideration due prisoners of war, which was promptly and gracefully acceded to by Commodore Foote.

* * * * * * * * * *

Confident of having performed my whole duty to my government in the defence of Fort Henry, with the totally inadequate means at my disposal, I have but little to add in support of the views before expressed. The reasons for the line of policy pursued by me are, to my mind, convincing.

Against such overwhelming odds as sixteen thousand well-armed men (exclusive of the force on the gunboats) to two thousand six hundred and ten badly armed, in the field, and fifty-four heavy guns against eleven medium ones, in the fort, no tactics or bravery could avail. The rapid movements of the enemy, with every facility at their command, rendered the defence, from the beginning, a hopeless one. I succeeded in doing even more than was to be hoped for at first. I not only saved my entire command outside the fort, but damaged, materially, the flotilla of the enemy, demonstrating thoroughly a problem of infinite value to us in the future. Had I been reinforced so as to have justified my meeting the enemy at the advanced works, I might have made good the land defence on the east bank. I make no inquiry as to why I was not, for I have entire confidence in the judgment of my commanding general.

*   *   *   *   *   *   *   *   *   *

Respectfully, your obedient servant,
LLOYD TILGHMAN, Brig.-Genl. Comdg.

Official.
ED. A. PALFREY, A. A. Genl.
A. and I. G. Office, *Aug. 29th, 1862.*

End Notes

Chapter VI

[1] Stanley F. Horn. *Tennessee' War 1861-1865*.

[2] Nathaniel Cheairs Hughes, Jr. & Roy P. Stonesifer, Jr. *The Life & Wars of Gideon J. Pillow*.

[3] Robert Selph Henry. *First With The Most Forrest*.

[4] Steven E. Woodworth. *Jefferson Davis and His Generals,* page 80.

[5] M. F. Force. *From Fort Henry to Corinth*, page 35.

[6] Ibid, page 38.

[7] OR Series I, Vol. 7, page 411.

[8] Ibid, page 296.

[9] Ibid, page 237.

[10] Ibid, page 370.

[11] Ibid, page 364. Undoubtedly some of the men in the fort were the Alabama volunteers who had enlisted to help build the fort.

[12] Chuck Lawliss. *The Civil War Sourcebook*, page 115.

Chapter VII

[1] B. Franklin Cooling. "Henry & Donelson Campaign", page 273. *Simon & Schuster Encyclopedia of the Confederacy. MacMillian Reference USA.*

[2] OR Series I, Vol. 7, page 364.

[3] Mauriel Joslyn. *Immortal Captives*, page 9.

A Dual Biography: General Lloyd Tilghman & General Francis Shoup

[4]Hershel Gower. *Pen & Sword*, "The Life and Journals of Randal W. McGavock, Colonel CSA", page 596.

[5]Ibid, page 597.

[6]OR Series II, Vol. I, page 169.

[7]Hershel Gower. *Pen & Sword*, "The Life and Journals of Randal W. McGavock, Colonel CSA", page 598.

[8]Ibid, page 601.

[9]William B. Hesseltine. *Civil War Prisons*, page 35.

[10]Hershel Gower. *Pen & Sword*, "The Life and Journals of Randal W. McGavock, Colonel CSA", page 601.

[11]William B. Hesseltine. *Civil War Prisons*, page 35.

[12]Hershel Gower. *Pen & Sword*, "The Life and Journals of Randal W. McGavock, Colonel CSA", page 602.

[13]Ibid, page 602.

[14]William S. McKeely. *Grant: A Biography.*

[15]Hughes and Stonesifer, Jr. *The Life and Wars of Gideon J. Pillow*, page 246.

[16]Alfred Roman. *The Military Operations of General Beauregard*, page 229.

[17]Mauriel Joslyn. *Immortal Captives*, page 11.

[18]Hershel Gower. *Pen & Sword*, "The Life and Journals of Randal W. McGavock, Colonel CSA", page 656.

End Notes

[19] Ibid, page 657.

[20] Ibid, page 658.

[21] Ibid, page 659.

[22] Stewart Sifakis. *Who Was Who In The Civil War*, page 654.

[23] Hershel Gower. *Pen & Sword*, "The Life and Journals of Randal W. McGavock, Colonel CSA", page 660.

Chapter VIII

[1] OR Series I, Vol. 24, page 450.

[2] Hershel Gower. *Pen & Sword*, "The Life and Journals of Randal W. McGavock, Colonel CSA", page 673.

[3] Ibid.

[4] Henry Davenport Northrop. *Pictorial History of the United States*, page 690.

[5] OR Series I, Vol. 24, page 450.

[6] OR Series I, Vol. 17, Part II, page 729.

[7] Ibid.

[8] Ibid.

[9] Peter Cozzens. *The Darkest Days of the War*, page 160.

[10] OR Series I, Vol. 17, Part II, page 728.

[11] Monroe F. Cockrell. *The Lost Account of the Battle of Corinth*, page 23.

[12] Peter Cozzens. *The Darkest Days of the War*, page 160.

[13]James Willis. *Arkansas Confederates in The Western Theatre*, page 273.

[14]Monroe F. Cockrell. *The Lost Account of the Battle of Corinth*, page 28.

Chapter IX
[1]OR Series I, Vol. 17, Part II, page 268.

[2]OR Series I, Vol. 27, Part II, page 450.

[3]Ibid.

[4]OR Series I, Vol. 17, Part II, page 507.

[5]Stephen Z. Starr. *Jennison's Jayhawkers*, page 222.

[6]Ibid, page 100.

[7]Ibid, page 222.

Chapter X
[1]OR Series I, Vol. 17, Part I, page 486.

[2]Stephen Z. Starr. *Jennison's Jayhawkers*, page 222.

[3]James Willis. *Arkansas Confederates In The Western Theatre*, page 288.

[4]OR Series I, Vol. 17, Part I, page 486.

[5]OR Series I, Vol. 27, Part II, page 787.

[6]OR Series I, Vol. 17, Part II, page 495.

Chapter XI
[1]OR Series I, Vol. 27, Part II, page 846.

[2]OR Series I, Vol. 24, Part III, page 592.

End Notes

[3]Ibid, page 61.

[4]Ibid, page 61.

[5]Stephen Z. Starr. *Jennison's Jayhawkers*, page 237.

[6]OR Series I, Vol. 24, Part III, page 61.

[7]Map by Donald S. Frazier, Abilene, Texas.

[8]OR Series I, Vol. 24, Part III, page 61.

[9]OR Series I, Vol. 27, Part II, page 846.

Chapter XII

[1]OR Series I, Vol. 24, Part I, page 377.

[2]W. A. Gillespie. *Confederate Veteran Magazine*, Volume 16, 1908.

[3]OR Series I, Vol. 24, Part III, page 629.

[4]John Fiske. *The Mississippi Valley in the Civil War*, page 216.

[5]OR Series I, Vol. 24, Part I, page 389.

[6]OR Series I, Vol. 24, Part III, page 656.

[7]Grady H. Howell, Jr. *For Dixie Land I'll Take My Stand*, page 74.

Chapter XIII

[1]OR Series I, Vol. 27, Part II, page 847.

[2]Ibid.

[3]Ibid.

[4]John C. Pemberton. *Pemberton Defender of Vicksburg*, page 10.

⁵Ibid.

⁶OR Series I, Vol. 27, Part II, page 847.

⁷"Confederate Veteran Magazine", Vol. IV, No. 9, Sept. 1896, page 314.

Chapter XIV
¹John K. Bettersworth. *Mississippi In The Confederacy As They Saw It*, page 108.

²OR Series I, Vol. 24, Part I, page 388.

³OR Series I, Vol. 24, Part III, page 649.

⁴Ibid, page 649.

⁵John Fiske. *The Mississippi Valley In The Civil War*, page 217.

⁶OR Series I, Vol. 24, Part III, page 649.

⁷OR Series I, Vol. 24, Part I, page 397.

⁸OR Series I, Vol. 24, Part I, page 412.

⁹OR Series I, Vol. 24, Part III, page 657.

¹⁰OR Series I, Vol. 24, Part I, page 379.

¹¹OR Series I, Vol. 24, Part III, page 667.

¹²Ibid, page 667.

¹³Dabney M. Maury. *Recollections of a Virginian*, page 178.

¹⁴OR Series I, Vol. 24, Part III, page 452.

¹⁵Ibid.

APPENDIX TO CHAPTER XIV.

ORDER OF BATTLE - YAZOO PASS EXPEDITION
February 3-April 10, 1863

UNION FORCES

Commanding Expedition, Brig. Gen. Leonard F. Ross (Feb. 15-March 21); Brig. Gen. Isaac F. Quinby (Mar. 21-April 10)

Thirteenth Division, Brig. Gen. Leonard F. Ross
  1st Brigade, Brig. Gen. Frederick Salomon
    43d Indiana Infantry. Col. W. E. McLean
    46th Indiana Infantry, Col. T. Bringhurst
    47th Indiana Infantry, Lt. Col. J. A. McLaughlin

2d Brigade, Brig. Gen. Clinton B. Fisk
    29th Iowa Infantry, Lt. Col. R. F. Patterson
    33d Iowa Infantry, Col. S. A. Rice
    36th Iowa Infantry, Col. C. W. Kittredge
    33d Missouri Infantry, Col. W. A. Pile
    28th Wisconsin Infantry, Lt. Col. C. Whitaker

Artillery
  Company A, 1st Missouri Artillery (6 guns),
    Capt. G. W. Schofield
  3d Battery, Iowa Light Artillery (6 guns),
    Capt. M. M. Hayden

Seventh Division, Brig. Gen. Isaac F. Quinby
  1st Brigade, Col. John B. Sanborn
    72d Illinois Infantry, Col. F. A. Starring
    48th Indiana Infantry, Col. N. Eddy
    59th Indiana Infantry, Lt. Col. J. N. Scott
    4th Minnesota Infantry, Lt. Col. J. E. Tourtellotte

  2d Brigade, Col. Charles L. Matthies
    56th Illinois Infantry, Col. G. B. Raum
    17th Iowa Infantry, Col. D. B. Hillis
    10th Missouri Infantry, Lt. Col. L. Harney
    Company F, 24th Missouri Infantry, Lt. D. Driscoll

80th Ohio Infantry, Col. M. H. Bartilson

3d Brigade, Col. George B. Boomer
93d Illinois Infantry, Col. H. Putnam
5th Iowa Infantry, Lt. Col. E. S. Sampson
10th Iowa Infantry, Col. W. E. Small
26th Missouri Infantry, Maj. C. F. Brown

Artillery, Capt. F. C. Sands
  Company M, 1st Missouri Artillery (6 guns),
    Lt. J. W. McMurray
  11th Battery, Ohio Light Artillery (6 guns),
    Lt. F. E. Armstrong
  6th Bathery, Wisconsin Light Artillery (6 guns),
    Capt. H. Dillon
  12th Battery, Wisconsin Light Artillery (6 guns),
    Capt. W. Zickerick

Cavalry, Capt. Samuel P. Tipton
  Company E, 2d Illinois Cavalry
  Company C, 5th Missouri Cavalry

Unattached
  1st Indiana Cavalry, Maj. T. A. Pace
  24th Indiana Infantry, Col. W. T. Spicely
  34th Indiana Infantry, Col. T. A. Cameron
    Commanding Gunboats, Lt. Cmdr. Watson Smith
    (Medically Surveyed); Lt. Cmdr. James P. Foster

Baron De Kalb, ironclad, Lt. Cmdr. J. G. Walker; *Chillicothe,* ironclad, Lt. Cmdr. J. P. Foster; *Rattler*, tinclad, Act. Master W. E. H. Fentress; *Marmora*, tinclad, Act. Master, R. Getty; Master John V. Johnston; *Petrel*, tinclad, Act. Lt. G. P. Lord; *Forest Rose*, tinclad, Act. Master G. W. Brown; *Dick Fulton*, ram, 1st Master S. Codman; and *Lioness*, ram, 1st Master T. O'Reilly.

O.R.N.

Appendix to Chapter XIV

CONFEDERATE FORCES

Commanding Confederate Forces, Maj. Gen. William W. Loring
- 1st Brigade, Brig. Gen. Lloyd Tilghman
  - 54th Alabama Infanctry, Col. A. Baker
  - 8th Kentucky Infanctry. Col. H. B. Lyon
  - 20th Mississippi Infantry, Col. D. Russell
  - 23d Mississippi Infantry, Col. J. M. Wells
  - 26th Mississippi Infantry, Col. A. E. Reynolds
  - Company C, 14th Mississippi Artillery Battalion (4 guns), Capt. J. Culbertson

- 2d Brigade, Brig. Gen. Winfield S. Featherston
  - 3d Mississippi Infantry, Co. T. A. Mellon
  - 22d Mississippi Infantry, Lt. Col. H. J. Reid
  - 31st Mississippi Infantry, Col. J. A. Orr
  - 33d Mississippi Infantry. Col. D. W. Hurst
  - 1st Mississippi Sharpshooter Battalion, Maj. W. A. Rayburn
  - Company C, 1st Mississippi Light Artillery (4 guns), Capt. L. A. Collier

- Moore's Brigade, Brig. Gen. John C. Moore
  - 37th Alabama Infantry, Col. J. F. Dowdell
  - 42d Alabama Infantry, Col. J. W. Portis
  - 35th Mississippi Infantry, Col. W. S. Barry
  - 40th Mississippi Infantry, Col. W. B. Colbert
  - 2d Texas Infantry, Col. Ashbel Smith
  - Bledsoe's Missouri Battery (4 guns), Capt. H. M. Bledsoe

Not Brigaded
- 37th Mississippi Infantry, Col. O. S. Holland
- 7th Tennessee Cavalry, Col. J. G. Stocks
- Waul's Texas Legion, Col. T. N. Waul
- Company B, Pointe Coupée Artillery (4 guns), Capt. W. A. Davidson
- Company A (Thompson's Section), Pointe Coupée Artillery (4 guns), Lt. J. J. Thompson
- Tobin's Tennessee Artillery (4 guns), Capt. T. F. Tobin

Detachment, 21st Louisiana Infantry
Company A. 22d Louisiana Infantry, Lt. J. E. Lambert
Naval Detachment, Lt. F. E. Shepperd
2d Missouri Cavalry, Col. R. McCulloch
2d Arkansas Cavalry, Col. W. F. Slemons
Blythe's Battalion, Mississippi State Troops,
  Maj. G. L. Blythe

3d Brigade, Mississippi State Troops, Brig. Gen. J. Z. George

Chapter XV

[1] OR Series I, Vol. 24, Part I, page 739.

[2] Ibid, page 206.

[3] Alexander D. Brown. *Grierson's Raid*, cover page map.

[4] OR Series I, Vol. 24, Part III, page 777.

[5] OR Series I, Vol. 24, Part I, page 544.

[6] Patricia L. Faust. *Historical Times Illustrated Encyclopedia*, page 326.

Chapter XVI

[1] Grady H. Howell, Jr. *For Dixie Land I'll Take My Stand*, page 188.

[2] OR Series I, Vol. 24, Part I, page 255.

[3] Ezra J. Warner. *Generals in Gray*, page 309.

[4] OR Series I, Vol. 24, Part III, pages 804 & 805.

[5] Ibid, pages 816 & 817.

[6] Ibid, pages 812 & 813.

End Notes

[7]Ibid, page 815.

[8]Ibid, page 815.

[9]Ibid, page 829.

[10]OR Series I, Vol. 24, Part I, pages 655 & 669.

[11]Ibid, page 655.

[12]Ibid, page 259.

[13]OR Series I, Vol. 24, Part III, page 841.

Chapter XVII
[1]OR Series I, Vol. 24, Part III, page 864.

[2]OR Series I, Vol. 24, Part I, page 215.

[3]Ibid, page 261.

[4]Edwin C. Bearss. *Decision in Mississippi*, page 226.

[5]OR Series I, Vol. 24, Part I, page 262.

[6]Alfred Roman. *The Military Operations of General Beauregard,* Volume 2, page 10.

Chapter XVIII
[1]Letter, William Augustus Drennan.

[2]"Confederate Veteran Magazine", Vol. 1, No. 9, Sept. 1893, page 285.

[3]OR Series I, Vol. 24, Part I, page 263.

[4]OR Series I, Vol. 24, Part III, page 88.

[5] Francis Vinto Greene. *The Mississippi, Campaigns of The Civil War*, page 154.

[6] James W. Raab manuscript, page 458.

[7] OR Series I, Vol. 24, Part II, page 32.

[8] Ibid, page 70.

[9] James Willis. *Arkansas Confederates In The Western Theatre,* page 353.

[10] OR Series I, Vol. 24, Part II, page 72.

[11] James G. Spencer - Private Cowan's Battery.

[12] E. T. Eggleston. "Confederate Veteran Magazine", Vol. I, page 296.

[13] Variations in the death of General Tilghman.
"as he careened and fell, he said to his son, who caught him: 'Tell your mother; God Bless her.'"
(L. S. Flatan, St. Louis, *Confederate Veteran*, Volume XVIII, No. 9, September 1910.).

[14] E. T. Eggleston. "Confederate Veteran Magazine", Vol. I, page 296.

[15] Fred G. Neuman. *Paducans in History.*

Chapter XIX

[1] Father A. J. Ryan, Chaplain, Confederate Army.

[2] "Confederate Veteran Magazine", Vol. XVIII, No. 7, July 1910, page 318.

[3] "Confederate Veteran Magazine", Vol. IV, No. 10, 1896.

End Notes

⁴"Confederate Veteran Magazine", Vol. XVIII, No. 7, July 10, 1910, page 319.

⁵OR Series II, Vol. 6, page 234.

Chapter XX
¹Richard & James Owen. *Generals At Rest,* page 161.

²"Confederate Veteran Magazine", Vol. XVIII, No. 7, July 1910, page 318.

³"Terrence J. Winschel Battlefield Guide".

⁴The Tilghman Heritage Foundation's goal is the restoration of the historic landmark home and the creating of a Civil War Interpretive Center for the time line 1852-1865. Phase I of the Restoration Plan was completed in 1998.

A Dual Biography: General Lloyd Tilghman & General Francis Shoup

Select Bibliography

Allen, Hall. *Center of Conflict - Civil War History Timeline.* Paducah, Kentucky booklet.

Battle, J. H., W. H. Perrin and G. C. Kniffin, *Part II, Kentucky: A History of the State,* 1st Edition 1885.

Battles & Leaders of The Civil War - by Castle - A Division of Book Sales, Secaucus, New Jersey.

Bearss, Edwin C. *The Vicksburg Campaign, Volume I, II, & III.* Morningside House, Dayton, Ohio.

The Fall of Fort Henry, reprint. "The West Tennessee Historical Society", Volume XVII, 1963.

Decision in Mississippi - Mississippi Commission on The War Between The States. Jackson, Mississippi, 1962.

Bettersworth, John K. *Mississippi In The Confederacy As They Saw It.* Louisiana State University Press. Kraus Reprint Co. 1970. The Mississippi Dept. of Archives and History, Jackson, Mississippi.

Bender, A. B. *New Mexico Historical Review,* Volume IX, No. 4, Santa Fe, New Mexico.

Black, Robert C. III. *The Railroads Of The Confederacy.* Broadfoot Publishing Co., Wilmington, North Carolina. 1987 Reprint (The University of North Carolina Press, 1952).

Boatner, Mark Mayo III. *The Civil War Dictionary* revised. David McKay Co., Inc. New York, New York. 1987.

Bonekemper, Edward H. III *How Robert E. Lee Lost The Civil War.* Sergeant Kirkland Press, Fredericksburg, Virginia. 1997.

Broadfoot Publishing Co. *Tilghman's Service Records.* 1907 Buena Vista Circle, Wilmington, North Carolina.

Brown, A. F. *Southern Historical Society Papers,* Volume VI. Richmond, Virginia. 1888.

Brown, D. Alexander. *Grierson's Raid.* University of Illinois Press. Reprint. The Morningside Hosue, Inc. Dayton, Ohio.

Bush, Bryan S. *The Civil War Battles Of The Western Theatre.* Rutner Publishing Co. Paducah, Kentucky.

Catton, Bruce. *Never Call Retreat, Vol. III, The Centennial History Of The Civil War.* Doubleday & Company, Inc. Garden City, New York. 1965.

Cockrell, Monroe F. *The Lost Account Of The Battle Of Corinth.* Broadfoot Publishing Co. Wilmington, North Carolina 1987.

Confederate Military History Extended Edition. Kentucky. Broadfoot Publishing Co. Wilmington, North Carolina. 1987.

Connelly, Thomas Lawrence. *Army Of The Heartland. The Army of Tennessee, 1861-1862.* Louisiana State University Press. Baton Rouge, Louisiana. 1967.

Cooling, Benjamin Franklin. *Forts Henry and Donelson, The Key To The Confederate Heartland.* The University of Tennessee Press. Knoxville, Tennessee. 1987.

Cozzens, Peter. *The Darkest Days Of The War, The Battles of Iuka and Cornith.* The University Press of North Carolina Press. 1997.

Crute, Joseph H., Jr. *Confederate Staff Officers, 1861-1865.* Derwent Books. Powhatan, Virginia. 1982.

Select Bibliography

Daniel, Larry J. *Cannoneers in Gray.* The University of Alabama Press. 1984.

Davis, William C. *The Cause Lost, Myths and Realities Of The Confederacy.* University Press of Kansas. Lawrence, Kansas. 1996.

Drennan, William Augustus. Letters. Mississippi Dept. of Archives & Records. Jackson, Mississippi.

Eastern Acorn Press. *The Struggle For Vicksburg.* Historical Times, Inc. Harrisburg, Pennsylvania.

Eggleston, E. T. "Confederate Veteran Magazine", Volume I.

Faust, Patricia L. *Historical Times Illustrated Encyclopedia Of The Civil War.* Harper & Tow Publisher. New York. 1986.

Fiske, John. *The Mississippi Valley In The Civil War.* 1900. Houghton, Mifflin & Co. The Riverside Press. Cambridge.

Flatan, L. S. "Confederate Veteran Magazine", Tribute To General Tilghman. Volume 28, No. 9. September, 1910.

Force, M. F. *From Fort Henry To Corinth.* Charles Scribner's Sons. New York. Fascimile reprint. Edition by The Archive Society. Harrisburg, Pennsylvania. 1991.

George, Henry. *History of the 3d, 7th, 8th and 12th Kentucky, CSA.* Reprinted by Simmons Historical Publications. Melber, Kentucky.

Gillespie, W. A. "Confederate Veteran Magazine", Volume 16. 1908.

Gower, Herschel. "Pen and Sword", The Life and Journals of Randal W. McGavock, C.S.A. Tennessee Historical Commission, Nashville, Tennessee. 1959.

Greene, Francis Vinton. *The Mississippi Campaigns Of The Civil War.* VIII. Charles Scribner's Sons. New York. 1882.

Henry, Robert Selph. *First With The Most Forrest.* Reprint. Broadfoot Publishing Co. Wilmington, North Carolina. 1987.

Hesseltine, William B. *Civil War Prisons.*
    McLain, Minor H. *The Military Prison at Fort Warren.*
    Downer, Edward T. *Johnson's Island.*
Kent State University Press, Kent, Ohio. 1962.

Holland, Richard. *Paducah History Time Line.* Paducah, Kentucky.

Horn, Stanley F. *Tennessee's War, 1861-1865.* Tennessee Civil War Centennial Commission. The University of Tennessee Press. Knoxville, Tennessee.

Howell, Grady H. Jr. *For Dixie Land I'll Take My Stand.* Chickasaw Bayou Press, Madison, Mississippi. 1998.
    To Live And Die In Dixie: A History Of The Third Mississippi Infantry. 1991. (Ibid)

Hughes, Robert M. *General Johnston.* 1893. C. Appleton & Co. New York.

Hughes & Stonesifer, Jr. *The Life & Wars Of Gideon J. Pillow.* The University of North Carolina Press. 1993.

Joslyn, Mauriel P. *Immortal Captives.* White Mane Publishing Co. Shippensburg, Pennsylvania. 1996.

Keegan, John. *Fields Of Battle - The Wars For North America.* Alfred A. Knopf, New York. 1996.

Kinkead, Elizabeth Shelby. *History of Kentucky.* American Book Co. 1909.

Select Bibliography

Lawliss, Chuck. *The Civil War Sourcebook, A Traveler's Guide.* Marmony Books. New York. 1991.

Leech, Margaret. *Revelille In Washington.* Carroll & Graf Publishers, Inc. New York. 1991.

Martin, David G. *The Vicksburg Campaign.* Gallery Books. New York. 1990.

Maury, Dabney M. *Recollections Of A Virginian.* Charles Scribner's Sons. New York. 2nd edition. 1894.

McKeely, William S. *Grant: A Biography.* New York. 1981.

Merrius, F. W. "Confederate Veteran Magazine", Volume I, No. 9. September, 1893. Career and Fate of General Lloyd Tilghman.

Myers, Raymond E. *The Zollie Tree.* The Filson Club Press. Louisville, Kentucky. 1964.

Neuman, Fred G. *Paducans In History.* 1922. Young Printing Co. Paducah, Kentucky.

Northrop, Henry Davenport. *Pictorical History Of The United States.* J. R. Jone. 1893.

Owen, Richard and James. *Generals At Rest.* White Mane Publishing Co., Inc. Shippensburg, Pennsylvania. 1997.

Paducah McCracken County Convention & Visitors Bureau booklet.

Pemberton, John C. *Pemberton Defender of Vicksburg.* The University of North Carolina Press. 1942. Chapel Hill, North Carolina.

Phillips, Herb. Champion Hill Battlefield Foundation, Inc. Edwards, Mississippi.

A Dual Biography: General Lloyd Tilghman & General Francis Shoup

Phillips, Philip L. The Tilghman Heritage Center & Civil War Interpretive Museum. 631 Kentucky Avenue. Paducah, Kentucky 42001.

Raab, James W. *Florida's Forgotten General, W. W. Loring.* Sunflower Univeristy Press. Manhattan, Kansas. 1997.

Roman, Alfred. *The Military Operations of General Beauregard.* Da Capo Press. New York. 1994.

Rowland, Dunbar. *Military History of Mississippi, 1803-1898.* The Official & Statistical Register of the State of Mississippi. 1908.

Sifakis, Steward. *Who Was Who In The Civil War.* Facts on File Publications, Inc. New York. 1988.

Simon & Schuster. *Encyclopedia of the Confederacy.* MacMillan Reference USA. 1993.

Spencer, James G. Private Cowan's Battery. Regimental Files, First Mississippi. Vicksburg National Military Park. Vicksburg, Mississippi. September 18, 1910.

Starr, Stephen Z. *Jennison's Jayhawkers.* Louisiana State University Press. Baton Rouge, Louisiana. 1973.

Tatum, George Lee. PhD. *Disloyalty In The Confederacy.* The University of North Carolina Press. Chapel Hill. 1934.

Warner, Ezra J. *Generals In Gray - Lives Of The Confederate Commanders.* Louisiana State University press. 1959.

Willis, James. *Arkansas Confederates In The Western Theatre.* Morningside Press. Dayton, Ohio. 1998.

Winschel, Terrence J. *Champion Hill: A Battlefield Guide.* Jackson Civil War Roundtable, Inc. Jackson, Mississippi.

Select Bibliography

Vicksburg National Military Park Historian. Provided reference material on Tilghman's monuments.

Woodworth, Steven E. *Jefferson Davis and His Generals.* University Press of Kansas. 1990.

The War of The Rebellion:
A compliation of the OFFICIAL RECORDS of the Union and Confederate Armies.
Published under the direction of The Honorable Daniel S. Lamont, Secretary of War. Washington: Government Printing Office. 1894.

A Dual Biography: General Lloyd Tilghman & General Francis Shoup

Part II

Confederate General Francis Asbury Shoup

A Dual Biography: General Lloyd Tilghman & General Francis Shoup

Table of Contents

Preface .... 153 - 154

CHAPTERS

1. Early life and U.S. Military Service;
   Fort Morgan, Alabama; Generals Hardee and
   Arkansas; The Central Army of Kentucky at
   Bowling Green; Shiloh .... 155 - 164

2. Little Rock, Arkansas;
   Canehill & Prairie Grove, Arkansas .... 165 - 172

3. Vicksburg, Mississippi;
   Siege, Surrender and Parole .... 173 - 180

4. Mobile, Alabama; Dalton, Georgia;
   Chief of Artillery; Fabian Policy;
   Building Fortifications; Advance To Atlanta;
   Kennesaw Mountain;
   Chattahoochee River Fortifications .... 181 - 196

5. The Battle of Atlanta and Retreat;
   Chief of Staff under General Hood;
   Lovejoy Station; Leave of Absence;
   Negro Enlistments at Richmond; End of War .... 197 - 208

6. University of Mississippi;
   Sewanee University of the South;
   Episcopal Church; Last Years .... 209 - 212

END NOTES .... 213 - 220

SELECT BIBLIOGRAPHY .... 221 - 225

INDEX .... 226 - 239

Illustrations

Shoup's Parole 178

Fortress Vicksburg 180

Roster of the Department of the Gulf, Feb. 1864 181

Shoup's Pay Voucher 182

Artillerymen Hauling Cannon to Top of Kennesaw Mountain 188

Shoups' Idea for Chattachoochee River Line 189

Scale Model of a Shoupade 194

MAPS

Shiloh 161

Battle of Prairie Grove 170

Fortress Vicksburg 180

Advance to Atlanta 185

Battle of Kennesaw Mountain 186

The Chattachoochee River Line 190

Photographs

General Shoup 150

Rev. Francis A. Shoup - Library of Congress 209

Burial - Sewanee University Cemetary 211

Preface

One may be surprised to learn that a significant number of West Point graduates of Northern birth, would cross over and join the newly formed Confederate States of America.

"Actually there were 306 graduates of the United States Military Academy at West Point, who used their training and skills to organize and lead the soldiers of the Confederate Army against the flag they had previously served.[1]

The influence and the achievements of these men were enormous. Without their assistance, there is no doubt that the Confederacy could never have fielded forces of the military caliber and proficiency of the Army of Northern Virginia and the Army of Tennessee.[2]

Fifty Northern born men rose to the rank of general in the Confederate Army, and many others filled the muster rolls at lesser ranks.[3]

This is the biography of one such Northerner, Francis A. Shoup, who graduated from West Point in the class of 1855. Out of a total of 34 graduates of that class, six cadets went on to join the Confederate cause.

The cadets were:[4]	CSA Rank:[5]
Frederick L. Childs	Lt. Colonel
Francis R. T. Nicholls	Brig. General
Francis A. Shoup	Brig. General
John R. Church	Deceased 1/8/63 in Service
James H. Hill	Major
Robert C. Hill	Colonel

As in most writings on the Civil War, The Army of Northern Virginia receives paramount attention. The author chose Shoup because he served with The Army of Tennessee and under eleven commanding generals:

(W.J.) Hardee
(E.) Van Dorn
(P.G.T.) Beauregard
(T.C.) Hindman
(S.B.) Buckner

A Dual Biography: General Lloyd Tilghman & General Francis Shoup

(T.H.) Holmes
(J.C.) Pemberton
(M.F.) Maury
(L.) Polk
(J.E.) Johnston
(J.B.) Hood

He served them well and in the capacity of trouble-shooter, he was transferred from one crisis to another. A cautious, mild mannered man who rallied to meet the challenge of the day, this intellectual general could be depended on whether it was in battle or in building fortifications.

He worked with the slaves at times and seemed convinced they should become available to refurbish the shrinking Confederate commands. His advice, like Pat Cleburnes, was taken too little and too late. His life after the war reflected his intellectual and spiritual nature in service to religion and education. He did his duty as God gave him the light to see it.

James W. Raab
St. Augustine, Florida

Chapter I

Francis Asbury Shoup, a native of Indiana, was born at Laurel in Franklin County on March 22, 1834. He was the eldest son of nine children of George Grove Shoup and Jane (Conwell) Shoup; James Conwell, his maternal grandfather, was the founder of the town of Laurel.[1] George Shoup was a well-to-do merchant and was a member of the Indiana constitutional convention and served for many years in the state legislature.

Francis was educated in the local schools, and attended Asbury University (now DePauw University) in Greencastle, Indiana; then entered the United States Military Academy at West Point on July 1, 1851. He graduated in 1855 and was ranked 15th in a class of 34 cadets.

His personal letters reveal…

> Shoup was appointed Brevt Second Lieutenant of Artillery. Served in garrison at Key West. Promoted to 2nd Lieutenant and ordered to Fort Moultrie, South Caroline, December 6, 1855. His company ordered to Fort Myers, Florida and then recalled back to Fort Moultrie.
>
> On account of the death of his parents and he being the oldest of eight children he felt it his duty to resign and look after them. He went back to Indianapolis. During his leisure time in the army he began reading the law. He entered the law offices of Barbour and Howland and was shortly after admitted to the bar and began the practice. He resigned his commission with the army on January 10, 1860.
>
> He gained considerable reputation by organizing a military company of Zouaves of which he was captain. He was a candidate for District Attorney on the Douglas ticket and made speeches during the campaign. "If I failed to convince other people, I at least convinced myself that the election of Lincoln would lead to a war of the sections." He had been brought up a Jeffersonian Democrat and had a great horror of abolitionism. "With my military education and love of that sort of thing, I felt that I should be compelled to take up arms on one side or another. My whole nature rebelled

against the Republican party and it seemed to me that the one thing to do was to change my residence." With the courage of his convictions, he began to make arrangements and set out for the south before South Carolina seceeded.

"I knew at the time that I was abandoning immense advantages. I had had the most flattering assurance that I could have anything I wanted on the northern side in the event of hostilities including Adjutant General of the state and would have had the organizing of the troops with prospects of high command.

I say this to show you that it was not personal advancement that moved me. I have been bitterly condemned for my actions, but my conscience has never annoyed me. I went to Charleston and was present at the time the ordinance of secession was passed."

Heeding to the call of the drum and bugle, Shoup traveled south to St. Augustine, Florida where a "secession flag" had already been raised. On the morning of January 6, 1861, the Quincy Guards seized the arsenal near Chattahoochee, Florida, and the next day, across the state, a company of 125 state artillerymen at St. Augustine, marched resolutely on Fort Marion. The entire garrison of the fort, consisting of one sergeant, delivered up the keys. On January 10, the State of Florida seceded and declared its independence from the Union. Shoup recalled his service in Florida...

> Shoup assisted in mounting the guns at the water batteries of Old St. Marks (Fort Marion) in St. Augustine. Shortly thereafter, he received an order from the governor to erect a battery at Fernandina, Florida on Amelia Island.[4]

At this time, Fernandina was the principal east coast port of Florida because it contained a deep water harbor which could be used by the U.S. Navy. It was also the eastern terminus for the Florida Railroad. Shoup said little was accomplished at this early date because of limited manpower and lack of cannon.

On March 11, Shoup sent a letter to the Hon. L.P. Walker, Secretary of the War, at Montgomery, Alabama, requesting a commission to the artillery of the Confederate States. Shoup had a hard time about getting the appoint-

Chapter I

ment since the secretary declined to put his name on the list of appointments, thinking he was a Yankee and perhaps a spy! Shoup approached President Jefferson Davis, who went to the war office, and under the objections of Walker, put Shoups name down with his own hand. Shoup remarked, "Say what they will, Mr. D. is a brick." Within days Shoup was appointed and assigned to duty at Fort Morgan, Alabama, March 16, 1861.[5]

Fort Morgan, Fort Gaines, as well as the arsenal at Mount Vernon, north of Mobile, had been seized by the Alabama state militia on January 5 of 1861. The militia had held the position for two months until they were relieved by Confederate troops under the command of Col. J. W. Hardee.[6] Fort Morgan, named in honor of Gen. Daniel Morgan, a Revolutionary War hero, was an old brick fortress located at the tip of Mobile Point, about 40 miles south of the port city of Mobile. It's 107 cannon commanded the entrance to Mobile Bay. Colonel Hardee needed experienced field officers for training the new volunteers. Shoup traveled west across Florida and joined the garrison at Mobile.

Hardee soon discovered that with limited manpower it was next to impossible for the inexperienced Confederate forces to defend hundreds of miles of shoreline along the Gulf of Mexico. Lincoln's proclamation of a blockade on April 19 put Fort Morgan and others in a state of jeopardy. One of Hardee's first moves was to burn the building on Ship Island off Biloxi, Mississippi to prevent the island from being occupied by Union forces.[7] As the Confederacy became organized, Fort Morgan was placed under the command of a Military Department and Hardee and Shoup were ordered to the Upper District of Arkansas, on the western frontier of the Confederacy, an arduous trip by rail and waterways.

In Arkansas, Shoup was assigned to Col. T. C. Hindman to help in recruiting and training the Arkansas volunteers. After much political conflict the Arkansas militia, arms, and munitions now in the service of eastern Arkansas, were transferred to Hardee and the Confederate government, and Hardee was promoted to Brigadier General.

By September of 1861, Hardee had a force of five thousand infantry, eight hundred cavalry and twelve pieces of artillery. His artillery was commanded by Lieutenant Shoup. The small army prepared for an invasion of eastern Missouri. This invasion never materialized[8] as Hardee's forces, now under the jurisdiction of Gen. A. S. Johnston's Confederate Dept. No. 2, would be removed from Arkansas.

General Johnston was correct in thinking that the first Federal threat in the western theater would come through neutral Kentucky. With the aid of Kentucky Confederates, Johnston began to consolidate his forces near Bowling Green. Among these troops would be General Hardee and his artillery officer, Francis Shoup.

Hardee was advanced to Major General and placed in command of the Army of Central Kentucky on October 7, 1861. Shoup was promoted to Major on November 7, 1861, and made Chief of Artillery with a battalion of eight officers and 145 men.

Major Shoup, with his three company artillery battalion were posted at Cave City, Kentucky, northeast of Bowling Green. They were positioned to prevent a Union advance on the Louisville-Cave City pike that ran through Bowling Green to Nashville.[9]

Johnston's line of defense was not to be successful. An advance into eastern Kentucky at the end of the year by Gen. F. K. Zollicoffer's Confederate volunteers ended in defeat at Logan Cross Roads on January 19, 1862, with General Zollicoffer losing his life and his small army virtually destroyed.

Early in February, the two forts, Henry and Donelson on the Cumberland and Tennesee rivers, were surrendered to Grant's forces. Some twelve to fifteen thousand Confederates were captured and sent to military prisons and a great deal of scarce ordnance and ammunition and other military supplies were lost to the invading Union army.

The capture of the two forts was a major disaster for the Confederacy and for General Johnston; his defensive line broken and with no fall back defenses prepared. Johnston's forces left Kentucky, making their way towards Nashville. Nashville soon fell, making it the first Confederate Capitol seized by the Union. Johnston's army, severely reduced by sickness, straggling and desertions, moved thru Murfreesboro, Tennessee and continued moving towards Corinth, Mississippi. Here, the Confederates elected to concentrate their scattered forces from their large Department.

Joining Johnston's army at Corinth was General Polk from Columbus, Kentucky; Gen. Braxton Bragg's Corp. of 10,000 men from Pensacola, Florida; Gen. Daniel Ruggles from New Orleans with 5,000 infantry and three batteries. Gen. P.G.T. Beauregard was placed second in command of the new army called the Army of The Mississippi. By the 23rd of March, Johnston had amassed 40,000 infantry and cavalry; with the artillery corps

Chapter I

now comprising over twenty-three batteries with 122 guns and 2,000 men. Still with Hardee, Major Shoup observed that many of the cannoneers were inexperienced and because of a shortage of ammunition some of the gun crews had not ever fired their pieces.[11] It was also evident to Shoup the batteries were scattered among the various brigades instead of being formed into one fighting force; the result being the artillery would not be committed to the battle in mass.

This mob, as Bragg referred to the assemblage at Corinth, had only two weeks to be formed into a cohesive fighting army. Johnston would have to hurry to prevent the important rail center at Corinth from being seized and at the same time resist the Yankees from making anymore inroads into the heartland of Dixie.

It was no April Fool as Grant's army began landing and assembling twenty-five miles northeast of Corinth at Pittsburg Landing a few miles below the town of Savannah on the Tennessee River. They bivouacked around Shiloh Church.

Shoup reminisced:

> "The question was whether we should wait and receive the enemy or advance upon him? The Federals, under Grant though he did not select the place, had put themselves in a very exposed position. In the first place, they were on the wrong side of the river for a rendezvous encampment. In a beautiful open country, only a little over twenty miles from us, and without the slightest artifical protection in the way of field works or grand guards, they simply invited attack.
>
> "Our Generals saw this, and determined to take advantage of it. But there was a serious trouble at the start on the part of the corps commanders of the military capacity of Sidney Johnston. I came to know it through General Hardee, with whom I was on the most confidential terms. Johnston's loss of all that region from Bowling Green down to the Mississippi line had set the press howling to such an extent that he wanted to resign his command. There never was a grander man, and I love his memory, but his movements are open to serious criticism.[10]
>
> "He was not a man of expedients, and had been so long used to the slow routine methods of the old army that he did

not adapt himself readily to the new, extraordinary conditions of things. He was too magnanimous and modest, and did not know how to seize authority and knock people over. At any rate, the corps commanders were nervous about going into battle with him in command.[12]

"We patched up a curious expedient. They got Bragg appointed Chief of Staff with plenary powers. Bragg accepted upon condition that he should retain the immediate command of his own corps. No use of this extraordinary arrangement was made. I think every one was rather ashamed of the thing after the battle.

"Well, a plan of operation was worked out by Beauregard, and we were to surprise the enemy at once. It was known Buell was moving down from Nashville to join Grant on the Tennessee River. He was making a forced march, but his rapidity was very like ours. What could have been done, and would have been done toward the latter part of the war in a few days, took weeks."[11]

By April 3, 1862, all of the Confederate forces were in readiness and they began marching towards Pittsburg Landing. The narrow country roads were ill suited for the movement of 40,000 men, horses, cannon and caissons. On the 4th, rain fell heavily making the roads muddy and bogging down and delaying the Confederates.

On the 6th, the thunder was from the Confederate artillery, announcing the opening of the days battle which came to be named Shiloh, from a small country church in the vicinity. 30,000 Confederates swept out of the woods in three lines and surged into the unsuspecting Federal campsites and swept away a large portion of their defensive line as the bluecoats scattered, leaving behind all personal belongings, as they fled for their lives, heading for the Tennessee River.

The mud and rugged terrain and the absence of clearings for the placement of artillery, made it extremely difficult for the batteries to maintain the pace of the charging infantry. This resulted in the separation of the artillery from the infantry for a portion of the morning.

Arriving at the front, Shoup's and other batteries began lobbing shells into the Federal camps; their main objective was to fire on the Union

Chapter I

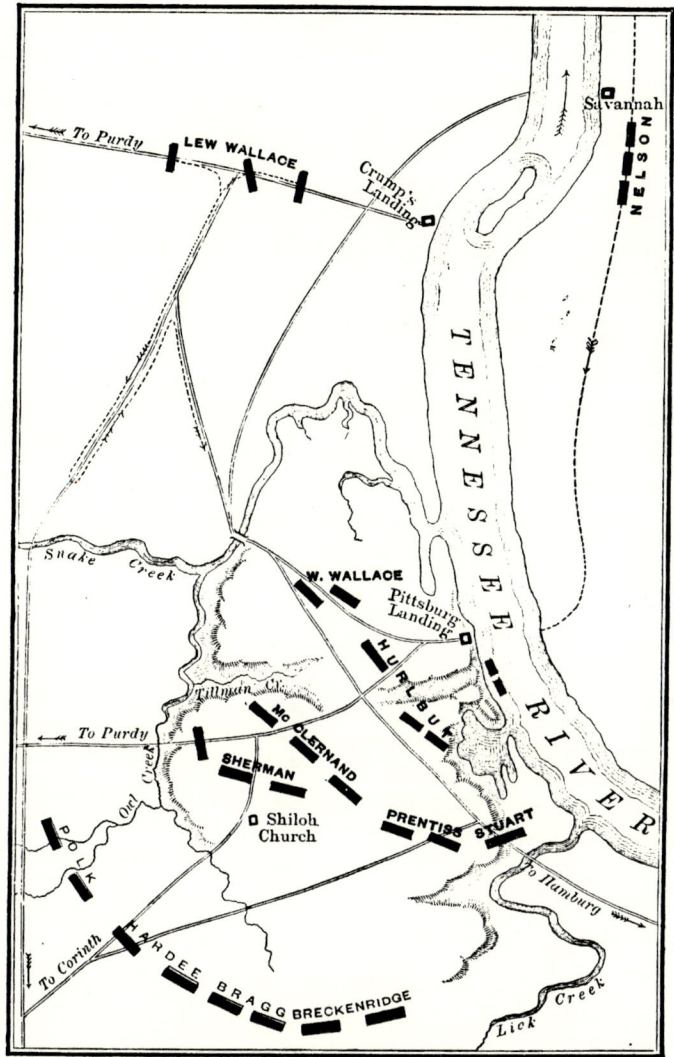

Shiloh, April 6, 1862, Morning

reserve units in an attempt to neutralize the Federal defensive capability.[12] "The inexperienced gunners fired too high and to often and the effect was minimal at first."[13]

It was also evident to Shoup's trained eye that the lack of direction given the artillery batteries by their respective generals who were preoccupied with their infantry, left the artillery to fend for itself while awaiting orders.

By noon the Federal forces launched a counterattack, but the

161

Confederate infantry held fast and swept away the charging unionists from the Shiloh Church vicinity, inflicting heavy loss of men and equipment as the casualties on both sides continued to mount.

The Confederate left encountered the entrenched division of Gen. W.H.L. Wallace, which was posted along a ridge under cover of heavy thicket and supported by active Union artillery. Throughout the early afternoon this bluecoat division unflinchingly held it's ground, repelling with slaughter every Confederate infantry attack made upon it; these frontal attacks appeared almost suicidal.

The Federal salient became known as the "hornet's nest" because the buzz from their concentrated fire of bullets and shells "buzzed" like a hornet. The shrill was unnerving, and it became apparent that the Federals could not be overwhelmed by infantry charges alone.

General Ruggles ordered all Confederate field guns that could be collected from the left and right to be assembled as rapidly as possible. His aides succeeded in rounding up the scattered artillery batteries and two separate concentrations developed.

On the left was Capt. S.P. Bankhead and to the right was Maj. F.A. Shoup, who for sometime had been massing and collecting guns in the woods.

> "On my own responsibility I massed the artillery on the position held by Prentiss."

A total of sixty-two guns were assembled, mostly of the six-pounder and twelve-pounder Howitzer type. The range was 500 yards across an open field. Around 4:30 p.m., both artillery groups began firing. It sounded like thunder as round after round roared and went sailing into the hornet's nest. A captain in the Union 2d Iowa wrote, "the shells and shot passed over us terrifically at about the height of a man's head from the ground while sitting down."[14] The sixty-two Howitzers quickly neutralized the "hornet's nest", inflicting great casualties on the unionists.. General Wallace was mortally wounded; his successor, Gen. B.M. Prentiss surrendered the remaining 2,200 Federals in the field. It was an artillery victory.

As the battle raged, General Johnston, riding in the battle, received a wound in the lower leg; not realizing it was lethal he bled to death on the battlefield. His own staff surgeon was not present, having been ordered to care for wounded union soliders. Beauregard took over and believing that

Chapter I

a well-supported infantry attack could win the day, ordered the tiring southerners to attack towards Pittsburg Landing.

Despite an extensive battle on one front, Grant's staff had amassed it's own line of artillery along a ridge covering Pittsburg Landing.[15] The Federal position on the bluffs was fronted by a deep ravine and creek which protected its front.

In support of the coming attack, Shoup moved his detachment of twenty-one guns on the road leading to Pittsburg Landing. Three-quarters of a mile along the road he met Gen. J.D. Breckinridge who was forming his infantry for one final charge of the afternoon. Shoup replenished his caissons from stacks of captured Federal ammunition and began a barrage in support of Breckinridge's attack.

Grant's artillery supported by the anchored Federal gunboats on the Tennessee made the first move and swept the whole Confederate field, inflicting staggering casualties. The Johnnies did press the attack, but it was not successful. Grant planned to unload D.C. Buell's Army of reinforcements at the landing when they arrived that night.

Exhausted from the long day's battle, the Confederates then retired and returned to the rear to encamp for the night and enjoy the captured food and other spoils they had gathered from the day's advance.

The Confederate command was elated over the success of the day. A half-disciplined army, poorly equipped, assailed an opposing army larger in numbers, better equipped, and had steadily driven them back to their last stronghold. The evening closed with heavy clouds and then cold rain.

As the exhausted Confederates slept, Col. N.B. Forrest's scouts, clothed in captured Federal overcoats, moved at night within the Federal lines and reported that large bodies of troops were crossing the river to Pittsburg Landing. Grant had not retreated across the river! These were Buell's 20,000 reserves who would be made available for the next day's battle.[16]

This landing information was conveyed to General Hardee, who for some unknown reason, failed to communicate this to Beauregard.[17]

The next morning the unsuspecting Confederates were blindsided as the fresh reinforcements drove home a new attack. The sheer mass of the onslaught crumbled the Confederate line and by early afternoon the Union advantage had become overwhelming and a general retreat was ordered by Beauregard.[18]

The retreat back towards Corinth was made on the same bad roads of mud, which slowed down both sides. Shoup, as well as other batteries, were experiencing a shortage of artillery horses since so many had been killed the day before; 200 cavalry troopers were ordered to dismount and the mounts were used to haul out the artillery. By late afternoon the Federal pursuit began to wane and Shoup was the last to leave the area. He wrote,

> "I looked to the rear and there was not an infantryman or cavalryman in sight."[19]

The fierceness of the fighting at Shiloh is reflected in the casualties of both sides. Union losses were 1,754 killed; 8,408 wounded, and 2,885 captured. Confederate had 1,723 killed; 8,012 wounded with 959 missing.

Grant later commented, "It was a high price to pay for a country church and a steamboat dock."[20]

Four days after Shiloh, on April 11, Union Gen. Don Carlos Buell's army moved eastward and captured Huntsville, Alabama, severing the Memphis & Charleston Railroad which ran through Corinth to the east. Northern Alabama was now lost to the Union forces.

Chapter II

Long columns of shattered grayclads tramped back to Cornith with the need for recuperating and regrouping. It was apparent to Beauregard there was now a great deficiency in experienced senior field officers and a shortage of animals and ordnance.

On the 10th of April, Beauregard assigned Major Shoup as his acting chief of Artillery for The Army of The Mississippi.[21] His duty was to refurbish the artillery. Shoup reported that fourteen pieces of the Federal's artillery and one caisson had been brought from the battlefield while the Confederates had abandoned on or near the field, for want of horses, nine pieces and thirty-five caissons.[22]

On the 14th Shoup wrote to Gen. Braxton Bragg that he would require four hundred and fifty horses to equip and pull the light batteries. Since the batteries were short of men, Shoup thought that many of the cavalrymen would be willing to transfer to the artillery. Other suggestions were made by Shoup and which were adopted for the army. "Deficiences in men and horses can be rectified by reducing the batteries from six pieces to four pieces."[23] He further supported that the artillery ordnance should be separated from the infantry and cavalry ordnance.

Gen. H. Halleck was placed in charge of the Union Forces after Shiloh. During May and June he continued to build up his forces until he had 125,000 Federal troops in the vicinity of Corinth.

After this two months of "a bloodless standoff" between the two armies, Beauregard decided to abandon the strategic city of Corinth. Part of the army retired to selected defensive positions which were prepared for them at Tupelo, Mississippi, while others were sent elsewhere to refill depleted ranks.

Beauregard, faced with a full-scale Union invasion in Arkansas because almost every force had been removed from the state and sent east, ordered Gen. T.C. Hindman on May 31 to take charge there. Shoup would accompany him.

On June 8, 1862, Shoup was relieved as Chief of Artillery, promoted to Colonel, and became Acting Inspector General to Hindman.[25] Upon arriving in Little Rock, they discovered the state arsenal had been emptied out of most of it's arms and munitions, thus requiring a search of the Dept. to inventory it's military capabilities. Shoup traveled to South Arkansas, North Louisiana and even part of Texas to prepare a report for President Davis on the mineral and manufacturing resources for casting guns, shot, and shell. Shoup reported back:

- In Quachita County there were salt deposits for the manufacture of about 200 bushels a day.
- The specimens of lubricating oil in the coal beds on the Quachita River, two miles from Camden, are almost inexhaustible.
- At Arkadelphia there was a saw mill and a foundry with all kinds of patterns of machinery, lathes prepared to cast iron cannon. The iron was smelted at Jefferson, Texas.
- Another foundry was found at Camden; they could smelt 30,000 pounds of iron at a single heat and have lathes to bore a cannon.
- A powder mill was located on the Quachita River and capable of making 200 pounds of powder a day.
- There was a foundry at Shreveport, Louisiana; at Monroe there was a quantity of quicksilver; and at Marshall, Louisiana, there was a small cloth factory.
- There were a large number of tanneries in the area but few shoe manufacturers.

In a letter, at a later date, to Gen. T.H. Holmes, President Davis wrote:

"A very interesting report of General Shoup on the mineral and manufacturing resources of a section of your Dept. indicated the practicability of casting guns and shot and shell. The difficult and uncertainty of transporting heavy articles from the East makes it especially desirable that such resources should be developed to the full limit. I know that

Chapter II

>you will not expect skilled workmen, and do not expect therefore all which your necessities require; but hope that you will be able to do something, particularly in the manufacture of siege guns."[26]

Hindman took measures and began a military factory system at Arkadelphia to produce small arms, percussion caps, and other goods to supplement the state penitentiary's production of clothing, shoes, wagons, harnesses, tents, knapsacks, cartridge boxes, and wooden drums. At the textile mills at Royston in Pike County he increased output to meet the needs of the soldiers.

It was while Shoup was at Little Rock that he had Infantry Tactics published in 1862.

> "After the battle of Shiloh, Cleburne, Marmaduke and I in consultation agreed that we ought to have a less cumberson and less artificial system of tactices and Shoup was appointed to prepare it and within a few days at Cornith had it finished. While it was being approved by Richmond, Shoup moved to Arkansas. The hundred page manual simplified things and was published at Little Rock, Arkansas as Infantry Tactics."

Hindman's proclamation of martial law and the assumption of other authorities not within his realm of command, provided much criticism by the citizens of Arkansas and a political crisis developed within the Arkansas delegates to Congress, the result being that Hindman was ultimately relieved of his command. Despite this, Shoup praised Hindman and said

"He just missed being a military genius."

Regardless, Hindman was re-assigned to Fayetteville, Arkansas to recruit a new army of volunteers in northwestern Arkansas.[27] A mature Gen. T.H. Holmes took over the department.

> The arrival of old Holmes knocked out Shoup's tactics and everything else. Shoup later said Holme's administration was a complete fiasco. Hindman assigned Shoup to a division and the newspapers supported Shoup's nomination for Brigadier General. In a week, news came that Shoup had

not been confined by the Arkansas Delegates, declaring that Shoup was probably an abolitionist. Shoup wished to resign on this news but General Holmes would not permit it.

Hindman and Shoup traveled up the Arkansas River to the mountains of northwestern Arkansas and established headquarters around Van Buren. They were now on the frontier of the Confederacy, and in Indian Country. Hindman, still the well-liked politican, rather quickly recruited 20,000 Arkansas volunteers for his new army. Unfortunately, time did not permit him and Shoup to adequately train or equip the raw recruits. Hindman's position was to be a defensive one, but Hindman had one thing in his mind, and that was to rectify his former actions. If he could regain the former Confederate position at Pea Ridge (Elkhorn Tavern) north of Fayetteville on the Missouri border, that had been lost to the Federal's in the spring of 1861, he would again be lauded by his constituents.

Hindman began to unite his scattered army. Col. J.S. Marmaduke's 8,000 Confederate cavalry unit, accompanied by Shoup with Bledsoe's battery of two iron, six-pounder cannon plus four small Howitzers, marched north of Van Buren on November 28, to the small village of Canehill where they encamped on an elevated position, next to the town's college. This movement was quickly reported to Union Gen. J.G. Blunt's Army of the Frontier. Blunt, suspecting this was the vanguard of Hindman's army moving up for another invasion of Missouri, marched south with 5,000 Federals, including a brigade of Cherokee Pin Indians, and soon found and surprised Shoup and Marmaduke at Canehill.

The dismounted Confederates formed to do battle while the advancing Federals, supported by twelve guns, opened fire upon the Confederate line. Bledsoe's cannon and Shoup's Howitzers answered and an artillery duel developed and was kept up by both sides for half-an-hour. Overwhelmed by the sheer number of charging Federals, the Confederates began to retire into the Boston mountains. Bledsoe's two guns had gone down the road and did not unlimber but Shoup's battery of four Howitzers made a stand and gallantly defied and stopped the advancing forces. In this skirmish Shoup's guns were partially disabled and were quickly packed upon cavalry horses and carried to the rear.[28]

Blunt's forces pursued a short distance and then withdrew as they detected a large body of Confederates hidden and waiting for them in

Chapter II

ambush. As the Federals retired, the rebels cheered at having stopped the invaders. For the day there was a loss of 40 Federals and 435 Confederates.[29]

Colonel Shoup was promoted to Brigadier General on September 13, 1862, and made Chief of Artillery. However, the confirmation of his promotion had not been made until after Canehill. Thus at Canehill, he was ranked as Colonel as mentioned, but two weeks later at the Battle of Prairie Grove he was listed as Brigadier General Shoup, Second Division, First Corp., Gen. T.C. Hindman commanding.[30]

> Second division, Brig.-Gen. Francis A. Shoup; First brigade, Brig.-Gen. James F. Fagan – Col. A. T. Hawthorn's Arkansas regiment; Twenty-second Arkansas, Col. J. P. King; Twenty-ninth Arkansas, Col. J. C. Pleasants; Thirty-fourth Arkansas, Col. W. H. Brooks; Capt. W. D. Blocher's Arkansas battery. Second brigade, Col. Dandridge McRae – Twenty-eighth Arkansas, Col. D. McRae; Twenty-sixth Arkansas, Col. A. S. Morgan; Thirtieth Arkansas, Col. A. J. McNeill; Thirty-second Arkansas, Col. C. H. Matlock; West's and Woodruff's Arkansas batteries. Unattached, Cheek's battalion of sharpshooters; Venable's Arkansas cavalry.[31]

Timely intelligence revealed that Blunt's small force remained encamped 20 miles southwest of Fayetteville. Despite freezing rain and snow, gallant Hindman with 11,000 men, on December 3, marched north from Van Buren looking to trap Blunt's force and destroy it. Blunt, realizing his exposed position, requested help. His closest support at the time was Gen. F.J. Herron's Federals, encamped 150 miles away in Springfield, Missouri at Wilson's Creek. Answering Blunt's call for help, Herron collected his 6,000 men and 30 guns and force-marched his troops for four days and nights, arriving exhausted at Fayetteville on December 6th.

Early in the morning the next day, the Confederate cavalry confronted and routed the advance units of Herron's force heading to Cane Hill to join Blunt's command. The Southern horsemen pursued the Union Cavalry across the Illinois River where they skirmished with Herron's men. Meanwhile, about ten o'clock, Hindman came up with his infantry and artillery to a ridge chosen by Shoup which overlooked the river. Once the

Federals were reinforced, they chased the Confederate Cavalry back towards the ridge and began wading across the freezing cold Illinois River.

The Federals managed to place their artillery and began returning the Confederate fire about 11 a.m. The more accurate Federal rifled cannons quickly silenced the Southern smoothbores.[32] Seeing movement on the ridge which would threaten the Union flanks, General Herron ordered two charges up the ridge. Shoup and Marmaduke received them at short range, and using shot guns, rifles, and muskets, drove the wilting Federals back toward the river, where they took a position behind the remnants of a fence at the foot of the ridge.

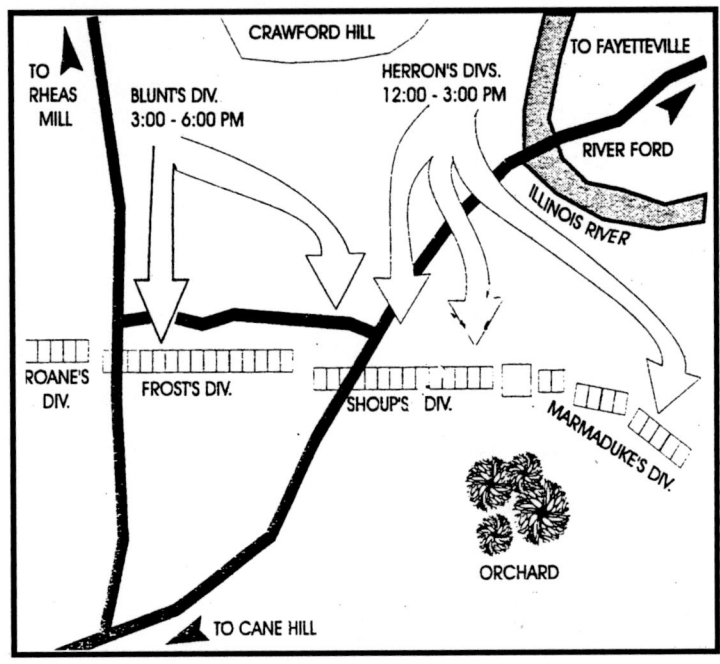

The battle of Prairie Grove, Arkansas[33]

The Federals rallied and renewed their attack, but were again repulsed. Each time the Confederates mounted counterattacks but were driven back by the Federal artillery.

General Blunt, some miles away, hearing the sound of cannon and battle, marched to Herron's relief, arriving in early afternoon. Blunt fell on Shoup's left; a Confederate reserve was brought up and received the attack. Intense fighting in the western woods continued for over an hour before

Chapter II

Blunt's forces were replused.[34] As darkness descended on this cold December day, the Confederates launched one final attack to win the day with Blunt being routed by Shoup and Herron by Marmaduke.[35] Again, the heavy Union artillery compelled the brave Southerns to return to the protection of the wooded ridge and the battle ended with neither side gaining a clear advantage. Out of an estimated 10,000 soldiers on each side, casualties were about equal with a total of over 2,700 men killed, wounded, and missing.

Lacking food, shelter and ammunition, with his supply train parked thirty-nine miles to the rear of his army, Hindman at mid-night decided to withdraw from the barren Ozark mountain, leaving the day's bloody battlefield to General Herron, who claimed a stategic victory. Herron was promoted to a Major General, and remarked, "I think this section is rid of Hindman."[36] Prairie Grove was the last major battle in northwest Arkansas. Hindman's failure to secure a victory on this expedition closed the door on his career. Shoup's notes on the battle:

> "At Prairie Grove I did splendid work and saved us from total defeat. Hindman told me on the field at the close of the day that I should have the full credit for it. But he forgot about it and made no report of it. When I got back to camp, I demanded to be relieved on the ground of the injustice to General James Fagan and the rest. Hindman telegraphed General Holmes. The old gentleman came up and finally I was relieved. The day after I was relieved, General Fagan appeared before my headquarters with a most extraordinary battalion of assorted officers who came to thank me for my services with the division. I was wholly taken by surprise and was pretty nearly knocked out."

General Shoup was relieved from duty on the 20th of December and ordered back across the state to headquarters at Little Rock, where Gen. T.H. Holmes appointed him Acting Inspector General on his staff on January 2, 1863.[37]

Another Confederate loss at Arkansas Post (January 4-12, 1863) just about erased Arkansas as part of the Confederate western military strategy. "I would assist the Confederacy in other ways."

Shoup was sent to Arkadelphia to examine the public manufacturing establishments and also to Camden and report on those at that place. He was to make suggestions for improvement and to increase their capacity of production of war goods, which he did.

> "After making a report on the resources of the country to the President, Mr. Davis often spoke to Colonel Lamar and others that he had made many mistakes during the war, but the greatest was that he had not put me in command of the Trans-Mississippi Dept.! Maybe so. Affairs could not have been much worse anyway."

Again, more changes as Richmond juggled their manpower in the west. Holmes was relieved of duty; Hindman reassigned to the Army of Tennessee and General Shoup was ordered to Mobile to relieve Gen. J.E. Slaughter, Chief of Artillery.

> "General Polk borrowed me for the Mississippi command but this was no better and I was allowed to return to Mobile. I was then ordered to Vicksburg."

Chapter II

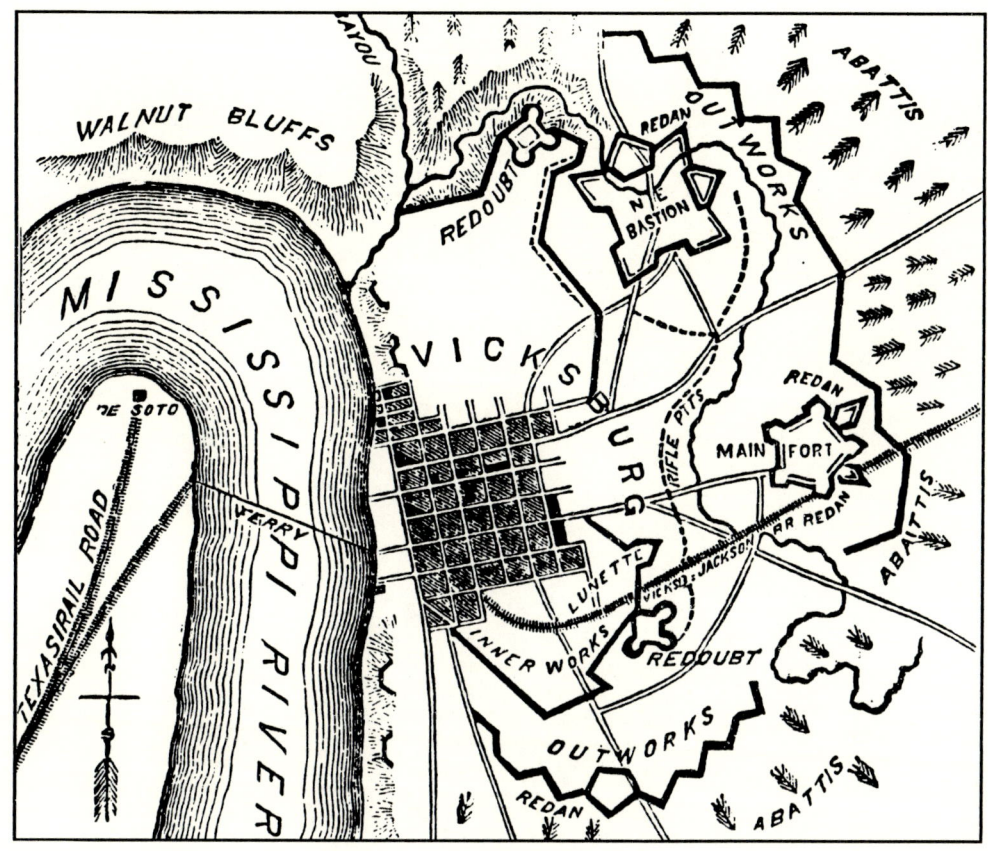

Fortress Vicksburg, 1863

"The achilles heel of The Mississippi's defense of The Mississippi Valley was the configuration of its river system. Unlike Virginia, whose Potomac-Rappahannock-York James ladder of east-west rivers afforded natural lines of defense, Mississippi's rivers were essentially north-south systems which virtually invited the Federal invasion."[1]

A Dual Biography: General Lloyd Tilghman & General Francis Shoup

Chapter III

"Fortress" Vicksburg, gatekeeper of the Mississippi River defense system, is located upon a slope of broken and complicated range of bluffs and ravines which lent themselves to a strong defensive fortification. Since 1862 Gen. M.L. Smith had been in charge of developing a line of defenses around the city. It consisted of a system of detached works (redans, lunettes, and redoubts) on prominent and commanding points, which were connected in most cases by rifle pits and was eight miles in length. It would be defended by 18,000 men and 128 pieces of artillery. In addition to these land defenses, the circuit was made complete by a series of water batteries, extending from Fort Hill in the north through Vicksburg and along the Warrenton ridge until they met the land batteries of the south.[2] (See map page 89.)

The early months of 1863 had seen one disaster after another for the Union forces as they tried desperately to reach Vicksburg. By late April they had successfully moved forces down the Louisiana side of the Mississippi River, bypassed the Vicksburg river defenses with their flotilla of transports and gunboats and had established a bridgehead over the river south of the city at Bruinsburg. Now across the river in force by May 1st, the Federals began moving on Confederate defense at Grand Gulf, which they overran after a bitter battle. The outnumbered Confederates retreated towards Hankinson's Ferry and Vicksburg.

Pemberton assigned Shoup to Gen. S.D. Lee's Louisiana brigade now at Hankinson's Ferry on May 3.[4] Shoup arrived in the middle of the Confederate retreat, assumed command and became a part of the 9,000 Confederates that retreated into Fortress Vicksburg.

General Grant avoided the error of moving straight on Pemberton at Vicksburg without defeating the Confederate forces in the field that could come to Pemberton's assistance. Moving around Vicksburg's defenses, he attacked and captured Raymond on the 12th of May and then on the 14th captured Jackson, the capital of Mississippi.[5]

Flushed with an unbroken series of victories after so many disappointments in the early part of the year, Grant turned his forces southeast and made a rapid advance towards Vicksburg. On the 16th, in the bloody battle of Champion Hill, where Gen. Lloyd Tilghman was killed, Grant routed the unprepared Confederates. The next day at the battle of the Big Black River bridge he forced the Confederates to seek cover in their fortress of Vicksburg.

Both wings of Grant's army started crossing the Big Black River on their own pontoon bridges on the 18th[6] and by noon of the 19th they had closed in and around Vicksburg. Pemberton and his army were invested in the fortress.

Local topography was such that the Vicksburg's works and defenses could only be approached by certain roads. Confederate Gen. M.L. Smith's Division held the left part of the defensive line. It was made up of Shoup's brigade a mile to the west on the Graveyard Road; W.E. Baldwin's brigade on his left and J.C. Vaughn's brigade on the extreme left, extending to Fort Hill.[7] (See map page 89.)

By early afternoon, Grant's forces, flushed with success and wanting to finish this battle, were opposite Fort Hill and the Graveyard Road.[8]

Pemberton ordered Smith to rush one of Shoup's regiments out on Graveyard Road; the unit sent was the 27th Louisiana, and when it marched, General Shoup rode with the regiment. At the stockade, Shoup was cautioned by the Confederate pickets that the enemy was nearby. Shoup deployed and threw out skirmishers; but, before they reached the commanding ridge, they encountered the Federals.[9] Shoup alerted General Smith to the danger, and, as the bluecoats worked their way slowly westward along the road, Shoup called up Col. W. Hill and his 26th Louisiana sharpshooters. They posted themselves in the thick woods at the head of Mint Spring Bayou.

The bluecoats replied with their own sharpshooters and the action became a standoff. Then the Federals brought up some artillery support for the infantry, but still the Confederate works could not be entered. The fresh Confederate troops from Vicksburg gave up nothing and the May 19th attack netted the Unionists little except heavy losses.

The momentum of Grant's advance upon Vicksburg began to slow. The very hot weather, shortage of drinking water, plus the huge clouds of dust stirred up by both sides as they moved, brought the armies to a standstill for a few days.

By the morning of May 22, Union Gen. F.P. Blair, Jr. had 27 cannon arrayed in carefully protected emplacements on either side of Graveyard Road. At about 2 p.m., the fire from the mortar fleet, plus Blair's artillery,

Chapter III

opened up and kept up a continuous and heavy bombardment of Vicksburg on Shoup's position.[11] Blair's guns knocked Shoup's parapets to pieces faster than the Louisianans repaired them. "Then as Shoup was becoming reconciled to seeing his earthworks battered down, Blair's artillery fire dwindled and ceased. Shoup was puzzled! The reason was simple; the Yankees had all but run out of artillery ammunitions, and had to wait until the roads to the Yazoo were opened before more could be brought up."[12]

It was now apparent to Grant that the Confederates had recovered from the demoralization of their early defeats and that Fortress Vicksburg was too strongly fortified to be taken in an open assault by his infantry.

Grant recalled taking Forts Henry and Donelson in early 1862 and that the forts became mere traps for ensnaring their defenders. If the Confederates stayed outside the city with their arms and additional troops from Vicksburg, they may have made themselves more formidable by joining Gen. J.E. Jonston's Army of Relief being formed at Canton.

General Grant, on the 25th of May, issued orders for the beginning of a siege of Vicksburg. Twelve miles of trenches ringing the city were prepared while 89 batteries were constructed and armed with over 200 field pieces. Grant had sealed the tomb and as the days of May and June passed, the hopes of the soldiers and inhabitants of the fortress faded.

The siege of Vicksburg lasted 47 days. General Smith, in his final report said, "The history of one day is pretty much the history of all."[13] General Shoup, with his men on the front lines, portrayed a much different story. Just a few excerpts from his report tell the bitter story of how ten to one hundred men daily were killed in and around Vicksburg.

> Picking up after the battle on May 22nd:
> "Enemy entrenching energetically at night, keeping up a continuous fire during the day. He has an almost continous line of circumvallation. We are ordered not to expend ammunition."
> May 31st:
> "A furious cannonade. Enemy has established a new battery opposite the center of my line and some additional rifled guns opposite redan."
> June 3rd:
> "Fire as usual. We lose a number of men each day."
> June 4th:

"Enemy opened on my left this morning with artillery and musketry."

June 5:

"During the night the enemy kept up an incessant artillery fire and occasionally musketry. The enemy is pushing forward his approaches on the Graveyard Road. Sharpshooting is maintained with great activity and bitterness. Sharpshooters take aim at exposed points, and when one exposes himself in the least, a number of guns are discharged simultaneously."

June 6:

"Enemy fired nearly all night."

June 10th and 11th:

"Heavy rain. Enemy is running a regular zig-zag and sap-roller in front of redan."

(SAP-ROLLER – to avoid being hit by Confederate's small arms fire, the bluecoats constructed a great roller made of saplings about six foot long and four high, which is pushed along in front of a soldier digging a trench.)

"The sharpshooters are extremely vigilant, and within 60 or 70 yards, excellently covered."

June 13:

"Sharpshooting very bitter."

June 14:

"Enemy disabled our 12-pounder gun at this point. Have organized my artillerists into a hand-grenade and thunder barrel corps, since our guns are of no service."

June 15:

"Sap at redan very close, within ten paces of ditch."

June 17:

"We are on speaking terms with the enemy. The picket parties agree upon short truces, during which neither party is to fire. Some trading going on in coffee, etc. Notes are thrown across from one party to another. Brothers, relations, and friends are constantly inquiring after each other."

June 19:

"Enemy now using a double sap but he can accomplish

Chapter III

nothing with it."
June 20:
"Furious cannonading began at daylight and continued a good part of the day."
June 21:
"Asked for more hand-grenades; find that they work excellently well."

Shoup's report on the fighting at Vicksburg, constantly refers to the men and officers that are killed daily, sadly reducing his brigade.[14]

Shoup also recalled that the Federals were very industrious under ground.

"We had run galleries out in all directions of their possible approach, and soon we could hear them working underground, and after awhile we could almost hear what they said. The question was which would get the move on the other in the explosion. We worked very silently and allowed them to get very close to us. So long as they were working we felt pretty safe, but it was rather uncanny in those galleries, not knowing at what moment they might fire their mines.

"At last we thought it best to put in our charges, and we got them all tamped while they were still working and only a few feet distant. At last we touched the match, and the earth trembled. I have never heard how much damage we did, though really the object was not so much to kill as to stop their operation."[15]

With dwindling food supplies and the onset of summer heat, Pemberton asked his division commanders their opinion as to the ability of the troops to make a march and undergo the fatigures necessary to accomplish a successful evacuation and join Johnston's Army of Relief. Most of Pemberton's Generals didn't think this could be accomplished, leaving only surrender as an option. It was decided that a surrender proposal would be made. After a truce was offered, Pemberton himself met with Grant but received little respect. After the meeting, Pemberton urged his generals that a decision be made soon, or else Grant was likely to assault them and inflict more casualties. On July 4th Pemberton, with the approval of all of his

179

generals except S.D. Lee, accepted Grant's terms of unconditional surrender. By nine o'clock in the morning, white flags were flying all along the line. Guns were stacked inside of the parapets, and the Confederates retired to town. Grant sent in his troops and a bedlam reigned for several days while the rebel paroles were prepared. The Southerners were dejected and indignant at being surrendered. Mighty Vicksburg, The Gibralter of The Mississippi, had fallen and Confederate hopes of ultimate success were diminished.

General Grant's conditions of surrender were the same as his initials, Unconditional Surrender. On the same day, Robert E. Lee began his retreat from bloody Gettysburg; the coincidence was tragic that two mortal blows had struck the Confederacy on the same date.

The old exchange and parole system was still in effect with both sides holding thousands of captured officers and volunteers.

Most of the captured Confederate Generals at Vicksburg, which included General Shoup, were released on parole on July 4, 1863.[16] On July 16, they were exchanged for Federal prisoners taken at the battle of Chancellorsville May 1-4, 1863.[17]

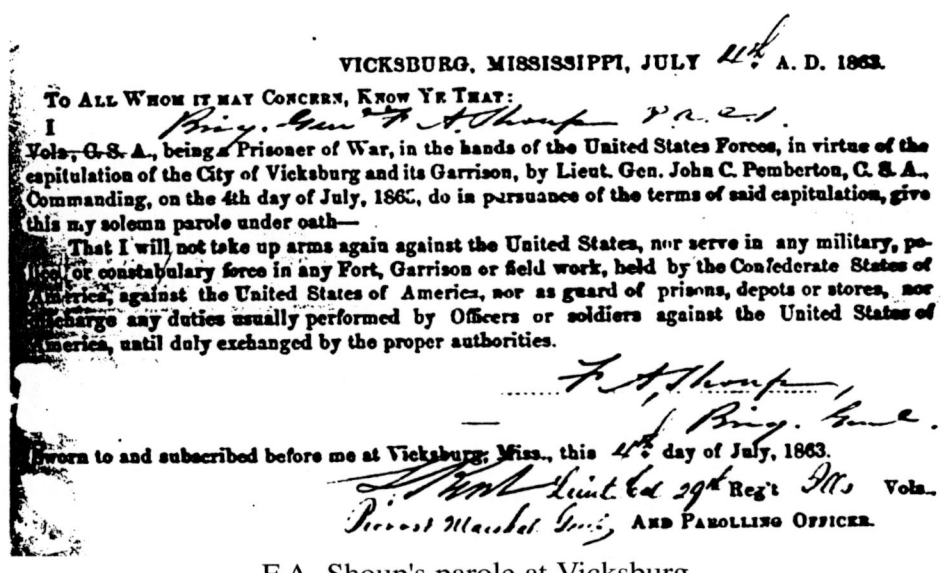

F.A. Shoup's parole at Vicksburg

Gen. M.L. Smith remained at Vicksburg to grant leave of absences to the sick and disabled and have the infirmed transferred by boat to New

Chapter III

Orleans. They numbered around 3,600 at the surrender.[18]

At 4 a.m. on the 11th of July, all the Confederate forces that signed paroles and were fit for duty, were marched out of Fortress Vicksburg, moving east toward Enterprise, Mississippi. General Shoup accompanied his brigade on the 120 mile march.

The long line of demoralized troops reached Raymond on the 12th; by the 13th they crossed the Pearl river at Bryam, just south of the heavy fighting going on at Jackson between Sherman and Johnston's Army of Relief. It was a gauling situation; they could not go to the relief of their comrades who had hoped to relieve them from their encircled fortress.

During the march, the men and animals suffered from the intense July heat, lack of suitable drinking water and half rations from the Federals. On the 14th they bivouacked in the fields south of Brandon.

Keeping south of the railroad, the long weary procession straggled into Enterprise on the 21st of July. Because General Pemberton had been insistent with President Davis, the men were granted mass furloughs for thirty days.

Pemberton himself continued to Demopolis, Alabama, where camps were to be established for the reception of the soldiers reurning from their leaves of absence. Many never returned to the army.

It's impossible to trace where Shoup went after Enterprise. There were many places in the south that showed little traces of the war where he could spend his thirty-day furlough.

On the 25th of September, 1863, Shoup received orders to proceed to Fort Morgan at Mobile Bay and assume command of the Third Brigade.[18] It is doubtful he ever arrived. Gen. D.H. Maury at Mobile said, "General Shoup is still without a command because there is no vacant command within the Department that he will accept. He has expressed a preference to join General Hardee and the Army of Tennessee.[19] His leave was extended because of ill health?[20]

A Dual Biography: General Lloyd Tilghman & General Francis Shoup

Chapter IV

The day after the surrender of Vicksburg, Sherman's forces were dispatched towards Jackson to drive Johnston's Army of Relief out of the state. In blistering July heat, the men in blue pursued the rebels eastward retreat for over a hundred miles until they were convinced the Confederates were worn out and would disperse. The persistent Confederate cavalry, and then the infantry, however, returned as rapidly as the Federals passed and by years end the Confederates were back occupying central Mississippi in towns such as Canton, Morton and Meridian.

On February 3, 1864, Grant ordered Sherman to again sweep the state and drive the rebels out once and for all. This action became known as Sherman's Meridian Expedition and would be carried out against the fighting Episcopal bishop, Gen. Leonidas Polk. A small band of stubborn Confederate defenders bitterly resisted Sherman's juggernaut as it headed

Abstract from return of the army in the Department of the Gulf, Maj. Gen. Dabney H. Maury, C. S. Army, commanding. February 20, 1864: headquarters Mobile, Ala.

Command.	Present for duty. Officers.	Present for duty. Men.	Effective total present.	Aggregate present.	Aggregate present and absent.	Pieces of field artillery.
General staff	14			14	14	
Cantey's brigade:						
Brigade staff	6			6	8	
Infantry	160	2,305	2,428	2,890	3,637	
Cavalry	16	154	188	215	288	
Shoup's brigade, artillery	120	1,296	1,371	1,587	2,869	24
Total	302	3,755	3,987	4,698	6,802	24
Baldwin's brigade, infantry	114	1,323	1,403	1,618	2,925	
Mackall's brigade, infantry	56	503	538	635	1,908	
Total	170	1,826	1,941	2,253	4,833	
Quarles' brigade, infantry	150	1,137	1,218	1,423	2,130	
McNair's brigade, infantry	104	803	927	1,073	2,012	
Total	254	1,940	2,145	2,496	4,142	
Higgins' brigade:						
Artillery	54	887	1,004	1,105	1,307	
Cavalry	6	206	218	238	333	
Total	60	1,093	1,222	1,343	1,640	
Grand total	800	8,614	9,295	10,804	17,431	24

Abstract from return of the army in the Department of the Gulf, Maj. Gen. Dalmey H. Maury, C.S. Army, commanding. February 20, 1864: headquarters Mobile, Ala.

across central Mississippi in the dead of winter, to capture Meridian. In hopes of stemming this tide of blue, Polk ordered Gen. J.H. Forney at Enterprise, Mississippi to send Shoup's brigade at once to Morton to help halt Sherman.[21] Once Sherman was moving, he spread the rumor that he was really heading for Mobile to capture the port city. Believing Sherman's rumor, Polk countermanded his orders requesting Shoup be sent to Morton; instead he rushed Shoup's command and battery south to Mobile by rail.[22]

Sherman's trick worked as other units were dispatched south to Mobile. On March 5, he sacked and burnt to the ground the town of Meridian, destroyed the railroad and communications in all directions. Polk abandoned Mississippi and retreated to Demopolis, Alabama while Shoup's brigade of artillery remained resting at Mobile.

"At Mobile I was placed in charge of the cities defenses."

Shoup's brigade enjoyed a rather quiet February and March. Shoup got paid for the month of January at Mobile. He made $301 a month as a

Chapter IV

Confederate General. The reproduced pay slip is from his Confederate Service Record.

After the Meridian campaign, Sherman's army returned to Vicksburg. U.S. Grant, now general-in-chief of all Union armies, in a determined effort to end the war in 1864, ordered all Union armies on the offensive with the strategy to kill the Confederates in such prodigious numbers that the ones left alive would lose all will to continue fighting.

Sherman was ordered to Chattanooga on the Tennessee-Georgia border to invade the central portion of Georgia and capture the rail-center at Atlanta with it's commissary and quartermaster depots. The Battle of Chickamauga in November 1863 was a smashing Confederate victory, but did not produce the results hoped for by the Confederates. In spite of terrible casualties of 16,000 Union and 18,000 Confederates, General Bragg had not been able to shake the Union control of Chattanooga and snatched defeat from the jaws of victory by withdrawing into northern Georgia.

The Confederate army recuperated in winter quarters at Dalton, Georgia, where General Bragg finally was replaced by General Joseph E. Johnston, who was encouraged by President Davis to make a spring offensive campaign back into Tennessee and Kentucky. Johnston had an aggreate of around 55,000 troops to confront approximately 90,000 Federals gathered in camps for miles around Chattanooga.[24]

With the call for additional Confederate troops at Dalton, Shoup was ordered from Mobile to report to Johnston at Dalton on the 19th of March.[25] As the assembled forces enlarged, Johnston decided he needed a chief of artillery for the army. Johnston passed over the obvious selections, i.e. those of long overdue promotion; he remained undecided.

President Davis ended the speculation by appointing a compromise candidate, Brig. Gen. F. A. Shoup as the chief of Artillery for the Army of Tennessee.[26]

The six foot tall Shoup had ably commanded Hardee's batteries at Shiloh; was an artillery officer in the regular U. S. Army and enjoyed seniority in rank as well as ability. Everything in his record suggested he could fill the new office with distinction.[27]

Shoup could control the tactical maneuvers of the batteries as well as handle executive and administrative duties between Richmond and the Army of Tennessee. As a member of Johnston's staff, Shoup would enjoy the highest possible standards of respect as a field officer plus enjoying the general's table and having his own staff and servants.

General Johnston, with years of military experience, knew that one soldier on the defensive in the trenches was equal to three or four of an attacking enemy, and that entrenchments would spare the lives of his men. He therefore, adopted the Fabian strategy of retreating to carefully prepared entrenched lines. His aim was to wear out and neutralize the numerical superiority of Sherman's three armies as they began moving south, following the Western and Atlanta railroad to Atlanta.

Shoup became privy to Johnston's strategy, as there would be eleven retreats and entrenchments on the way to Atlanta. Each stand would mean a battle. And each battle saw Johnston retire to the next prepared position.

With most of the white southerners in the army, slaves were impressed and served in labor brigades on the front line in order to build these positions. In effect the slaves service and loyalty increased and strengthened the south's military power.

ARMY OF TENNESSEE
General Joseph E. Johnston
General John B. Hood[442]
Present for Duty, April 30, 1864 - 54,500 men and 144 guns.
Present for Duty, June 30, 1864 - 69,946 men.

CHIEF OF STAFF - *Brig. General William W. Mackall*
CHIEF OF ARTILLERY - *Brig. General Francis A. Shoup*[443]
CHIEF OF ARTILLERY - *Colonel Robert F. Beckham*[444]
CHIEF ENGINEER - *Lt. Colonel Stephen W. Pressman*
CHIEF ENGINEER - *Maj. General Martin L. Smith*[445]
MEDICAL DIRECTOR - *Surgeon-Major A. J. Foard*
CHIEF ORDNANCE OFFICER - *Captain W. D. Humphries*
CHIEF ORDNANCE OFFICER - *Lt. Colonel James M. Kennard*[446]   [28]

During the winter of 1864, a wave of religious revivalism swept the Confederate Army of Tennessee encamped in and around Dalton. When Shoup arrived at Dalton, his life was enriched when he became a member of the Episcopal Church.[29]

The opening action for 1864 was near Dalton at Rocky Face Ridge on the 5th of May. Sherman's orders were to turn Johnston's position from the

442 Commanded from July 18.
443 Chief of Staff from July 21
444 From July 21.
445 From July 20.
446 From July 29.

Chapter IV

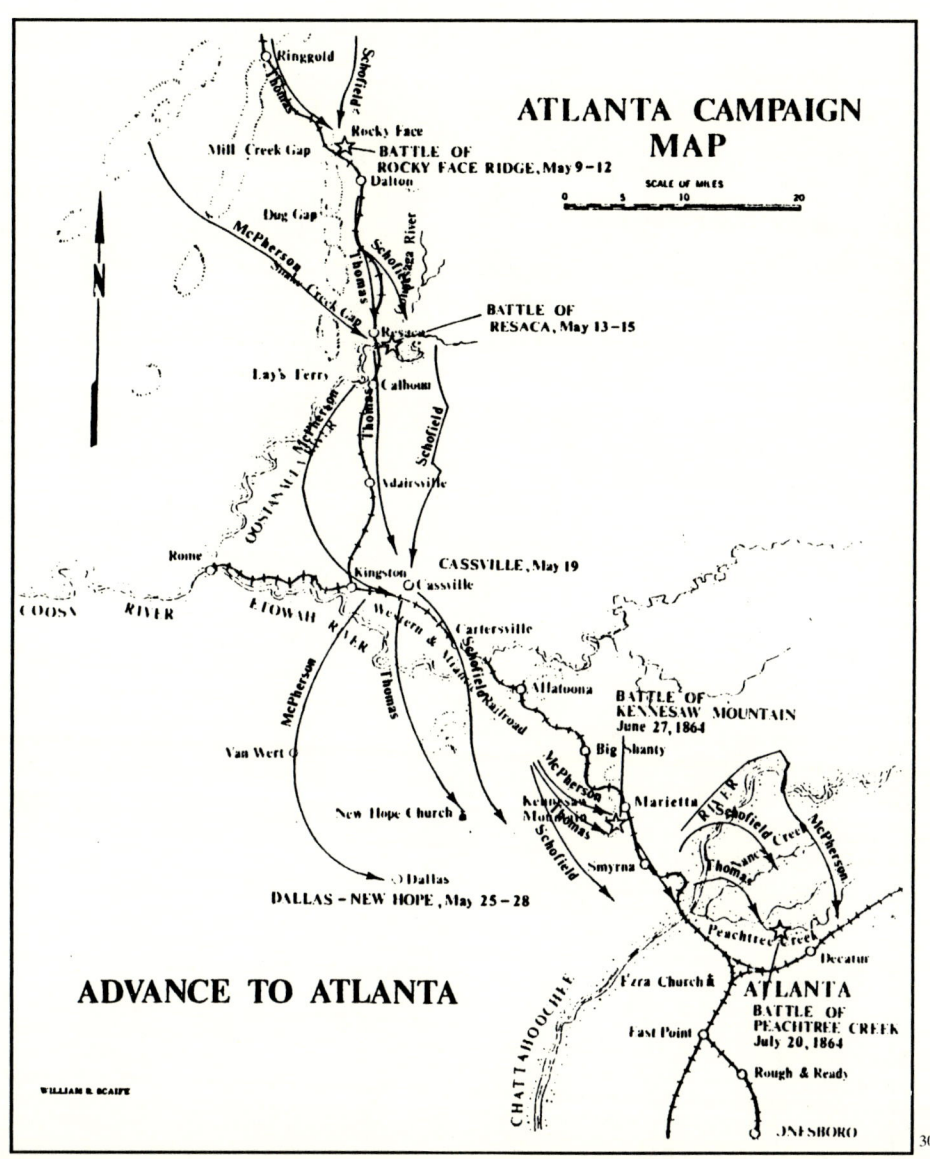

west; the maneuver failed, but his superior numbers forced Johnston to make a retreat on May 13 to the next town of Resaca, Georgia.

Shoup's location and actions during the Atlanta campaign are too numerous to report. Some of the more important decisions that he took part in are documented.

May 19 - Cassville, Georgia. The Confederate army was drawn up in a position on a ridge south of Cassville, with a broad open, elevated valley in front of it completely commanded by the fire of their troops occupying a crest of a hill.

The hill was long enough to position Hood's, Polk's, and half of Hardee's corps. Shoup pointed out to Johnston an apparent weak point near Polk's right, a space of one hundred and fifty yards, which, in Shoup's opinion, might be enfiladed by the Union artillery now placed on a hill more than a mile off beyond the front and to the right. "So far, it seemd to me," said Johnston, "as to make the danger trifling."[31]

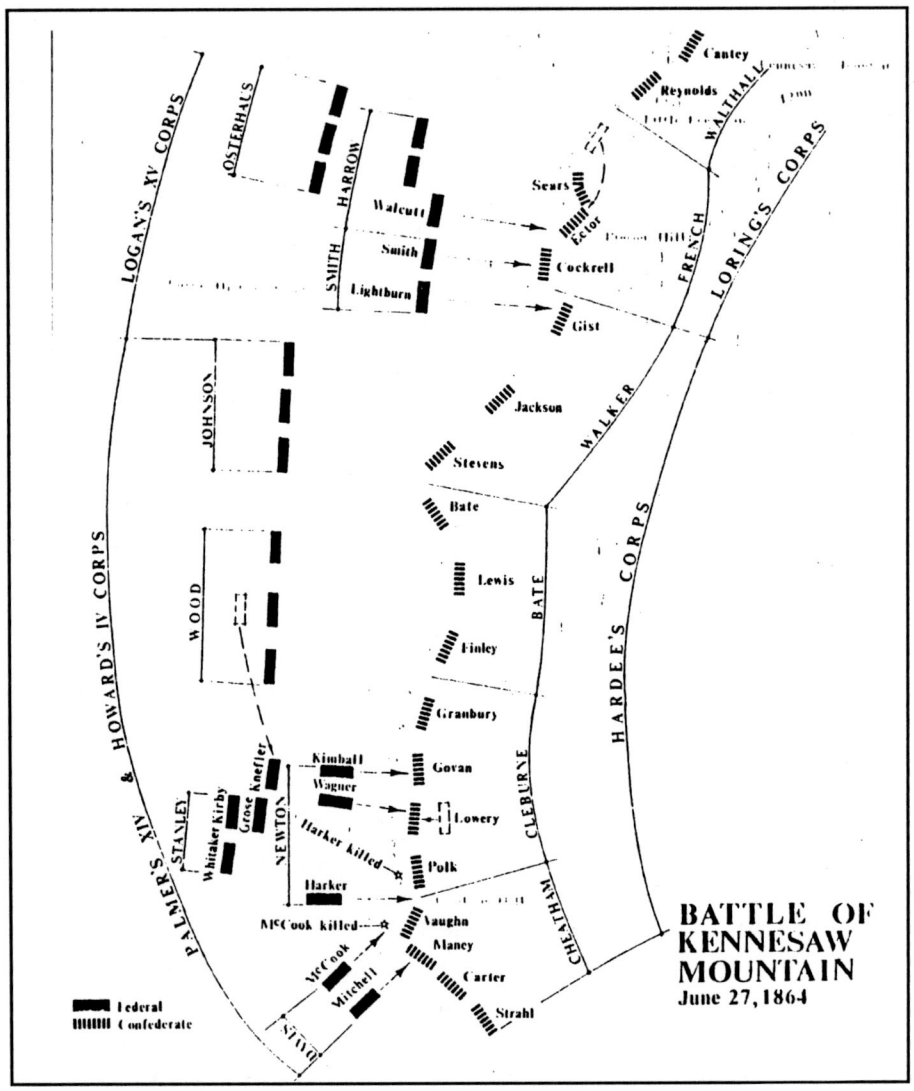

Chapter IV

The Federal's artillery commenced firing upon Hood's and Polk's forces soon after they had formed, and continued the shelling until darkness. At least forty Union cannon pounded the Confederate positions. Shoup's warning about the vulnerability of being enfiladed was becoming a reality.

That evening both Hood and Polk told Johnston they could not hold their part of the line in the morning. After more than an hour of discussion, Johnston decided to order a retreat, starting at once, moving south to the Etowah River.

On June 11, 1864, north of Marietta, Georgia, Johnston established the "Lost Mountain Line" which extended ten miles from Lost Mountain eastward across the W. & A. Railroad to Brush Mountain. He soon realized that this ten mile line stretched his outnumbered forces too thinly; he again withdrew his army two miles to the southeast where on the 18th he formed the heavily entrenched Kennesaw Mountain line.

Although this line put Johnston's forces in a better military position, it also enabled Sherman's forces to gain two miles of difficult country without even having to fight for it. Johnston was running out of time and terrain.

Sherman had put together an army of approximately 100,000 men and over 250 pieces of artillery. This force included Thomas' Army of the Cumberland, McPherson's Army of the Tennessee, and Schofield's Army of the Ohio. Furthermore, Sherman believed he knew more of Georgia than the rebels did because he had become familiar with the area while stationed near Atlanta in the 1840's.[32]

At the battle of Kennesaw Mountain, the artillery positions were designated by the divisional commanders. Shoup was to supply the reserve artillery as he found necessary to add to the artillery of Generals Polk and Hardee.[34]

On the morning of June 14, Generals Hardee, Johnston, and Polk rode forward to Pine Mountain to examine the ground. Down below, Generals Sherman and Howard spotted the group on the mountaintop. Sherman ordered a battery to fire at them. The third shot struck Polk. He was dead before he toppled from his rearing horse.

Because of the steep incline of Kennesaw, the Confederate engineers advised against planting artillery on the crest. But Maj. G. S. Storrs, commanding General French's cannon, found a spur in the rear of Little Kennesaw, cut a roadway through the brush up the mountainside.

A Dual Biography: General Lloyd Tilghman & General Francis Shoup

Southern artillerymen haul a field piece to the summit of Kennesaw Mountain during the Atlanta campaign. *(Mountain Campaigns in Georgia)*

"Pulled upward by a hundred men tugging on ropes, the first gun reached the summit within thirty minutes. The ammunition chests were dismounted and carried up empty, along with the ammunition. Several batteries were moved to the top in this manner."[35]

The combination of heat, rain, mud, rough terrain, and the strong natural defensive positions made Kennesaw Mountain impregnable to Sherman's frontal attacks. After three weeks of heavy losses and frustration, Sherman decided to abandon his supply line and began a movement to flank Johnston out of his position.

The wily Johnston knew when to move. On the 3rd, the mountain line was abandoned and the army moved four miles south of Marietta where a double line entrenchment, nearly six miles long, had been prepared by the Georgia militia at the Smyrna Camp Grounds. This same day heavy shelling occurred across the whole front and Johnston realized he was in no position to contain the Federals who had seized the opportunity to rapidly

Chapter IV

move all their corps directly toward Smyrna. This line held 48 hours before

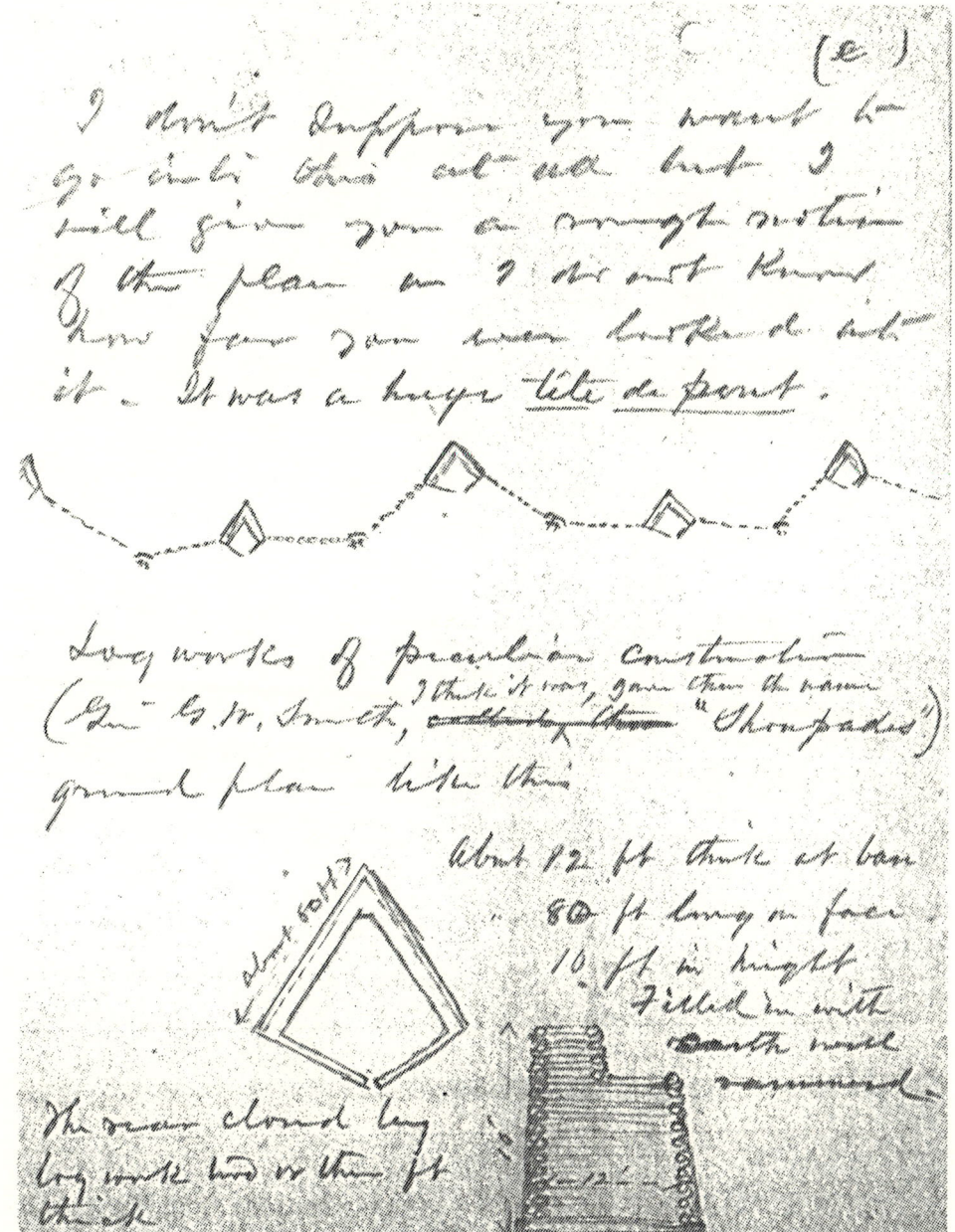

Shoup's sketch of idea for Chattachoochee River line.

A Dual Biography: General Lloyd Tilghman & General Francis Shoup

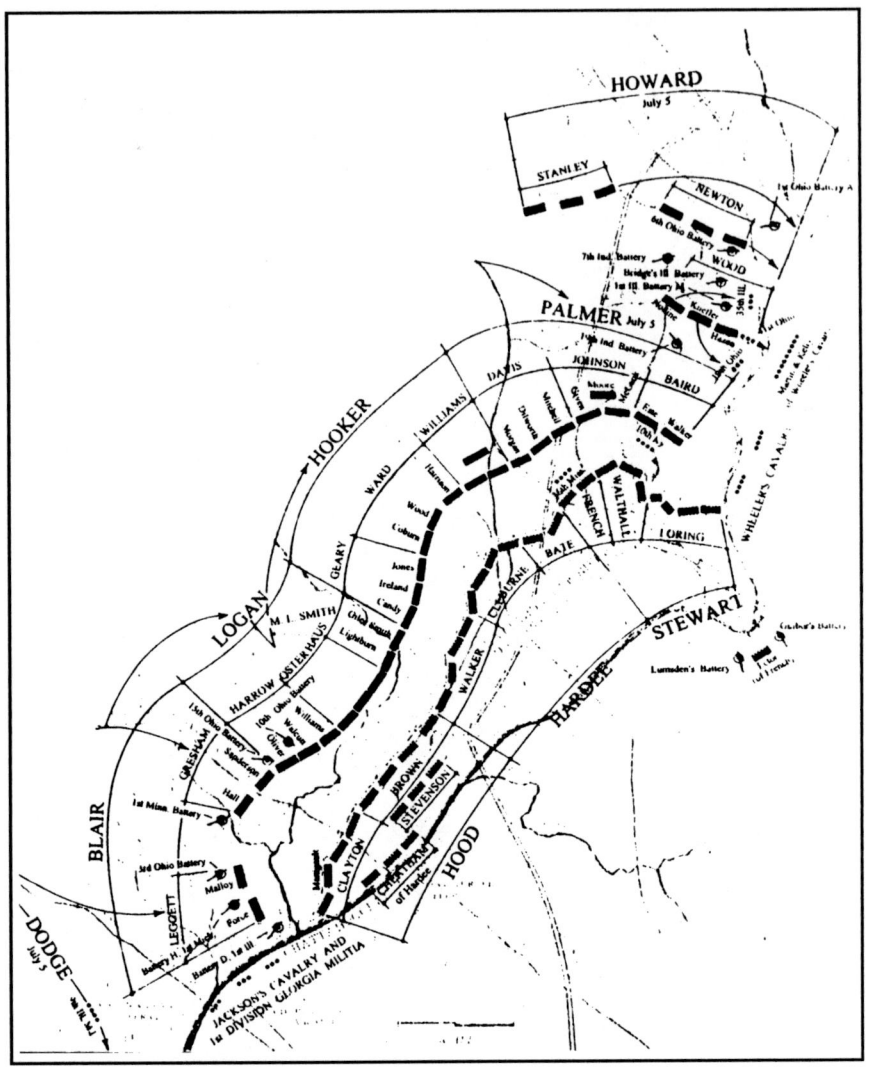

*The Chattachoochee River Line An American Maginot
by William R. Scaife*

Joe Johnston had to call it quits and retreat again.

The battle of maneuver had been going on for seven weeks, yet with all of the confidence in the world Johnston moved his weary army towards the Chattahoochee River. Here on the north bank of the river Johnston would have his last chance to defend Atlanta. Sherman hoped to catch Joe Johnston in the act of trying to cross such a broad and deep river as the

Chapter IV

Chattahoochee.

Shoup had not spent much time with the army for the last three weeks. At the onset of the Kennesaw Mountain campaign, which lasted three weeks, Shoup had approached Johnston with an idea for an innovative defense system to be built on the banks of the Chattahoochee River, where the Western & Atlantic Railroad crossed the river.

Johnston accepted Shoup's plan and ordered a special locomotive to take Shoup to Atlanta to begin construction. Shoup hired slaves from their owners numbering as many as 1,000, from nearly plantations. He was assisted by Maj. W. B. Foster, Chief Engineer of W. W. Loring's division.

Shoup begain laying out his transitional defense line on the north bank of the Chattahoochee River. It was four miles long, crescent shaped line enclosed by a powerful bridgehead protecting the train and wagon road bridges and was built large enough to shelter the entire Confederate army.

General Shoup's design was a radical departure from the then accepted method of digging in and embarced a system of log forts built above grade. Each fort was diamond shaped in plan with its two outer faces pointing in the direction of the enemy like an arrowhead. The forts were constructed after the fashion of log cabins, using double walls of logs filled with compacted earth. The exterior face walls were 10 to 12 feet thick at the base and extended to a height of 10 to 12 feet - surmounted by an infantry parapet or banquette for riflemen, for a total height of some 16 feet. These massive earthen structures could readily absorb the impact of artillery fire and were therefore virtually impregnable. Each fort was designed to be manned by a company of 80 riflemen. Georgia Militia commander, Gen. G.W. Smith, coined the term SHOUPADE to describe these strange looking structures.[36]

As Sherman's forces approached the river, they were astounded to see the retreating rebels enter the gigantic entrenchment that ran in length beyond ones sight. Sherman later admitted he had not learned beforehand of the existence of such a strong fortification.

While Sherman paused for his railroad supply line to catch up with him, Johnston sent his cavalry to the south side of the river to operate on the flanks of this mighty fortification. Wheeler's cavalry moved some 20 miles from the place and burnt the bridge at Roswell. The swollen Chattahoochee and its tributaries would provide few places for the Federal juggernaut to ford and get to the south bank and behind Johnston. Shoup was sure the line and the river constituted a formidable obstacle to Sherman's forces.

"Shoup told General Johnston that he could put up this works in ten days without calling on Johnston for men. That it would be such that one division could hold them for days against the whole of Sherman's Army. That Johnston could then concentrate without fear on either flank or at the center for attack. Johnston said, "Suppose the enemy should cross the river above or below?" Shoup replied, "In that case he could move on Sherman's supplies at Marietta and make Sherman fight his way back, or march for Tennessee and Kentucky and have him followed. In any event Johnston would be on his rear and could attack him with every advantage in our favor. General Johnston said, "I wish to God I had such a system of works!" The result of the conference was that the General gave me full authority and ordered an engine at once to take me to Atlanta.

I made good all I proposed, and the line nearly three miles in length was ready when Johnston fell back and could have been held by three thousand men for any reasonable time against a hundred thousand.

Johnston had confidence in the works as he wanted me to construct a like system about Atlanta. This I could have done as I agreed in one week, but when it came to raising the Negroes, Johnston would not give the necessary orders on the ground that his department did not extend below Atlanta! I tried to induce Gov. Brown to supply the Negroes, but failed to induce him to act. Thus was Atlanta lost."

On July 8, Sherman began an exploratory probing of the river line to satisfy himself as to the strength of Johnston's position. McPherson's army was sent to threaten a crossing at Turner's Ferry six miles downstream while General Thomas in support of this move, began demonstrations on the front of the river line, more-or-less bottling up the three Confederate Corps now inside their fort.

General French's diary notes, "This morning I rode along the lines with

Chapter IV

Generals Loring and Shoup. The enemy kept up a sharp fire on our skirmish line until night. On the 9th, the enemy attacked the line in front of Sear's Brigade with force."

On this same date, Schofield's army made a surprise crossing at Soap Creek using pontoons to cross to the south side; by the 9th, a strong bridgehead had been established. To add to Confederate problems, Garrard's Federal cavalry crossed over the river to the north at Roswell.

The booming of Sherman's cannons announced that his army had been supplied, watered and fed, and was ready to move around the SHOUPADES and begin crossing the Chattahoochee.

Faced with Thomas's ponderous army in his front and with two well-established bridgeheads across the river, General Johnston thought he had no choice but to order the evacuation of this strong position on July 9, 1864.

Later, Shoup said, "I need not attempt to say what a blow this was to me. I took a long look at the works into which my heart had gone to such a degree and felt that the days of the Confederacy were numbered. I could not then, and have never been able since, to see why the position should not have been held indefinitely."[37]

The only contemporary reference to the abandmonment of Shoup's River line concept was found in General French's journal under the date of July 10, 1864:

> "The works of General Shoup, with its stockades, did not give Johnston spare troops enough to prevent this movement of the enemy across the Chattahoochee River. Thus we were constantly outflanked by a superior force not disposed to attack us behind any kind of works."[38]

On July 9, 1864, orders were given to withdraw across the Chattahoochee River and make a stand at Peachtree Creek line, which had been previously constructed north of Atlanta. Johnston was at the end of the line in more than one way.

On July 17, Johnston was dismissed as commander of The Army of Tennessee and was succeeded by Gen. John Bell Hood. Johnston did not accept the dismissal very gracefully. So to speak, he left Hood holding the bag, left the command and never once helped Hood on any part in defending Atlanta. In the shadow of Shoup's career is a possibility he informed

President Davis that Johnston had made a major mistake in abandoning the Chattahoochee River line. How much hurt on Johnston's part? Edward G. Longacre in American National Biography records, "In early 1865 Johnston, under who Shoup had served faithfully on the road to Atlanta, took the unusual step of protesting Shoup's assignment to his undermanned command, which could have used all the senior-officer experise he could get." Shoup was relieved from command of the artillery on July 25[39], and was assigned to duty as chief of staff for Hood.[40]

In a confidential letter to President Davis, General Hood mentioned "I have assigned General Shoup as chief of staff. This may strike you as inexpedient, but it is evidently the best. He is decidedly fond of this kind of work and is very efficient at it while he was not satisfied with his position at the head of the artillery and had on my former visit desired transfer to an infantry command."[41]

The Confederate forces had been in the immediate presence of Sherman's three armies for 74 days, laboring and fighting daily. There had been rain and mud and lately, excessive heat. Exhausting marches, day and night, had been forced upon them by Johnston's Fabian policy. All month long they had been subjected to an almost continuous cannonading and heavy casualties; but all the time loyal to the cause. Would Atlanta be any different?

Model by William R. Scaife   *Photography by Jack Melton, Jr.*

54 Millimeter Scale Model of a Shoupade

Chapter IV

Atlanta Developer To Save Rare Shoupade Earthwork

By Joe Kirby

MARIETTA, Ga — A "Shoupade" that had been in danger of being bulldozed will be preserved instead.

The Shoupade is one of seven unique earthworks that still exist of 36 originally constructed as part of Johnston's River Line to shield Atlanta from the onslaught of Union Gen. William T Sherman.

Developer John Wieland Homes obtained permission from the Cobb County Board of Commissioners in April to build 260 townhomes and condos on a 34.5-acre tract on Log Cabin Road just inside Interstate 285 (Atlanta's Beltway). Wieland planned to level the Shoupade site as part of the development, but changed its mind after a series of stories, columns and editorials in the Marietta Daily Journal and Atlanta Journal-Constitution.

In addition, members of local Sons of Confederate Veterans camps, including Marietta lawyer Martin O'Toole, pleaded with at a commission meeting to require the developer to save the Shoupade.

"A socially responsible and historically minded development can be done here," O'Toole told commissioners. "One Shoupade on this property can be saved with a half-acre."

Also weighing in was retired architect and author Bill Scaife, who has written extensively about the Atlanta Campaign and first brought the existence of the Shoupades to light. Scaife, who lives in nearby Allatoona, reminded the Commission in a letter that only a handful of the Shoupades remain and that they are in danger of being lost to commercial and residential development.

The county's preservation planner was prepared to require Wieland to pay for an archaeological excavation of the Shoupade if he received permission to level it.

But Wieland ultimately decided to build around the earthwork and the   of nearby trenches, incorporating them into the project. Wieland's   were then the stipulation the Shoupade be protected.

Due to the fact the development will be a "gated" community, the Shoupade will not be open to the public at large. But that beats seeing it demolished. As O'Toole noted, "Since the developer could have simply cranked up the bulldozer and removed the fortification at any time, it was a good compromise for all concerned."

Non-residents who wish to view the Shoupade will be allowed to do so on an appointment basis.

The Shoupade squabble marked the fourth time that Marietta-area developers have worked with local preservationists and the SCV in the past year or so to minimize the damage to Civil War sites.

Said O'Toole: "With the stakes so high and extinction being forever, it is felt that these 'half-loaf' measures of compromise do offer the best way of piquing the interest of the developers to work within reason."

The Shoupades were designed by Gen. Joseph Johnston's chief engineer, Col. Francis Mitbury Shoup. Built with slave labor, they were arrowhead-shaped two-story log-and-dirt forts. Soldiers standing behind the rampart would pass their rifles down to those on the lower level for reloading, thereby allowing for a near-continuous stream of fire at an approaching enemy.

The Shoupades were linked by trenches and interspersed with two-gun artillery forts and helped create interlocking fields of fire that were considered nearly impregnable.

According to Scaife, no other such system of fieldworks was constructed until the French built the Maginot Line after World War I. Like the Maginot Line, Johnston's River Line and its Shoupades served its purpose—deterring an assault by an enemy.

But as in the case of the Maginot Line, the enemy instead outflanked the line and forced its evacuation. Johnston's River Line was occupied before Sherman upstream on the Chattahoochee

A Dual Biography: General Lloyd Tilghman & General Francis Shoup

Chapter V

Atlanta's irregular circle of fortifications made it one of the best-protected cities in the world at the time. The city had a ten-mile circumference of high breastworks, redoubts, cannon emplacements, and rifle pits that for a year had been prepared for just this eventuality. No sooner had Sherman got to the Peachtree Creek fortifications than General Hood embraced at the opportunity to strike out against the invaders. In scarcely over a week, Hood would attack three times.

The morning of July 20 found Thomas's army crossing south of Peachtree Creek. Hood embraced the opportunity to strike, thinking he had caught Thomas in an isolated position. He soon learned that Schofield and McPherson were approaching Atlanta from the east.

The Confederates advance at Peachtree Creek became disjointed and in a seesaw engagement, the day proved a complete failure for Hood, although a success as far as mere fighting was concerned. Casualties were in the thousands for both sides. Hood had no time to rest.

The next battle was at Decatur, also referred to as the Battle of Atlanta, though it took place outside the city. This again was a poorly coordinated offense by the southerners which had been badly miscalculated by the aggressive Hood. Shoup was active in the fray, "Hardee and Shoup's artillery pounded the hill from what seemed like all directions, leveling whole sections of parapets, mangling the men behind them."[43]

By nightfall, the Federal line was restored to essentially the same position it had held 24 hours earlier. General Hardee's opinion was that this battle was "one of the most desperate and bloody of the war." Federal casualties were over 3,700, including General McPherson. Hood lost 8,000 men.

Hood continued his impetuous attack. The slaughter continued at Lickskillet Road at the battle of Ezra Church, July 28, 1864. This unsettling blood bath brought no benefit to Hood's army, but cost him 5,000 more casualties plus a host of Confederate Generals being wounded, including S.D. Lee; J.C. Brown; W.W. Loring; A.P. Stewart; R.L. Gibson; and M.D. Ector. Ector had his left leg amputated.

General Shoup, as chief of staff, begged the president of the Macon and Western Railroad, in the "name of humanity" to assit in the task of removing the wounded. "Those who managed to find space in the filthy boxcars often were subjected to the horrors of a 70-hour ride to Macon, 100 miles to the south, with great suffering and loss of life."[44]

Admist all of the fighting, Sherman's engineers and pioneers built a new bridge over the Chattahoochee River; the sound of the locomotive's whistle could be heard in Atlanta. The rebs used to joke that Sherman carried his own tunnel with him because he built the railroad so fast. Sherman's supply line was now to the rear of the Army of the Cumberland. The extension of the railroad to the fighting front meant Sherman's army would be more efficient and quickly supplied with food, ammunition, and equipment.

It was August 1st, and the scorching heat slowed down the tempo on both sides. Sherman ordered forts and siege guns to be mounted all within easy range of Atlanta. He told his commanders to fire 10 to 15 shots from every gun they had in position that would reach any of the houses in Atlanta. Eight, four-and-a-half inch rifled siege guns were brought down from Chattanooga with 1,000 shells, which began firing continuously into the city at an average of one shell every 20 minutes.[45]

"Today," General Shoup wrote in his memoranda of daily movements and events in Army of Tennessee, "good news has flowed in from all distant points. We have just completed the killing, capturing, and breaking up of the entire raiding party under Gen. E. McCook and routed G. Stoneman and his cavalry."[46]

These token victories mattered little as Atlanta, bit by bit, began to be destroyed during the month of August. Hood did manage to keep the Macon railroad open, thus enabling him to receive supplies from south of the city.

On August 25, 1864, Sherman's cannons stopped firing. This was the first signal that Sherman's armies were ready to move again. The forty-day siege was over and the impatient Sherman ordered his armies to move around the western side of the city and south towards Jonesboro.

Shoup records in his journal for August that the Confederates thought the Federals "were falling back across the Chattahoochee River". He added, "no reliable information has been received in regard to the intention of the enemy as he may plan to make another attempt to reach the Macon railroad by extending southward."[47]

With this news, Hood decided to abandon Atlanta. Shoup instructed his chief quartermaster, commissary, and ordnance officers to be ready by day-

Chapter V

light to ship out of the city all locomotives, cars, food stores, ammunition and heavy artillery.[48]

On August 31, Sherman's forces seized Rough and Ready, cut the telegraph lines linking Hood and Hardee. The Union army, in great strength, crossed the Flint River, and by September 1 Sherman began to maneuver Hood out of Atlanta.

The Confederates began evacuating Atlanta at 5 P.M. Hood and his staff (Shoup) left for Lovejoy's station on the short stretch of the Macon railroad still in Confederate hands. Shoup issued orders, "General Hood desires the men to go at the enemy with bayonets fixed, determined to drive everything that may come against them."[49]

Hood rejoined Hardee at Jonesboro, the Confederates again evidenced the old fighting spirit that had sustained them all year long; enough so to make Sherman's commanders hesitate, causing them to wait for O.O. Howard corps to catch up to them so they could attack Hood's strong position.

When Sherman received word that Howard could not re-enforce in time, he became disgusted. Sherman never cared for the devout church-going Howard and once remarked, "he ought to have been born in petticoats and ought to wear them."[50]

Sherman, tired and weary of this terribly long campaign, envisioned that he might have to pursue Hood all the way to Macon. In a surprise move on September 8, he began to move his army back towards Atlanta to rest his forces. He then proposed an armistice of ten days between the armies to reorganize, recruit and to exchange prisoners.

Sherman's failure to use the strength of his forces at hand enabled Hood to get a reprieve from total destruction and Sherman lost one of the most favorable opportunities ever to destroy and eliminate the Army of Tennessee.

Before the armistice had expired, the greater part of Hood's army moved out on September 18, marching in a northwesterly direction toward Palmetto Station, near the Chattahoochee River. This location became the summit for a meeting between President Davis and General Hood, where they developed a strategy to checkmate Sherman with an offensive on his communications and supply line north of Atlanta, and eventually into Alabama and Tennessee for an invasion into Ohio.

"I did agree with Hood and the feasibility of his project,

but I did not dream that Sherman would be so obliging as to march away from the theatre of war with the best part of his army, or I should have thought better of it. If Sherman had held his forces together, Hood would have been wiped out. As it was, he came near a brilliant success."

At his own request, Shoup was relieved from duty as chief of Hood's staff on September 14.[51] A court of inquiry in regard to the loss of stores to Sherman at Atlanta was settled with Shoup receiving a mild censure.[52] Already on leave, Shoup took leave which was extended by 30 days on October 25.[53]

Perhaps because of his Northern birth, Shoup was criticized at times, but Jefferson Davis wrote that, "the only very clear information communicated to him regarding the establishments of munition manufactures in the Trans-Mississippi, was in the report of this much abused officer, Brigider General Shoup."[54]

"I went to Richmond during this interval and wrote a letter to Senator Hemming for permission on the subject of raising Negro troops which was published in pamphlet form and provided Congress and the Virginia Legislature. I had been partially assured that the matter be brought up in both bodies and actions in favor of the measure."

With Confederate resources dwindling, the proposal to enlist negroes was brought up in November in Jefferson Davis' presidential message.

Even before the widespread publication of General Lee's views, the Richmond *Enquirer* (February 18, 1865) thought that the tide of opinion had turned, and the *Enquirer* began to emphasize the necessity of discipline for Negro recruits:

The question of negro soliders, we consider as settled. Public opinion has definitely declared in favor of arming the negroes; the resolution introduced in the Virginia Legislature, giving the consent of the State to the measure, will pass, and may be followed, and should be, by instructions to [Confederate] Senators to vote for the measure and thus put the matter at rest. As to giving the slaves their free-

Chapter V

dom, this should be the reward for faithful service, at the end of the war, if desired by the slaves. To some it may be a boon, a reward – others may not even desire freedom. Negroes are divided in opinion as to whether they would prefer freedom to slavery, but by all means leave the choice with them, let them decide the matter. We do not expect the reward to make soldiers of them; *discipline* only will do that. It must be a discipline differing, very much, from that which now holds together, with loosened bands, the armies of the Confederate States. It must be a discipline sharp, severe, exacting, which first teaches them their duty and then compels them to perform it. There never has been discipline in the armies of this Confederacy, but instead thereof a kind of universal suffrage, which fights when it chooses and straggles when it feels like it. All this must be changed with the negro troops; they have not the motives that impel the white man to this fight; they must be kept up to the mark by *fear of punishment* more than by hope of reward.[55]

General Lee, in a letter to Honorable E. Barksdale, House of Representatives, "I can only say that in my opinion, the negroes will make efficient soldiers." Lee's young artillerist, William R. J. Pegram sensed that the recruitment of slaves would meet with general approbation in the entire army and that some of the best officers under Lee would be trying to get commands in the Corps D'Afrique.[56] The impressment of slaves began in February of 1864, when the Confederate Congress permitted the impressment by states of twenty thousand free Negroes and slaves for menial service in the Confederate Army. Shoup suggested recruitment.

Lee had emphasized emancipation, but the *Enquirer* seemed more interested in discipline for the Negro soldiers. Another high Confederate officer, Brigadier General Francis A. Shoup, shared the disciplinary emphasis in an article that appeared in the Richmond *Whig* (February 20, 1865):

The proposition to put negroes in the army has gained favor rapidly of late, and promises, in some form or other, to be adopted. So far from exciting the repugnance on the part of the army a first apprehended, it has been called for by the resolves of many regiments and brigades, and is known to be favored by nearly all the principal officers. We [the *Whig*'s editors] do not profess to be very sanguine of good results from the measure, but we do not feel that, as civilians, we would be justified, in the present emergency, in opposing the use of any means which our leading military men assure us can be made efficient. To them this cause is trusted, and especially to the General-in-Chief. It is known that he urges – with a warmth he has not, perhaps, exhibited in regard to any other matter of legislation – the passage of a law subjecting the negro element to military use. His opinion, at all times entitled to great weight, becomes imperative as to such a matter, when we reflect that the whole responsibility of our defence has been devolved upon him. . . .

. . . A paper on this subject, written by Bridadier General Shoup, presents the military view of the subject very clearly and forcibly; and as it is a matter in regard to which our people desire all the light that can be thrown upon it, we assure ourselves that we will meet their wishes in extracting largely from what he has written. After stating that the subject has engaged his earnest attention from the very beginning of the war, Gen'l S. says:

"Napoleon declares as a maxim that 'the first quality of a soldier is the power to endure hardships and fatigue.' It will not be denied, I take it, that the negro possesses this element in the highest degree. The common opinion is that courage is the highest quality, and, as if to meet that opinion, Napoleon goes on to say, in the same maxim, 'courage is altogether secondary.' It is to be understood, of course, that he here speaks of the private soldier. That courage is necessary in an army, and that of the highest order, is entirely manifest – but to understand this maxim it is necessary to consider the nature and organization of an army. There are, as everybody knows, three separate and distinct grades or

Chapter V

estates – the private soldier, the non-commissioned officer and the officer. . . . Real soldiers come to have no will of their own, but obey simply because they are ordered by proper authority. You will hear it said that this is a West Point notion; but in truth it is the notion underlying the whole military world. On this continent we are new hands at war. We are just beginning to learn what soldiers are. When discipline is properly enforced the soldier is so entirely in the hands of his officers, that the tone, character and courage of a command is entirely determined by these properties in the officers and non-commissioned officers. Whenever there is misconduct on, or off, the field, it is to be charged to misconduct or neglect on the part of the officers. All soldiers know this. Thus while courage may be dispensed with in the private, it is most important in the two higher classes. . . . There is no necessity to make anything but a private soldier of the negro. The officers and non-commissioned officers should be taken from the most gallant and meritorious officers and soldiers of the army. . . .

"So much for the theory. What has experience shown? It is by no means certain that the negro is so deficient in courage as is generally believed. If we are to credit the statements of travellers in Africa, the native negro is the most sanguinary warrior in the world. In their battles hand to hand, they fight till either party is almost annihilated; and our very slaves are in great part the descendants of prisoners captured in war. We see the negro altogether in his servile condition. He naturally shrinks, without regard to appearances. He, however, makes a fearless sailor and fireman. The English have long used him as a soldier, and he has done good service. But the experiences of this war are abundantly sufficient to show his adaptability as a soldier. The enemy has taught us a lesson to which we ought not to shut our eyes. He has caused him to fight as well, if not better than, have his white troops of the same length of service. Our prisoners from Ship Island and elsewhere declare that they are far the best sentinels and most thoroughly drilled of the federal troops. I have myself seen them, in the hands of a single engineer officer, entirely without organization, work under fire, where certainly he could not have held white men. Now, if the enemy has succeeded in making any kind of troops of these people, with all their non-commissioned officers and a great part of their officers black, how much better could we make with all these white!

". . . But it is alleged by those who oppose the measure, and here seems to lie the greatest difficulty, that they will not fight in our cause. Here again let us go to that highest of all authorities – Napoleon. He says in one of his maxims of war, 'a good general, good officers, commissioned and non-commissioned, good instruction, and strict discipline, make good troops without regard to the cause in which they fight.' By 'cause' we are to understand the particular sentiments or preferences of the troops. This is the broadest and most positive enunciation of a principle which goes to the very foundation of the whole matter. It is strictly true, and procceds from the very nature of army organization and discipline. It will be observed that he assumes the two higher orders, officers and non-commissioned officers, to be good. Such would be the case in the plan proposed. The truth is, troops always hold the sentiments and opinions of their officers, whatever they may be. **Even the negroes that have served with our armies as cooks and teamsters, are as thoroughly enlisted in our cause as are their masters; and in many cases have been known to fight as gallantly as they.** It is altogether a mistaken notion to suppose that it is pay or bounties that induce men to fight. These considerations may cause them to enlist, but once made soldiers, they find themselves in the hands of a giant that leaves them no power to escape – discipline. One who is not a soldier can hardly understand this, but it is not the less true. Nor is it patriotism, nor any other senitment, that holds a soldier at his post. Give our troops – brave and patriotic as they are – liberty to go home to-day – removing all influence of officers – and how much of an army would you have to-mor-

Chapter V

row? The negroes, however, should be given pay, etc.

... "I speak now of heavy infantry. With the other arms a somewhat different rule holds – since more individuality is required – but the same is substantially true throughout. Thus the negro is excellently adapted for a soldier.

"The negro does not fight for the enemy because he is free. He has been tricked and forced into his service, and he cannot help it. Those who have been re-captured say they would rather fight on our side, because we know better how to treat them.

"It is not true, then, that to make good soldiers of these people, we must either give or promise them freedom. On the contrary, it is my firm conviction that to do either would be to impair their efficiency and tractability. But the greatest possible advantage can be had by skilfully using their desire for freedom. The President should have power to declare free such of them as may from time to time be recommended for such reward, by their officers, for gallant or meritorious conduct. This would act as an ever-present spur. It should not be to take effect at the end of the war, but be declared at once in general orders, and the soldier should be given honorary chevrons to distinguish him during the remainder of his service. To say that all should be free at the end of the war would have little effect. The uncertainty and vagueness would altogether fail to impress a simple-minded negro beyond a week. As well might one promise to free one's cook at some indefinite period with the expectation of thereby securing good dinners. But if it be held out as a boon within his immediate grasp, and which he sees conferred upon others every day, it must have a most excellent effect. Besides, to either give or promise freedom wholesale, would have a most pernicious influence upon the whole race, it is wholly unnecessary, and should not be done, as a mere matter of expediency.

"But, it is alleged, he would desert. No soldier who understands the potency of discipline could hold such an opinion. . . .

"... It is said, again, they would revolt. Nothing could be more impossible. No scheme could be kept from the non-commissioned officers constantly at hand. Even if a regiment were to succeed sufficiently to come to an outbreak, others could not act in concert, and would be brought to crush the refractory ones at once. Besides, the cavalry and artillery (white) would be ever at hand to destroy any that might attempt it. Mutiny is scarcely known where discipline is maintained. . . .

"**. . . My proposition, then, is to let the slavery question remain just where it is – put into service as many negroes as we can provide with arms and equipments – organize them strictly as heavy infantry, to be held for the day of battle – convert the white troops into cavalry, artillery and *elite* infantry – take all officers and non-commissioned officers from the most gallant and meritorious of our present armies, and introduce the strictest possible system of discipline – all with the greatest rapidity. The time required to accomplish this would be less that at first thought. The greatest obstacle in making troops is to teach and give experience to the officers. In this case we would have them, in great part, already made. The soldier is taught everything so far as the drill goes when he knows the school of the company. All drill beyond that depends upon the officer almost entirely, so that the time required would be that necessary for experienced officers to drill one company. Thus an army would spring into existence in a remarkably short time.**"[57]

The Virginia Military Institute made an offer to the Confederate secretary of war to undertake the task of organizing and drilling the blacks:

On February 9, 1865, a resolution to enlist 200,000 negroes in the Confederate army was proposed. The Congress approved the incorporation of blacks into the army on March 13, and emancipation became part of the plan when President Davis issued General Order No. 14, ten days later.[58] General Shoup was in Richmond at this time, perhaps politicking for the

Chapter V

passage of the bill. A letter dated March, 1865 that was sent to Gen. S. Cooper, Adjutant and Inspector General, Shoup "requested to command Negro troops, if any such be organized. I should perfer service in the southern states – Mississippi or Alabama." Orders were issued for Shoup to join General Hardee in Georgia, on February 21, but he never left Richmond. On March 11, the order to report to Hardee was revoked and Shoup was assigned to Joe Johnston in the Field at Smithfield[59], but was rejected by the general. In the meatime the Negro Enlistment Bill was passed and hard-pressed Virginians placed their black population at the Confederate Government's disposal. Notices on March 15 in the Richmond newspapers carried copy authorizing recruitment of blacks.[60] They read, "We shall have a Negro Army. Letters are pouring into the department from men of military skill and character, asking authority to raise companies, battalions, and regiments of Negro troops. It is the desperate remedy for the very desperate case – and may be successful."[61]

General Shoup, on the 13th, was named to command some black troops that were being raised in response to the new law.[62] Shortly, a few companies of newly recruited Negro troops paraded in the Capitol Square.[63] Judah Benjamin watched from his window as they marched in a drill ceremony and remarked, "some were in new uniforms."[64] But it was too late by April 2, Lee's once mightly army, depleted by desertion, sickness, and death, faced a much larger Union Army at Petersburg, Virginia. The decisive struggle was at hand for the capitulation of Richmond and Lee's depleted army. The unthinkable had happened, Richmond must be abandoned quickly. Eight trains were formed and brought-up for the transportation for the fleeing government, including a special train for President Davis and his functionaries.[65] As the advancing Federal forces entered Richmond, the slow moving, over-capacity trains, containing the President and his cabinet, treasury and archives, slowly lumbered out of the city at midnight, chugging south towards Danville, Virginia in hopes of preserving the Confederacy. With the city burning, Lee's divided army moved towards Amelia Courthouse where they expected to find supplies and to use the Danville and Richmond Railroad to join Joe Johnston's forces in North Carolina. The arrival of Sheridan's cavalry at Jetersville cut the Confederate line of retreat south along the railroad, so when Lee's forces converged at Amelia Courthouse they had to proceed west. A running fight took place at Sayler's Creek on the 6th; rearguard action took place at

A Dual Biography: General Lloyd Tilghman & General Francis Shoup

Farmville on the 7th, with a final action at Appomattox Station on April 8th. With Lee's army surrounded, he had to surrender on April 9, 1865.[66]

General Shoup did not travel out of Richmond with Lee's Army. He may have accompanied President Davis' entourage, but most likely he was with the naval troops under Rear Admiral Semmes, which traveled from Richmond to Danville, and subsequently guarded the Piedmont railroad between Danville and Greensboro. They remained in the trenches before Danville for ten days. The first news they received of Lee's surrender came to them from the stream of fugitives which came pressing into their lines at Danville. It indeed was a rabble route Semmes reported.[67] As soon as the word reached Johnston of the surrender, there was a stampede from his fragmented army.[68] Admiral Semmes contended later on, that there never was a surrender of Johnston's army as prisoners to the enemy. He said the Sherman's and Johnston's second military meeting after hostilities had ceased and Sherman's first surrender agreement had been rejected by Federal Secretary of War Stanton, was a military convention, which main features were that Johnston should disperse his army, and Sherman should, in consideration thereof, guarantee it against molestation by Federal troops.[69] Regardless, the war was over and Shoup was surrendered at Durham Station, North Carolina on April 26, and paroled at Greensboro on May 2, 1865. After ten years of military life, Shoup would make a career change, and decided to serve a much higher authority than the Confederacy.

Chapter VI

Immediately following the war and upon reorganization of the University of Mississippi at Oxford in 1865, Shoup was elected professor of Applied Mathematics and Engineering.[1]

Here he studied for the ministry and was admitted to the orders of the Episcopal Church in 1868 and assumed the duties of rector of St. Peter's Parish in Oxford, Mississippi.[2]

In the same year he became chaplain and professor at the University of the South in Sewanee, Tennessee, where he taught Logic and Metaphysics, (1868-1870) and Mathematics (1870-1875).[3] He published "Elements of Algebra" in 1874.[4]

There were a number of Confederates now at Sewanee. General Edmund Kirby Smith from St. Augustine; Jason Fairbanks, one-time staff officer for General Hardee; and Gen. Josiah Gorgas, who later became president of the University of Alabama.[5]

In 1870, Shoup was married to Esther Habersham Elliott of Sewanee, the daughter of Bishop Stephen Elliott. Rev. Shoup resigned from the university to go into parish work. In 1875, he was rector successively of churches in Waterford, New York; Church of the Advent, Nashville, Tennessee (1878); and Jackson, Tennessee and New Orleans, Louisiana.[6]

He received an honorary Doctor of Divinity degree from Sewanee in 1879 and became a Tennessee Trustee to the University of the South (1879-1881).[7] He was conspicuous in the councils of the church, and several times was elected deputy to the general convention.

He was recalled to Sewanee in 1883 as professor of math, engineering, and physics (1883-1891); professor of metaphysics (1885-1892); and lecturer in constitutional law (1892-1893).[8] He published "Mechanism and Personality" (1891).[9]

Dr. Shoup was a man of fine presence and exquisite demeanor. His mind was clear, penetrating and wonderfully alert in its analysis. He was a graceful and ready writer, his style at times rising to great dignity and beauty. In his chosen department of mathematics and metaphysics he was both original and profound. His last book on the "Consideration of Modern Problems in Light of Recent Research" was pronounced by some of the foremost scholars in the country as the finest work of its kind that had appeared in recent years.[10]

Dr. Shoup was a teacher of great enthusiasm of passionate devotion to ideals, and for twenty-five years and more his heart and his love have been with the work and objects of the University of the South at Sewanee.[11]

Shoup was a long-time friend of E. Kirby Smith. At his passing over in 1893, Shoup wrote a memorial to Smith in the University of the South magazine.

Dr. Shoup died at Columbia, Tennessee, September 4, 1896, leaving his wife and three children. He was buried at Sewanee University Cemetery.

His great-grandson, David M. Shoup, gained fame as a World War II combat leader of the U.S. Marines. His career paralleled the rapid expansion of the U.S. military during World War II and the Cold War. He helped to prepare the marines to fulfill their role in the increasing number of U.S. interventions abroad.[3] He was awarded the Medal of Honor at Taraw and served as commandant (1960-1963).

Chapter VI

Sewanee
University Cemetery

BRIGADIER GENERAL FRANCIS ASBURY SHOUP

Born: 1834 – Laurel Indiana
Died: September 4, 1896 – Columbia, Tennessee

The Reverend-General Shoup is buried under two crosses: the Christian symbol, and the crossed cannons of the artillery service.

Inscription.

4

213

A Dual Biography: General Lloyd Tilghman & General Francis Shoup

End Notes

Preface

¹Patterson. *Rebels from West Point*, Preface.

²Ibid.

³Macmillan. *The Encyclopedia of the Confederacy*, page 403.

⁴Patterson. *Rebels from West Point*, page 162.

⁵Weinert, Jr. *The Confederate Regular Army*, child's page 120;
James H. and Robert C. Hill, page 122.
Nicholls. *Generals in Gray*, by Warner, page 224;
Church. *U.S. Military Academy*, page 621. (Did not list his rank).

Chapters I & II

¹*Dictionary of American Biography,* Vol. 17, page 130.

²Ibid.

³Boatner III. *The Civil War Dictionary*, page 758.

⁴Faust. *Historial Times Illustrated Encyclopedia*, page 685-686.

⁵Confederate Service Record of F.A. Shoup.

⁶Hughes. *General William J. Hardee*, page 74.

⁷Burns, Ned H. *Confederate Forts*, page 44.

⁸Hughes. *General William J. Hardee*, page 80.

⁹Confederate Service Record of F.A. Shoup.

¹⁰Davis. *The Confederate General*, Vol. 5, page 150.

[11] *Confederate Veteran Magazine*, Vol. II, June, page 137.

[12] Davis. *The Confederate General*, Vol. 5, page 32.

[13] Ibid, page 34.

[14] Ibid, page 38.

[15] Roman. *The Military Operations of General Beauregard*, Vol. I, page 299.

[16] Ibid, page 307.

[18] Daniel. *Cannoneers in Gray*, page 42.

[19] Ibid, page 43.

[20] Carvel. *The Kentucky Brave*, page 86.

[21] Confederate Service Record of F.A. Shoup, General Order No. 10.

[22] Ibid.

[23] Ibid.

[24] Carl H. Moneyhon. *To Live and Die In Dixie* by Archie P. McDonald, page 109, Arkansas.

[25] Ibid, General Order No. 10, Part I, Trans-Mississippi Dept., Par. II.

[26] Rowland, Dunbar, LL.D. *Jefferson Davis, Constitutionist*, page 357.

[27] Ibid, page 110.

[28] *Confederate Military History*, Vol. XIV, Arkansas, page 140.

[29] Boatner III. *The Civil War Dictionary*, page 119.

End Notes

[30]*Confederate Military History*, Vol. XIV, Arkansas, page 148.

[31]Ibid, page 153.

[32]Prairie Grove Battlefield State Park pamphlet.

[33]Ibid.

[34]*Confederate Military History*, Vol. XIV, Arkansas, page 146.

[35]Ibid.

[36]Faust. *Historical Times Illustrated Encyclopedia*, page 358.

[37]Confederate Service Record F.A. Shoup.

Chapter III, IV, & V
[1]Allen Dennis. *To Live and Die in Dixie* by Archie P. McDonald, page 13.

[2]Ibid, page 176.

[3]Confederate Service Record of F.A. Shoup. S.O. #102[19], A.G.O. dated April 27, 1863.

[4]Bearss. *The Campaign for Vicksburg*, Vol. II, footnote #59 on page 422.

[5]Raab. *Florida's Forgotten General*, page 106.

[6]Boatner III. *The Civil War Dictionary*, page 876.

[7]Greene. *The Mississippi Campaigns of the Civil War*, page 177.

[8]Ibid.

[9]Bearss. *The Campaign for Vicksburg*, Vol. III, page 748.

[10] Ibid, page 749.

[11] OR Series I, Vol. 24, Part I, page 276.

[12] Bearss. *The Campaign for Vicksburg*, Vol. III, page 794.

[13] OR Series I, Vol. 24, Part II, page 399.

[14] Ibid, pages 407-410.

[15] *Confederate Veteran Magazine*, Vol. II, Page 174.

[16] OR Series I, Vol. 24, Part I, page 232.

[17] Hattaway. *General Stephen D. Lee*, footnote, page 245.

[18] OR Series I, Vol. 24, Part III, page 493.

[19] OR Series I, Vol. 31, Part II, page 851.

[20] Ibid, page 852.

[21] OR Series I, Vol. 32, Part II, page 692.

[22] Ibid, page 701.

[23] Ibid, page 785.

[24] Govan. *A Different Valor*, page 254.

[25] OR Series I, Vol. 32, Part III, page 657.

[26] OR Series I, Vol. 38, Part III, page 742.

[27] Daniel. *Cannoneers in Gray*, page 121.

[28] Scaife. *Order of Battle*, page 29.

End Notes

[29] Daniel. *Cannoneers in Gray*, page 121.

[30] Scaife. *The Campaign for Atlanta*, Plate II.

[31] Johnston. *Military Operations of Civil War*, page 323.

[32] Bailey, Anne J. *To Live and Die in Dixie* by Archie P. McDonald, page 77 of Georgia.

[33] Scaife. *The Campaign for Atlanta*, Plate XII.

[34] OR Series I, Vol. 38, Part IV, page 770.

[35] Daniel. *Cannoneers in Gray*, page 151.

[36] Scaife. *The Chattahoochee River Line*, pages 2 & 15.

[37] Scaife. *The Chattahoochee River Line*, inside front cover.

[38] French. *Two Wars*, page 216.

[39] OR Series I, Vol. 52, Part II, page 616.

[40] OR Series I, Vol. 38, Part V, page 907.

[41] OR Series I, Vol. 52, Part II, page 643.

[42] Castrel. *Decision in the West*, page 410.

[43] Raab. *Florida's Forgotten General*, page 167.

[44] *Georgia Historical Review*, Vol. 50, Part 4, page 417-418. Article written by Errol MacGregor Clauss.

[45] Ibid, page 170.

[46] Castrel. *Decision in the West*, page 448.

[47] Ibid, page 486.

[48] Ibid, page 496.

[49] Ibid, page 498.

[50] Faust. *Historical Times Encyclopedia*, page 373.

[51] OR Series I, Vol. 39, Part II, page 836.

[52] Malone. *Dictionary of American Biography.*

[53] Confederate Service Record F.A. Shoup. Special Field Order #131, Headquarters Army of Tennessee, in the field dated October, 1864.

[54] OR Series I, Vol. 53, page 880.

[55] Durden, Robert E. *The Gray and the Black*, page 210.

[56] Carmichael, Peter. *Lee's Young Artillerist*, page 158.

[57] Durden, Robert E. *The Gray and the Black*, page 210.

[58] Carmichael, Peter. *Lee's Young Artillerist*, page 158.

[59] OR Series I, Vol. 47, Part II, page 1374.

[60] Faust. *Historical Times Encyclopedia*, page 64.

[61] Jones. *A Rebel War Clerk's Diary*, Vol. II, pages 451, 461, 462.

[62] Davis. *The Confederate General*, Vol. 5, page 151.

[63] Jones. *A Rebel War Clerk's Diary*, Vol. II, pages 456 & 457.

[64] Evans. *Judah P. Benjamin*, page 291.

End Notes

[65]Jones. *A Rebel War Clerk's Diary*, Vol. II, page 466.

[66]Boatner III. *The Civil War Dictionary*, page 22.

[67]Semmes. *Memoirs of Service Afloat*, page 818.

[68]Ibid, page 820.

[69]Ibid, page 821.

Chapter VI
[1]*U.S. Military Academy at West Point*, reprtin from the *Maury Democrat* Newspaper, page 31.

[2]Ibid.

[3]*American National Biography*, Vol. I, page 888.

[4]Owen. *Generals at Rest*, page 231.

A Dual Biography: General Lloyd Tilghman & General Francis Shoup

Select Bibliography

Books and Articles

Allardice, Bruce S. *More Generals in Gray*. Louisiana State University Press. Baton Rouge, Louisiana. 1995.

Burns, Ned H. *Confederate Forts*. Southern Historical Publications, Inc. Natchez, Mississippi. 1977.

Bearss, Edwin Cole. *The Campaign for Vicksburg*. Vols. I, II, and III. Morningside House, Inc. Reissued October 1991.

Boatner III, Mark Mayo. *The Civil War Dictionary*. Revised Edition. David McKay Co., Inc. New York. 1987.

Bradley, Mark L. *The Battle of Bentonville - Last Stand in the Carolinas*. Savas Woodbury Publishers. Campbell, California. 1996.

Buker, George E. *Blockades, Refugees and Contrabands*. The University of Alabama Press. 1993.

Carmichael, Peter S. *Lee's Young Artillerist*. William R. J. Pegram. University Press of Virginia. 1995.

Carvell, Frank R. Jr. *The Kentucky Brave*. S.B.C. Publishing Co. Paducah, Kentucky. 1999.

Castel, Albert. *Decision in the West - The Atlanta Campaign of 1864*. University Press of Kansas. 1992.

Connelly, Thomas Lawrence. *Army Of The Heartland - The Army of Tennessee, 1861-1862*. Louisiana State University Press. 1967.

Crute, Joseph H., Jr. *Confederate Staff Officers*. Derwent Books. Powhatan, Virginia. 1982.

Cullum, George W. Bvt. Major. *Biographical Register of the Officers and Graduates of the U.S. Military Academy*. Volume II, 3rd Edition. Houghton, Mifflin & Co. 1891.

Cutler, Harry Gardner. *History of Florida - Past and Present*. The Lewis Publishing Co. Chicago, Illinois. 1923.

Daniel, Larry J. *Cannoneers in Gray - The Field Army of the Army of Tennessee, 1861-1865*. The University of Alabama Press. 1984.

Davis, William C. *The Confederate General*. Volume 5. Francis A. Shoup by Edwin C. Bearss. A Publication of the National Historical Society. U.S. Army Military History Institute.

Durden, Robert E. *The Gray and The Black*. Louisiana State Univeristy Press. 1972.

Evans, Eli N. *Judah P. Benjamin - The Jewish Confederate*. The Free Press. A Division of Macmillan, Inc. 1988.

Fleming, Francis P. *Memoir of Capt. C. Seton Fleming of the Second Florida Infantry, CSA. 1881*. Reprinted 1985. Stonewall House. Alexandria, Virginia.

Futch, Ovid L. *History of Andersonville Prison*. University of Florida Press. 1988.

Gannon, Michael. *The New History of Florida*. University Press of Florida. Gainesville, Florida. 1996.

Govan & Livingood. *A Different Valor - The Story of General Joseph E. Johnston, CSA*. The Bobbs-Merrill Co., Inc. Indianapolis & New York. 1956.

Greene, F. V. *The Mississippi Campaigns Of The Civil War*. Charles Scribner's Sons. 1892.

Hattaway, Herman. *General Stephen D. Lee*. University Press of Mississippi. Jackson, Mississippi. 1976.

Hawk, Robert. *Florida's Army*. Pineapple Press, Inc. Englewood, Florida. 1986.

Hillhouse, Don. *Heavy Artillery & Light Infantry. A History of the 1st Florida Special Battalion & 10th Infantry Regiment CSA*. 1992.

Select Bibliography

Hughes Jr., Nathaniel Cheairs. *General William J. Hardee - Old Reliable.* Louisiana State University Press. 1965.

Johns, John E. *Florida During the Civil War.* University of Florida Press. Gainesville, Florida. 1963.

Johnson & Buel. *Battles & Leaders of the Civil War.* Castle Division of Book Sales. Secaucus, New Jersey. 1988.

Johnston, Joseph E. *General narrative of Military Operations during the Civil War.* De Capo Press, Inc. with the permission of Indiana University Press. 1959.

Jones, John B. *A Rebel War Clerk's Diary.* Vol. II. J.B. Lippincott & Co. 1866. Reprinted 1982 Times-Life Books, Inc.

McDonald, Archie P. *To Live and Die in Dixie. How the South Formed a Nation.* Southern Heritage Press. Murfreesboro, Tennessee. 1999.

Nash, Charles Edward, M.D. *Biographical Sketches of General Pat Cleburne and General T. C. Hindman.* 1898. Reprint 1977 by Morningside Bookshop. Dayton, Ohio.

Ness, George T., Jr. *The Regular Army on The Eve of the Civil War.* Toomey Press. Baltimore, Maryland. 1990.

Owen, Richard and James. *Generals At Rest.* White Mane Publishing Co., Inc. Shippensburg, Pennsylvania. 1997.

Patterson, Gerald A. *Rebels from West Point.* Doubleday. New York. 1987.

Prairie Grove Battlefield State Park pamphlet. P.O. Box 306, Prairie Grove, Arkansas, Department of Parks.

Robertson, Fred L. *Soldiers of Florida in the Seminole Indian and Spanish American Wars.* Board of State Institutions. 1903.

Rowland, Dunbar, LL.D. *Jefferson Davis, Constitutionist.* Volume 5. Mississippi Department of Archives and History. Jackson, Mississippi. 1923.

Scaife, William R.
Allatoona Pass. Etowah Valley Historical Society. 1995.
Order of Battle. Federal and Confederate Forces Engaged in the Campaign for Atlanta. 1992.
The Campaign for Atlanta. Second edition.
The Chattahoochee River Line - An American Maginot. 621 Old Allatoona Road, Cartersville, Georgia 30120.

Semmes, Raphael (Admiral). *Memoirs of Service Afloat.* Kelly, Piet and Co. Baltimore, Maryland. 1869.

Sifakis, Steward. *Who Was Who In The Civil War.* Facts on File Publications, Inc. New York, New York. 1988.

Symonds, Craig L. *Joseph E. Johnston - A Civil War Biography.* W.W. Norton & Co. New York, New York. 1992.

Thomas, George H. *Report of Major General George H. Thomas to the Honor Committee on the Conduct of the War.* 1865. Reprint.

Vandiver, Frank E. *Rebel Brass - The Confederate Command System.* Louisiana State University Press. Baton Rouge, Louisiana. 1984.

Warner, Ezra J. *Generals In Gray - Lives Of The Confederate Commanders.* Louisiana State University Press. 1991.

Weinert, Jr., Richard P. *The Confederate Regular Army.* White Mane Publishing Co. 1991.

Wingfield, Marshall *General A. P. Stewart - His Life and Letters.* The West Tennessee Historial Society. Memphis, Tennessee. 1954.

Select Bibliography

Encyclopedia

Patricia L. Faust. *Historical Times Illustrated Encyclopedia of the Civil War*. Harper & Row Publishers. New York. 1986.

The Encyclopedia of the Confederacy. Richard N. Current, Editor-in-Chief. Macmillan Reference USA. Simon & Schuster Macmillan. New York. 1993.

National Cyclopedia of American Biography. 63 Volumes. James T. White. Clinton, New Jersey. 1893.

American National Biography. American Council of Learned Societies. General Editors. John A. Garraty and Mark C. Carnes. Volume 1. Oxford University Press. New York. 1999.

Archives and Universities

Alabama Department of Archives and History. Montgomery, Alabama.

Confederate Service Record, provided by Broadfoot Publishing Co. 1907 Buena Vista Circle. Wilmington, North Carolina 28405.

Sewanee - The University of the South. Letters to author by Annie Armour, Archivist. 1999.

The Western Reserve Historical Society Library, Cleveland, Ohio. Shoup Manuscript Collection.

U.S. Army Historical Reference Institute, Department of the Army, Carlisle Barracks, Pennsylvania. Louise Arnold Friend, Archivist.

U.S. Military Academy at West Point, New York. Annual Reunion of the Association and Graduates. June 11, 1896. A reprint from the Maury Democrat. Columbia, Tennessee.

Index

"Abbeville, MS" 54
"Adams, Col. J." 86
Adams, Col. W. 102
"Africa" 203
"Alabama" 12, 14, 18, 21, 29, 41, 156, 157, 164, 179, 182, 199, 207, 209
"Albany" 41
"Alcorn, J.L." 5
"Alton, IL" 30, 40
"Amelia Courthouse" 207
"Amelia Island" 156
"Anderson, Adna" 12
"Appomattox Station" 208
"Arkadelphia" 166, 167, 171
"Arkansas" 1, 49, 55, 70, 157, 165, 166, 167, 168, 170, 171
"Arkansas Post" 171
"Asbury University" 155
"Atlanta, GA" 183, 184, 185, 187, 190, 191, 193, 194, 197, 198, 199, 200
"Bailey's Landing" 17, 20, 21
"Baker's Creek" 97, 98, 101, 103, 104
"Baldwin, Gen. W.E." 64, 90, 174
"Baldwin-Ferry Road" 92
"Baltimore" 42
"Bankhead, Capt. S.P." 162
"Banks, Gen. N.P." 92
"Barbour & Howland" 155
"Barksdale, Hon. E." 201
"Baron DeKalb" 79, 80, 81
"Bates, Edward" 10
"Baton Rouge, LA" 87
"Bayou Pierre" 91
"Beauregard, Gen. P.G.T." 91, 158, 162, 163, 165
"Beck's Ferry Landing" 71
"Belmont" 9, 15
"Benjamin, Judah P." 5, 9, 207
"Big Black River" 90, 91, 92, 93, 173, 174
"Blair, Gen. F.P., Jr." 174, 175
"Bledsoe" 168
"Blocher, Col. W.D." 169
"Blunt, Gen. J.G." 168, 169, 170, 171
"Bolivar, TN" 50, 52
"Bolton" 93, 98

Index

"Boston" 41, 168
"Bovina" 92
"Bowen, J.S." 51, 55, 90, 91, 92, 97, 103, 104
"Bowling Green, KY" 2, 5, 7, 8, 10, 14, 15, 16, 29, 43, 47, 158
"Bragg, Gen. Braxton" 45, 47, 49, 66, 85, 90, 96, 158, 159, 165, 183, 160
"Brandon" 179
"Breckinridge, Gen. J.D." 163
"Britton, C.P., Jr." 26
"Brooks, Col. W.H." 169
"Brown, Gen. J.C." 197
"Brown, Govenor" 192
"Bruinsburg, MS" 90, 173
"Brush Mountain" 187
"Bryam" 179
"Buchanan, President" 35
"Buckner, Simon Bolivar" 1, 3, 5, 16, 31, 32, 35, 37, 40, 41, 42, 43, 44, 45
"Buell, Gen. D.C." 163, 164
"Buffalo" 41
"Burbridge, Gen. S.G." 102, 103
"Cairo, IL" 3, 20, 30, 33, 37, 40
"Camden" 166, 172
"Camp Chase" 41
"Camp Daniel Boone" 2, 8
"Canehill" 168, 169
"Canton" 86, 96, 175, 181
"Cape Ann Advertiser" 42
"Capitol Square" 207
"Carondelet" 26
"Carroll, Anna E." 9, 10, 60
"Carthage" 87
"Cassville, GA" 185, 186
"Cave City, KY" 158
"Champion Hill" 98, 101, 103, 112, 173
"Chancellorsville" 178
"Charleston, S.C." 1
"Charlotte Road" 35
"Chattahoochee River" 190, 191, 193, 194, 198, 199
"Chattahoochee, FL" 156
"Chattanooga" 45, 49, 92, 183, 198
"Cheat Mountain" 64
"Cheek" 169
"Cherokee Pin" 168
"Chewalla" 52
"Chickasaw Bayou" 62

"Chilicothe" 79
"Cincinnati" 26, 28, 30, 125
"City Point" 44
"Civil War" 9
"Clarksville, TN" 2, 8, 15, 29, 31, 108
"Clayton Bayou" 72
"Cleburne" 167
"Clinton" 47, 49, 50, 85, 96, 97, 98, 99, 103
"Coffeeville, MS" 59, 60
"Coker House Ridge" 102
"Coldwater River" 70, 71, 72, 79
"Colt" 59
"Columbia, TN" 60, 210
"Columbiads" 13. 20, 26, 27, 32
"Columbus, Ky." 1, 3, 5, 9, 12, 14, 15, 29, 31, 43, 47, 60, 61, 92, 93, 124, 158
Columbus, Oh 41
"Conestoga" 13, 25
"Confederacy" 1, 2, 3, 5, 11, 13, 18, 32, 43, 44, 64, 66,
.... 112, 157, 158, 168, 171, 178, 193, 207, 208
"Confederate" 2, 3, 5, 7, 8, 9, 10, 11, 12, 15, 17, 18,
.... 20, 22, 28, 29, 30, 31, 32, 33, 34, 35, 37, 39,
.... 40, 41, 44, 45, 47, 48, 50, 51, 52, 54, 55, 56, 59,
.... 60, 61, 62, 63, 64, 69, 71, 72, 75, 79, 80, 81, 82, 84, 85, 87,
.... 92, 95, 96, 97, 98, 99, 101, 103, 104, 106, 107, 156,
.... 157, 158, 160, 162, 163, 164, 165, 168, 169, 170, 171, 173,
.... 174, 175, 178, 179, 181, 183, 184, 185, 187,
.... 191, 193, 194, 197, 198, 199, 200, 201, 206, 207, 209
"Conwell, James" 155
"Cooper, Gen. S." 207
"Corinth" 47, 48, 49, 50, 53, 54, 158, 159, 164, 165
"Cotton Hill" 104
"Court of Inquiry" 16, 53, 55, 60, 75, 200
"Cowan, Capt. J." 104, 105
"Crittenden, Gen. T.L." 30
"Crystal Springs" 105
"Cumberland River" 7, 9, 10, 11, 12, 13, 17, 29, 31, 33, 34, 35, 40, 158
"Cumberland City" 14
"Cumberland Gap" 17
"Cumberland Mountains" 5
"Cummings, Capt. E.H." 55
"Curtiss" 72
"Dalton" 45, 183, 184
"Danville" 2, 207, 208
"Danville & Richmond R.R." 207

Index

"Davis, Col." 52
"Davis, Pres. Jefferson" 7, 43, 50, 52, 96, 97, 157, 166, 179,
....183, 194, 199, 200, 206, 207, 208
"Decatur, AL" 197
"Demopolis, AL" 179, 182
"Dickens, E.V." 79
"Dillon" 97
"Dimick, Col. J.E." 41
"Dix, Gen. John A." 44
"Dix-Hill Exchange" 44
"Dixie" 43, 159
"Dixon, Joseph" 13, 14
"Donelson, Daniel W." 11, 12
"Donelson, John" 12
"Donelson, Rachel" 12
"Douglas" 155
"Dover Hotel" 37
"Dover Road" 28
"Dover, TN" 11, 31, 40
"Drennen, Lt. W.A." 101
"Duckport Landing" 69
"Dunbar" 2, 21
"Durham Station, N.C." 208
"Eakin's Landing" 44
"Ector, Gen. M.D." 197
"Edwards Depot" 90, 92, 97, 102
"Edwards Station" 90
"Elliott, Bishop Stephen" 209
"Elliott, Esther Haversham" 209
"Ellis, Powhatten" 105
"Ellison" 97, 98, 99, 101, 102
"English" 203
"Enterprise, MS" 86, 87, 179, 182
"Episcopal Church" 184, 209
"Essex" 26
"Etowah River" 187
"Ezra Church" 197
"Fagan, Gen. James F." 169, 171
"Fairbanks, Jason" 209
"Fayetteville, AR" 167, 168, 169
"Featherston, Gen. W.S." 82, 101
"Federal" 1, 3, 5, 10, 13, 17, 20, 21, 26, 28, 30, 32, 33, 34, 35,
....40, 41, 44, 47, 48, 49, 50, 51, 52, 54, 55, 59,
..............................60, 62, 63, 64, 69, 70, 71, 72, 79, 80, 81, 82, 83, 86, 87, 89,

231

....90, 92, 93, 95, 96, 97, 99, 102, 103, 104, 105,
....160, 161, 162, 163, 164, 165, 168,169, 170, 173, 174,
................................177, 178, 179, 181, 183, 187, 188, 191, 193, 197, 198, 207, 208
"Fernandina, FL"..156
"Flint River"..199
"Florence, AL"...12, 29
"Florida"..156, 157, 158
"Florida R.R."...156
"Floyd, Gen. J.B."...31, 32, 34, 35, 36, 39, 43
"Foote, Andrew H."...17, 20, 21, 25, 28, 34
"Forbes, Col. "...87
"Forney, Gen. J.H."...182
"Forrest, Col. N.B."...2, 33, 36, 60, 62, 91, 163
"Fort Donelson"...9, 12, 13, 14, 15, 20, 22, 28, 29,
....31, 32, 33, 35, 36, 37, 43, 50, 61, 64, 158, 175
"Fort Gaines"..157
"Fort Greenwood"..72
"Fort Heiman"..13, 14, 17, 18, 21, 29, 61
"Fort Henry"..........9, 12, 13, 14, 15, 17, 18, 20, 21, 22, 25, 28, 29, 31, 33, 61, 158, 175
"Fort Hill"...173, 174
"Fort Marion, FL"...156
"Fort Morgan, AL"...157, 179
"Fort Moultrie, S.C."...155
"Fort Myers, FL"..155
"Fort Pemberton"...72, 79, 80, 82, 84
"Fort Sumter"..1
"Fort Warren, MA"...41, 43, 44, 47
"Fortress Monroe, Virginia"..44
"Foster, Commander J.P."..82
"Foster, Major W.B."...191
"Fourteen Mile Creek"..95
"Franklin County, IN"...155
"Fry, Col. Speed S."...17
"Gaines Mills, VA"..44
"Garrard"...193
"George's Island"...41
"Georgia"..183, 185, 187, 188, 191, 207
"Gerry, Elbridge"...76
"Gettysburg"...178
"Gibson, Gen. R.L."...197
"Gilmer, Major J.F."...13, 21, 27, 32
"Goodwin, Col."...102, 103
"Gorgas, Gen. Josiah"..209
"Grand Gulf"..63, 90, 91, 92, 173

Index

"Grant, Gen. Ulysses S." 3, 4, 9, 17, 21, 25, 28, 30, 31, 33, 34, 35, 37, 39,
.... 43, 49, 51, 60, 61, 62, 63, 64, 66, 69, 70, 75, 79,
.... 83, 84, 85, 87, 89, 90, 91, 92, 93, 95, 96, 97, 98,
.... 102, 105, 158, 159, 163, 164, 173, 174, 175, 177, 178, 181, 183
"Grant's Pass" 79, 83
"Graveyard Road" 174, 176
"Greeg, Col." 41
"Greensboro" 208
"Greencastle, IN" 155
"Greenwood" 71, 82
"Grenada, MS" 60, 61, 64, 70, 75, 92
"Grierson, Col. B.H." 85, 86, 87, 96
"Griffith, Col. John S." 61
"Gulf of Mexico" 157
"Haines Bluff" 70
"Halleck, Gen. H.W." 41, 48, 165
"Hankinson Ferry" 91
"Hard Times, LA" 85, 89, 90, 93
"Hardee, Col. J.W." 157, 158, 159, 163, 179, 183, 185, 187, 197, 199, 207, 209
"Harris, Gov. Isham" 11, 12
"Hatchie River" 52
"Hawkins, Col." 52
"Hawthorn, Capt. A.T." 169
"Haxall's Landing" 44
"Hayes, Lt. Col. M.A." 14, 21, 29
"Heiman, Col. Adolphus" 12, 13, 20, 21, 22, 26, 27, 28, 29, 31, 41
"Helena, AR" 55, 70, 79, 82
"Hemming, Senator" 200
"Henry, Gustavus A." 12
"Herron, Gen. F.J." 169, 170, 171
"Hickman, KY" 3
"Hill, Col. W." 174
"Hill, Gen D.H." 44
"Hindman, Col. T.C." 157, 165, 167, 168, 169, 171, 172
"Holly Springs, MS" 49, 50, 52, 54, 61, 62, 64
"Holmes, Gen. T.H." 166, 167, 171, 172
"Home Guard" 1, 3
"Hood, Gen. John Bell" 186, 187, 193, 194, 197, 198, 199, 200
"Hopkinsville, KY" 5, 7, 8, 9, 15, 16
"Howard, O.O." 187, 199
"Huntsville, AL" 164
"Illinois" 3, 20, 30, 33, 40, 55, 169, 170
"Illinois Central R.R." 3
"Illinois River" 169, 170

233

"Indian War" 55
"Indiana" 33, 80, 155
"Indianapolis, IN" 41, 155
"Inspector General" 1, 165, 171, 207
"Iowa" 55, 162
"Iuka, MS" 47, 49
"Jackson R.R." 86
"Jackson, Andrew" 12
"Jackson, Col. H.W." 55
"Jackson, Col. Wm. ""Red" 61
"Jackson, Lieutenant" 41
"Jackson, MS" 45, 47, 50, 53, 54, 64, 80, 85, 86,
 .... 90, 91, 92, 93, 95, 96, 97, 105, 173, 179, 181
Jackson Road 104
Jackson, TN 61, 210
"Jackson's Creek" 103
"James River" 44
"Jawhawk" 56
"Jefferson, TX" 166
"Jetersbille" 207
"Johnson, Gen. Bushrod" 31, 37, 40, 105
"Johnson, Gov. George W." 10
"Johnston, Gen. Albert S." 3, 5, 7, 9, 11, 12, 13, 14, 15, 17,
 .... 30, 32, 43, 47, 48, 157, 158, 159, 162
"Johnston, Gen. J.E." 91, 92, 95, 96, 97, 98, 177, 179, 181, 183, 184,
 .... 185, 186, 187, 188, 190, 191, 192, 193, 194, 207, 208
"Jonesboro" 198, 199
"Kansas" 55, 56, 59, 64
"Kennesaw Mountain" 187, 188, 191
"Kentucky" 1, 2, 3, 5, 7, 8, 9, 10, 11, 12, 16, 17, 31, 60, 62, 112, 158, 183
"King, Col. J.P." 169
"Kirkman " 12
"Kittson, Henry H." 112
"Knickerbocker" 44
"Knoxville" 45
"La Grange, TN" 86
"Lake Providence, LA" 69
"Lamar, Col." 172
"Lang Park" 112
"Lanier, N.B." 92
"Laurel, IN" 155
"Lee, Col. A.L." 54, 59, 64, 66
"Lee, Gen. S.D." 62, 173, 177, 197, 201, 207, 208
"Lee, Robert E." 178

Index

"Lexington" 18, 19
"Lick Creek" 37
"Lickskillet Road" 197
"Lincoln, Abraham" 1, 9, 10, 106, 155, 157
"Lioness" 80
"Little Rock, AR" 165, 167, 171
"Lockett, Major S.H." 103, 104
"Logan Crossroad" 17, 158
"Logan, J.A." 90, 95
"Longacre, Edward G." 194
"Loring, Gen. W.W." 64, 70, 71, 72, 81, 82, 86, 87, 90, 91, 92, 93, 95, 97, 99,
.... 101, 102, 103, 104, 105, 107, 191, 193, 197
"Lost Mountain" 187
"Louisiana" 50, 63, 64, 69, 70, 85, 87, 89, 90, 92, 166, 173, 174, 175, 210
"Louisville & Nashville R.R." 2
"Louisville-Cave City Pike" 158
"Lovejoy Station" 201
"Lovell, Gen. Mansfield" 50, 51, 54, 59, 60, 75
"Mackall, Col. W.W." 29
"Macon & Western R.R." 197, 198, 199
"Macon, GA" 198, 199
"Macon, MS" 86
"Magoffin, B." 1
"Marietta, GA" 187, 188, 192
"Marmaduke, Col. J.S." 167, 168, 170, 171
"Marshall, LA" 166
"Maryland" 1, 9, 41, 42, 76
"Massachusetts" 41
"Matlock, Col. C.H." 169
"McCall, Gen. C.A." 45
"McClernand, Gen. John A." 33, 79, 85, 90, 93, 95, 102, 103
"McCook, Gen. E." 198
"McCulloch, Robt. ""Black Bob" 61, 72, 80
"McGavock, Randal W." 29, 42, 47
"McLendon" 102
"McNeill, Col. A.J." 169
"McPherson, J.B." 90, 93, 95, 96, 97, 187, 192, 197
"McRae, Col. Dandridge" 169
"McRaie, George" 79
"Memphis & Charleston R.R." 164
"Memphis & Ohio R.R." 29
"Memphis, TN" 2, 15, 70, 86
"Meridian, MS" 86, 181, 182, 183
"Merrin, Lt. F.W." 102

235

"Merriwether, Major...71
"Mexican War"..55, 76
"Milliken's Bend"..85
"Mint Spring Bayou" 174
Mississippi 1, 5, 7, 15, 45, 47, 48, 49, 50, 54, 55, 59, 60, 61, 62, 63, 64, 66,
....72, 75, 83, 85, 86, 87, 90, 92, 93, 114, 157, 158, 165,
....173, 178, 179, 181, 182, 207, 209
"Mississippi Central R.R." 54
"Mississippi River".....3, 5, 9, 10, 11, 12, 30, 40, 47, 49, 55, 60, 62, 63, 69, 70, 173, 179
"Missouri"...1, 33, 40, 79, 157, 168, 169
"Mobile & Ohio R.R." 62, 87
"Mobile Bay" 157, 179
"Mobile Point" 157
"Mobile, AL" 26, 45, 157, 172, 179, 182, 183
"Monroe, LA" 44, 166
"Mont Alban" 92
"Montgomery, AL"...156
"Moon Lake"..70, 71, 79, 83
"Moore, Gen. J.C." 82
"Moore, Gov. A.B." 14
"Morgan, Col. A.S." 169
"Morgan, Gen. Daniel" 157
"Morton, MS" 86, 181, 182
"Mount Vernon" 157
"Murfreesboro, TN" 158
"Murray Road" 18
"Muray, Gen. D.H." 55
"Muscle Shoals, AL" 29
"Myrick, Capt. J.D."..72
"Napoleon"...105, 202, 204
"Nashville, TN" 5, 7, 8, 11, 12, 15, 16, 31, 32, 33, 36, 37, 40, 47, 96, 158, 160, 210
"Negro Army" 207
"Negro Enlistment Bill" 207
"New Orleans" 60, 158, 178, 210
"Newton" 87
"North Carolina" 1, 207, 208
"Ocean Queen" 44
"Ohio" 33, 41, 187, 199
"Ohio River" 3, 4, 5, 33
"Old Blizzards" 81
"Oxford, MS"..55, 56, 59, 61, 209
"Ozark Mountain" 171
"Paducah, Ky." 1, 2, 3, 4, 30, 40, 112
"Palmetto Station" 199

Index

"Panther Island" 20, 21, 25, 26
"Parallel" 80
"Paris Landing" 17
"Parole of Honor" 40
"Parrott Guns" 59
"Pascagoula, MS" 157
"Pea Ridge (Elkhorn Tavern)" 168
"Peachtree Creek" 193, 197
"Pearl River" 87, 179
"Pegram, William R.J." 201
"Pemberton, Gen. J.C." 50, 52, 54, 55, 60, 61, 63, 66, 70, 71, 75, 76,
.... 81, 84, 85, 86, 87, 89, 90, 91, 92, 93, 95, 96, 97, 98, 99,
.... 101, 102, 103, 104, 106, 173, 174, 177, 179
"Peninsula Campaign" 44
"Pensacola, FL" 158
"Petersburg, VA" 207
"Pettus, Gov. John T." 93
"Philadelphia" 42, 75, 87
"Piedmont R.R." 208
"Pike County" 167
"Pillow, Gen. Gideon" 14, 31, 32, 35, 36, 39, 43
"Pine Mountain" 187
"Pittsburg Landing" 159, 160, 163
"Pleasants, Col. J.C." 169
"Point Coupee" 91
"Polk, Gen. Leonidas" 3, 9, 12, 14, 15, 31, 47, 158, 172, 181, 182, 186, 187
"Ponchatoula, MS" 49
"Pontotoc, MS" 86
"Port Gibson" 90, 91, 92
"Port Gibson-Raymond Road" 97
"Port Hudson" 47, 63, 64, 91, 92
"Porter, Admiral D.D." 62, 85
"Porter, Cap. W.D." 26
"Potomac River" 179
"Prairie Grove" 170, 171, 171
"Prentiss, Gen. B.M." 162
"Price, Gen. Sterling" 49, 50, 51, 53, 55
"Proclamation" 4, 157, 167
"Provisional" 8, 10
"Purnell" 72
"Quachita County" 166
"Quaker" 75
"Quimby, Gen. I.F." 82
"Randolph, G.W." 45

"Rappahannock River" 179
"Raymond" 93, 95, 97, 98, 99, 102, 103, 104, 105, 173, 179
"Red Hill" 59
"Red River" 64
"Resaca, GA" 185
"Revolutionary War" 157
"Reynalds, Col. A.E." 107
"Reynolds. Gen. J.F." 44, 91
"Richmond Enquirer" 200
"Richmond Whig" 201
"Richmond, VA" 5, 8, 9, 14, 15, 29, 44, 45, 50, 91, 114, 172, 183, 207, 208
"Ripley, MS" 49, 50, 52, 61
"Robinson, Capt. Powhaton" 72
"Rochester" 41
"Rocky Face Ridge" 184
"Ross, Gen. L.F." 79, 80
"Roswell, GA" 191, 193
"Royston" 167
"Ruggles, Gen. Daniel" 158, 162
"Russellville" 10, 31
"Rust. A." 51, 64, 85
"Savannah" 159
"Sayler's Creek" 208
"Sear" 193
"Searles" 105
"Semmes, Rear Admiral" 208
"Sewanee, TN" 209, 210
"Sharp" 59
"Shell Mound" 80
"Shepperd, Lt. F.E." 71
"Sherman, Gen. W.T." 30, 37, 60, 62, 75, 79, 89,
.... 92, 93, 96, 97, 108, 109, 179, 181, 182, 183, 184, 187, 188,
.... 190, 191, 192, 193, 194, 197, 198, 199, 200, 208,
"Shiloh" 47, 159, 160, 162, 164, 165, 183
"Ship Island" 157, 203
"Schofield" 187, 193, 197
"Shoup, David M." 210
"Shoup, Francis Asbury" 149, 155, 156, 157, 158, 159, 160, 161, 162,
.... 163, 164, 165, 166, 167, 168, 169, 170, 171, 172,
.... 173, 174, 175, 177, 178, 179, 182, 183, 184, 185, 186,
.... 187, 191, 193, 194, 197, 198, 199, 200, 201, 207, 208, 209, 210
"Shoup, George Grove" 155
"Shoup, Jane (Conwell)" 155
"Shoupade" 191, 193, 194

"Shreveport, LA"...166
"Sievers, F. William"..114
"Slaughter, Gen. J.E."..172
"Smith"..59
Smith, A.J. 97
"Smith, Gen. C.F."..17, 18, 21, 33, 35,97
"Smith, Gen. G.W."..191
"Smith, Gen. M.L."..173, 174, 175, 178
"Smith, Gen.Edmund Kirby"..209, 210
"Smith, W."...79, 82
"Smithland"...40, 207
"Smyrna"...188
"Snyder's Bluff"..89
"Soap Creek"...193
"South Carolina"...1,156
"Southern R.R."..87, 91
"Spring Hill, TN"..85
"Springfield, MO"..169
"St. Augustine, FL"..156, 209
"St. Louis"...10, 26, 30, 40, 41
"St. Peter's Parrish"..209
"Stanton"..10, 30, 42, 208
"Starkville, MS"..86, 87
"Stevenson, Gen. C.L."..97, 101, 104
"Stewart, Gen. A.P."..197
"Stewart's Hill"..13
"Stoneman, G"..198
"Storrs, Major G.S."..187
"Tallahatchie River"..54, 55, 70, 72, 79, 80, 82, 84
"Taylor, Capt. Jesse"..12, 13, 90
"Tennessee"..1, 2, 3, 8, 9, 10, 11, 12, 13, 14, 15, 18, 19,
....20, 21, 27, 31, 33, 37, 47, 49, 50, 61, 62, 66, 85, 96,
.....................108, 158, 163, 172, 179, 183, 184, 187, 193, 198, 199, 209, 210
"Tennessee River" 2, 10, 11, 12, 13, 14, 17, 20, 28, 29, 159, 160
"Terre Haute, IN"..41
"Texas"..41, 52, 61, 64, 83, 166
"Thompson Station, TN"..85
"Thompson, Martha"..75
"Tilghman, Augusta"..2, 108, 112
"Tilghman, Frederick B."..111, 114
"Tilghman, Lloyd"..2, 5, 55, 60, 103, 107, 112, 114, 173
"Tilghman, Lloyd, Jr."..108
"Tilghman, Matthew"..76
"Tilghman, Sidell"...111, 114

239

"Tracy, Gen. E.D." 90, 91
"Trans-Mississippi" 62, 172, 200
"Tullahoma, TN" 66, 85, 96
"Tunnel Hill" 45
"Tupelo, MS" 49, 165
"Turner's Ferry" 192
"Twin Rivers Fort" 11
"Tyler" 25
"U.S. Army" 42
"U.S. Star of the West" 72
"Union" 1, 2, 3, 9, 10, 11, 17, 18, 20, 26, 27, 28, 33,
.... 41, 43, 44, 48, 55, 61, 63, 70, 71, 79, 80, 81, 83, 84,
.... 85, 87, 90, 95, 97, 191, 102, 103, 156, 157, 158,
.... 160, 162, 163, 164, 165, 168, 169, 170, 171, 17, 174, 183, 186, 187
"University" 155, 209, 210
"Utica" 41
"Van Buren, AR" 168, 169
"Van Dorne, Gen. Earl" 49, 50, 51, 52, 53, 54, 55, 60, 61, 62, 63, 64, 66, 85, 97
"Vaughn, J.C." 174
"Venable" 169
"Vicksburg, MS" 45, 47, 60, 62, 63, 64, 69, 0, 75, 82, 84, 85,
.... 87, 89, 90, 91, 92, 96, 97, 104, 105, 111, 112, 114,
.... 173, 174, 175, 177, 178, 179, 180, 181, 183
"Villepigue, J.B." 51, 52
"Virginia" 1, 3, 31, 36, 43, 44, 47, 64, 114, 179, 206, 207
"Walker Hon. L.P." 156, 157
"Walker, Gen. W.H.T." 95, 96
"Wallace, Gen. W.H.L." 162
"Wallace, Gen. Lew" 33, 35
"Warrenton" 90, 173
"Washington, D.C." 42
"Water Valley" 56, 59, 60
"Waterford, NY" 210
"Waul, Col. T.N." 64, 80
"Weakley, S.D." 14
"Weldon, Thomas" 72
"West & Woodruff" 169
"West Point" 11, 59, 75, 155
"Western & Atlantic R.R." 191
"Wheeler" 191
"Whitfield, Gov. Harry L." 114
"Willow Springs" 92
"Wilson, Forcyethe" 26
"Wilson's Creek" 169

A Dual Biography: General Lloyd Tilghman & General Francis Shoup

"Winona" 86
"Wither, Col. W.F." 104, 105
"Woodpecker" 51
"Yalobusha River" 60, 61, 70
"Yazoo City" 70, 71, 72, 8081, 82
"Yazoo Pass" 69, 70, 79, 82, 175
"Yazoo River" 70, 71, 72
"Yerger, Capt. William S." 96
"York James River" 179
"Zollicoffer, Felix Kirk" 17, 158
"Zouaves" 155

Printed in the United States
1240200003B/318